Architectural Guide
Dhaka

Architectural Guide
Dhaka

Sayed Ahmed

DOM
publishers

Contents

Left page:
Fruit vendor in front of a construction site next to the
Shaheed Shuhrawardhy Medical College and Hospital (2023)

I don't find you in Veda and Purana,
But I know that you are the ornament of Bengal,
In eastern Bengal. You are dazzling in this place,
The way a flower in a vase is, the way
a queen on a throne is.

Michael Madhusudan Dutt, 1873

নাহি পাই নাম তব বেদে কি পুরাণে,
কিন্তু বঙ্গ অলঙ্কার তুমি যে তা জানি,
পূর্ববঙ্গে। শোভ তুমি এ সুন্দর স্থানে
ফুলবৃন্তে ফুল যথা, রাজাসনে রাণী।
- মাইকেল মধুসূদন দত্ত

Dhak or palash (*Butea frondosa*) blossoms in the spring

The Urban Development of Dhaka

Sayed Ahmed

Dhaka (known in English as 'Dacca' until 1983) has grown from a small Hindu trading centre in between the River Dholai (not to be confused with the Dholai Canal) and the River Buriganga to become today's metropolis. It is a beta-global city with an urban area of approximately 300 square kilometres; Greater Dhaka occupies more than 2000 square kilometres and has a population estimated to be 22 million (2022), making it the sixth largest megacity on this planet and one of the most densely populated cities in the world, with around 50,000 people per square kilometre. Dhaka generates a third of Bangladesh's total economic production.

How did the city get its name?

The most common species of vegetation in this region was the dhak tree, commonly known as 'palash' (*Butea frondosa*); one theory is that this is where the name

'Dhaka' comes from. Another legend has it that when the Mughals conquered this river port, they beat their drums so that the city's boundaries could be marked out at the limits of the drums' audibility; drum is *dhak* in the Bangla language, and *dhak* became 'Dhaka'. Other scholars, however, believe that Dhaka's name derives from its leafy canopy: *dhaka* in Bangla means 'covered'. Yet the origin theory that to this day seems to have the best scientific basis is associated with Dhakeshwari Temple in Dhaka. The temple's missing deity was discovered in the jungle by King Ballal Sen in the late twelfth century; the king erected the temple here to pay homage to the goddess.

Why did Dhaka grow here?

This could not be a more suitable place on this planet for establishing a city. The world's largest mountain ranges, the

Himalayas, are to Dhaka's north; they are rich in minerals. A network of 700 rivers forms the planet's largest and most fertile delta and gives access to the largest bay in the world, the Bay of Bengal. Dhaka is surrounded by flood plains and luxuriant greenery growing on alluvial soils; and yet its slightly elevated position on the southern edge of the Madhupur Tract, a place known as Bhawal Garh, protects it from the recurrent flash floods occurring in the Ganges/Bhammaputra basin. Interestingly, Dhaka's older parts are often the driest lands as they were built on higher ground with an elevation of at least six metres. This region is known for its clay of a red/brown colour, formed by the Pleistocene Age 2.6 million years ago. The climate here is also favourable: Dhaka straddles the Tropic of Cancer. The access to wild nature all around, the presence of waterways and canals, and the landforms created by the marshy land were all crucial for survival. The fish in the rivers and canals and the animals in the jungles to the north helped maintain a healthy ecological balance. In fact, this is the only city in the world, along with Rome in Italy, to be surrounded by five major rivers. In 1865 a local newspaper reported that youngsters had captured three tiger cubs at Mogbazar, just 5.5 kilometres away from today's old town. Their eyes were not yet open, and they were given

Dhakeshwari Temple in 1904

Fritz Kapp, British Library

cow milk to eat! The corpus cotton culture ensured the Kapasia region's economic success. Here some of the finest possible cloths were woven, including muslin, the first global clothing brand in human history and one of the most notable 'treasures' of the Silk Road.

How old is the city of Dhaka?

There are thought to have been six major phases of socio-economic and political fluctuation in Dhaka's continuous urban existence. Most historians believe that Dhaka was a prosperous trade centre in the early Gupta age (280–550 AD) as gold coins from this time have been found in Pilkhana Pond (a site previously occupied by a stable for the Mughals' elephants and now home to today's BGB HQ). Further evidence of Dhaka's ancient existence is to be found in *Rajtarangini* (Royal River), a royal chronicle written in Sanskrit by

Old Dhaka

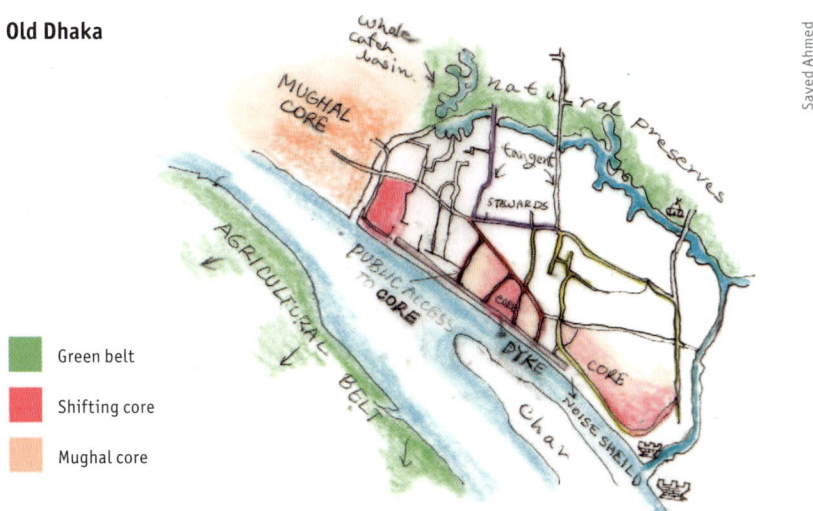

Sayed Ahmed

Green belt

Shifting core

Mughal core

The core of the ancient city on the River Buriganga: the agricultural belt and areas of nature all around ensured successful global trade.

Muslim lady wearing muslin, painting by Francesco Renaldi, Dhaka, 1789

Kalhana, a priest from Kashmir (780 AD). Kalhana mentions a place called Debekka where a watch tower was erected on high land in the vicinity of the then capital, Bikrampur. The history of urbanised settlement in Dhaka probably dates to the seventh century and is possibly connected with the Buddhist kingdom of Kamarupa (Assam). This kingdom was subsequently followed by the rules of the Hindu Chandra and Sena dynasties (Southern Indians) from the ninth to the twelfth centuries. A Bashudev (supreme icon of Krishna) sculpture at Churihatta Mosque, a Harishakar (a hybrid of Shiva and Bishnu) sculpture at a pond in Tejgaon, and a Nateshwar (Dancing Shiva) sculpture at Sharangadhar Jeu Akhra in Chowkbazar are all evidence that craftsmen from the Chandra Hindu

Mir Jumla Gate, slave market, 1875

community of Bikrampur had started to settle in this area, especially in the lower parts in the south of the city near the River Buriganga. Ancient legends also link archaeological ruins found in a peripheral belt stretching through Wari-Bateshwar, Rampal, Durduria, Dhamrai in Savar, and Dhapa in Narayanganj. Most historians think that the temple of the Hindu Goddess Dhakeshwari functioned as the hub of a rapidly developing trade centre established by King Ballal Sen II, who found a statue of the goddess concealed here and drove the last peg into the heart of the Pala dynasty. A stone inscription found in a pond in Manda records the establishment of the powerful Sena dynasty. Surprisingly, no similar black-stone sculptures have been found in Bengal's middle region since 1200. When Hindu statues and inscriptions are discovered in ponds, this indicates that they were hidden to protect them against the destruction of the Turkish invasion. After the fall of the Sena dynasty, various independent Muslim dynasties of Turkish and Pathan (Afghan) origin, such as the Khiljis, Mameluks, Shahs, and Khans, took power and developed this area during the period from 1204 to 1608. An

Afghan fort was also constructed during this period in the vicinity of what is now the Central Jail, to reinforce security. Trade in pre-Mughal Dhaka was mainly confined to the area between today's Sadarghat district and Bahadurshah Park – as has been proven by the discovery of two fourteenth-century Persian inscriptions at Binot Bibi Mosque. Another stone inscription in Persian found in a mosque in Shatgaon (now Greater Kolkata) in Persian indicates that the son of a revenue collector from Dhaka established this holy prayer space in 1467. This means that Dhaka had by this time already become an important river port and been made subject to tax collection. Misled by Mughal myth, written chronologies and official documentation of Dhaka start only with the Mughal conquest and the establishment of the new capital city of Islam Khan Chisti in 1609. Islam Khan Chisti named his capital 'Jahangirnagar' ('the city of the Emperor Jahangir'); this results in a very fragmented history. In this period Dhaka's boundary was extended almost 18 kilometres from the River Buriganga to the River Tongi. But the city's populous core remained within four kilometres of the riverbank. From *Baharistani-Gaibi*, a book by a Mughal lieutenant called Mirza Nathan, we learn that administration and defence were functions later added to western parts of the city, especially in the Lalbagh area, while the city's east was always the centre of commercial activity. In 1608–1610 the Mughal governor Islam Khan offered tax privileges to various crafts as a means of attracting their members to settle in his new capital of Dhaka. The city acquired a proto-industrial character and a pluralistic governing system. Half of the Mughal Empire's GDP came from the province of Bengal, while the empire itself had the largest GDP in the world at that time – nearly 12 per cent of global GDP. The main commodities and industries were textiles (silk, cotton, muslin),

A Mughal-era (17th century) painting showing an Eid procession in Dhaka

Aerial view of old Dhaka (2023)

Dholai Canal, 1905. The bridge and canal no longer exist.

Weaver of Dacca, Charles D'Oyly, early 19th century

shipbuilding using steel (the hull deck technique), saltpetre, calcium carbonate, rice, betel leaf, elephants, and slaves. Dhaka also served as a strong naval base, from which the Mughals were able to conquer Jessore (Mahmudabad), Barishal (Bakla), and Noakhali (Bhulua) during the 1640s. A document called 'Ain-an-Akbari' (The Administration of Akbar) refers to Dhaka at this stage of its development as an important *thana* (military or police post). The Old Afghan fort (today's Central Jail) was the largest of all the *garazs* (Afghan river forts) and had thick mud walls. Dhaka was a key stronghold in the game of empire expansion. The later Mughal conquests were a result of agricultural production and land reform in low-lying Bhati regions, such as Mymensingh, Comilla, and Sylhet. Living in the delta area formerly inhabited by Muslim farmers, the Bhatis cleared jungles and cultivated paddy fields without having to pay taxes. They mastered the hybridisation of wet-rice species. This blooming food production from its vast hinterland gave Dhaka the benefit of food security. It was the Mughals' wish to secure Dhaka and its waterways from Arakanese and Portuguese pirates by building nine river forts. They also dug a ditch cutting through Dhaka's urban fabric to connect the River Buriganga and create a short cut to the River Lakhya from the navy base at Chandnighat. Ten bridges over this artificial ring canal (today's English Road) gave the city connections with the surrounding territory. The central core of Dhaka was now protected by a system of defences that included nine river forts in districts immediately to its south.

During his governorship from 1660 to 1663 Mir Jumla built two road networks and two bridges. Tongi Bridge connected Dhaka with the north-west; this road was called 'the Mymensingh road'. Pagla Bridge was part of a famous trunk road connecting Dhaka with important trade centres in the south-east, such as Sonargoan and Bikrampur. Finally, Lalbag Fort was intended to be a lavish palace fort and administrative centre but was never completed. Shaista Khan, uncle of the Mughal emperor Aurangzeb, presided over the most prosperous era (1664–1688) in the history of Dhaka. The city at this point was 19 kilometres long and 12 kilometres wide with a population of one million, including 80,000 skilled weavers of silk and muslin. Shaista Khan even developed his own style in architecture, known as 'the Shaista Khani style'. He organised the successful Chittagong expedition in 1666. His Assam expedition in 1671, however, failed decisively. A natural harbour bounded by the River Bouriganga and Dholai Khal, Banglabazar-Sutrapur was a supportive trade outpost for the nearby medieval capital of Sonargaon. Betel leaf, the royal business, was subject to a Mughal monopoly; it was harvested in Bajuha (Rajshahi), the largest revenue-generating region in Mughal Bengal. The product was collected through Dhaka's 'Sanchi paan Dariba' port. Elephants were hunted in the jungles of Sylhet and Kachar Mohal and sent to the imperial capital, Delhi. Together, elephants and the betel leaf give birth to new forms of Dhaka craftsmanship: the making of carved-ivory and brass or metal *paandani* (leaf-holders) and *haman dista* (pestles and mortars). Dhaka's shop

Prof. Q.A. Mowla, BIP publication, 2012

Dhaka City Across the Buriganga River, Frederick W. A. de Fabek, 1861

houses, the traditional form of urban development in the city from the pre-Mughal period to the present day, are another clue to the importance of the craft industry here, pointing to at least 1000 years of craft and trade heritage. Dhaka gained prosperity and uninterrupted commercial importance due to its position on the maritime Silk Road connecting south-east Asia, the Coromandel coast, the Persian Gulf, and Europe for trade in a great variety of commodities, including muslin, earthenware pottery, miniature arts, and conch-shell craftwork, as well as agricultural products. When Europeans started to arrive, they found this city a playground for oriental romance. The Portuguese traveller Tome Pires, who was in India around 1510, wrote that the people of Bengal were successful wholesalers and that large numbers of Persians, Turks, Arabs, and Armenian merchants lived here for the profitable clothing and salt trade. The neighbourhood of Narinda was, like Dabekka in Narayanganj and Sen Parbata in Dhaka, an ancient area of high land; this settlement was famous as the place where the best 'muslin washers' took advantage of the perfect water and environment of the Dholai Canal (the name itself means 'washing' in Bangla). The Italian traveller Manucci, who came to Dhaka in 1663, described the city as neither strong nor large. Nevertheless, Dhaka came to be known as 'the Venice of the East'. Its large population lived mainly in houses of baked earth. Typical early houses in Tantibazar were depicted as thatched huts in a picture by the British collector, explorer, and painter Sir Charles D'Oyly titled 'Indian Weaver of Dacca'. D'Oyly lived in Dhaka from 1808 to 1817. Following the British conquest in 1757, however, Dhaka started to decline as Kolkata, on the contrary, prospered, propelled by its status as the capital of British India. Visiting Dhaka in 1765, James Rennel, the English surveyor and father of oceanography, wrote that East Bengal was naturally the most convenient location for trade with any country in the world. Dhaka's central position and history as an urban settlement since ancient times enabled it to command a large number of major water routes. Early records kept by the East India Company describe Dhaka in 1786 as a city with boundaries determined by aquatic routes: Buriganga in south, Tongi in the north, Mirpur in the west, and Postogola in the east. The British subsequently converted the Old Afghan fort to the city's central prison in 1788 and in 1789 added barracks to Lalbagh Fort.

In 1825 a district magistrate called Charles Dawes cleared the district of Ramna. The Temple of Joy Kali and

A Bengal Atlas: Mapping Bengal: earliest map of Dhaka

Map prepared by James Rennel in 1776, showing development on the River Buriganga

Shahbaz Khan Mosque were two monuments that fortunately survived. Until the Sepoy mutiny of 1857, Dhaka's historical core consisted of lower-class residential quarters, whereas the upper classes and Europeans settled in the upper part of what is today Bahadur Shah Park. The Chawkbazar, initially a Mughal public square, was gradually transformed from a retail to a wholesale centre. To serve the British bureaucrats, new retail functions were extended northwards along Nawabpur Road and Islampur Road. In 1864 the same Charles Dawes cleared jungle northeast of Nawabpur (today's Shiddheswari) to create space for a cantonment (Purana Palton). The commissioner Charles Buckland built a dyke (Buckland Bund) on the riverbank. This was regarded as somewhere where local and foreign elites, landlords and businessmen, could show off their status in architectural forms. The area lying to the north of Mir Jumla's Gate (today the area occupied by Dhaka University) was, on the other hand, very sparsely populated. At this time the British consolidated their power and established a settlement along a single road called 'Johnson Road'. This area, known as 'the Civic Line', was closer to the river and the jute factory at Postagola. It included a court building, a magistrate's office, and a collector's office. Despite this, the city's population continued to decline, reaching its lowest ebb, 51,636, in 1867. When the Dhaka municipality was formed to convert the old town into a business hub in 1872, its population started to rise again. A rail line and an iron bridge connected Dhaka with Narayanganj. The station at Fulbaria (today's Nagar Vaban) opened in 1885. The residential area for civil servants providing local clerks to support the Civic Line was designed as a township by the collector Frederick Wyer and is today known as 'Wari' in his honour. Middle class settlements sprang up all around, including in areas such as Gandaria, Tikatuli, Swamibag, and Purana Paltan.

The railway separated the European civil station (Ramna) and the Civic Line from the city's indigenous settlements. The partition of Bengal in 1905 allowed Ramna Race Course to become the focus of the Civic Station. As capital of East Bengal, Dhaka had a cityscape shaped by massive civic structures such as Curzon Hall, the old High Court building, and the secretariat (now DMC Hospital and Medical College). The dissolution of the regime eventually facilitated the establishment of Dhaka University in Ramna in 1921.

Sir Patrick Geddes, a botanist who spent the period from 1915 to 1919 travelling through 50 Indian cities, was appointed in

Chawkbazar, 1885

Jute factory, Postagola

Curzon Hall, University of Dhaka, 1908

Nawabpur Road with mixed-use buildings, 1875

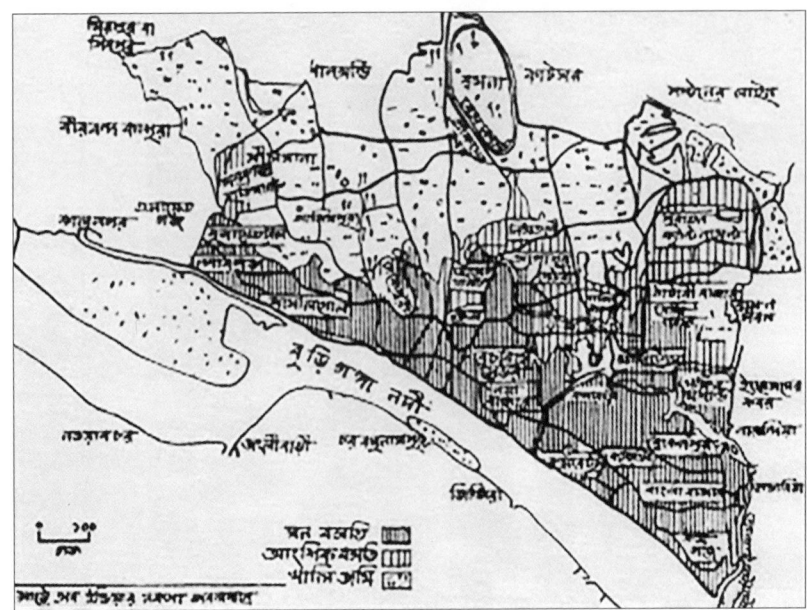

Map of Dhaka, *Survey of India*, 1850

1917 to design a master plan for Dhaka as a provincial capital following the partition of East Bengal in 1905. Well known for his theory of conurbations, Geddes looked to Dhaka's own morphology and natural garden belt to shape the city. Dhaka is thus one of the earliest examples of the garden city concept outside Europe. Geddes described his planning initiatives as the creation of 'a modern city' in the northern outskirts of the historical Mughal core. On the one hand, on the opposite bank of the River Buriganga, the palaces of nawabs in the district of Shahbag and the bungalows and recreational spaces in green Raman reflected the garden-city movement. On the other, business and administrative functions replaced the residential emphasis of the riverfront with a mixed-used pattern from the 1930s forwards. Small bazaars sprang up spontaneously, facing the streets in residential neighbourhoods. This is why Dhaka is called 'a city of 52 markets on 53 lanes'.

In a nutshell, Dhaka is a city of unique historical layers. Banglabazar developed in the Hindu Sena dynasty period from the tenth to the twelfth centuries.

Banglapedia

Palace of the Nawabs, Shahbag, 1890

Girdakilla was the Pathan central core from the thirteenth century forwards. Binot Bibi Mosque was a pre-Mughal centre from the thirteenth century. The west part of Lalbagh Fort was the Mughals' administrative centre from the seventeenth century forwards. Eastern expansion during British rule included industrialisation from the eighteenth century forwards. An English cotton factory was shown on a map of this area in 1735. The factory was probably built to compete with or even kill traditional crafts; the cruelty of European traders towards indigo producers is still evident in Bengal as a whole. This history has resulted in a multiplicity of different demographic groupings, found from medieval times around the historical cores in mosaics of ethnicities, such as Hindus, Pathans, Persians, Turks, Arabs, and, lastly, Mughals. Further marks on the city's fabric were left by the Armenians (the jute business in 1714 at Tejgaon), the Greeks (a church built in 1821 in the area of the TSC), the Portuguese (the Augustinian missionary church built at Narinda in 1628), the French (a factory built in 1740 at Islampur), the Dutch (a factory at Wari in 1660), the British (a factory built at Tejgaon in 1650), and, finally, migrating North Indian Muslims (following the partition of British India in 1947).

Interestingly, Dhaka is the only city in the world which has been awarded the status of capital city five times. It was named 'Jahangirnagar' and established as capital when the Mughals conquered Bengal in 1609. It was honoured as capital of the Eastern District in 1887. In 1905 it again became capital – this time of the newly formed province of East Bengal and Assam, following the partition of Bengal. It was declared legislative capital of East Pakistan in 1962. And finally, after Bangladesh gained its independence, it was declared capital under Article No. 5 of the republic's constitution, adopted in 1972. Yes, Dhaka is the most fascinating city in the eastern part of the Indian subcontinent, an important playground and cradle that witnessed the first British conquest in India and then the creation of Pakistan. Notwithstanding its civic and infrastructure problems, Dhaka is still the city that we love most. We will adore it forever!

Liberation war e-archive Flickr

The Pakistan Army surrendered on 16 December 1971 – a moment that has never been forgotten in Bangladeshi politics and culture.

Philipp Meuser

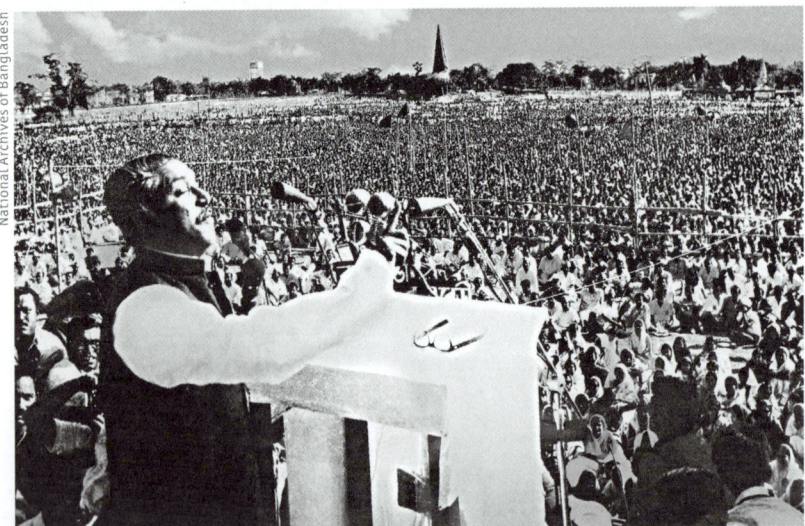

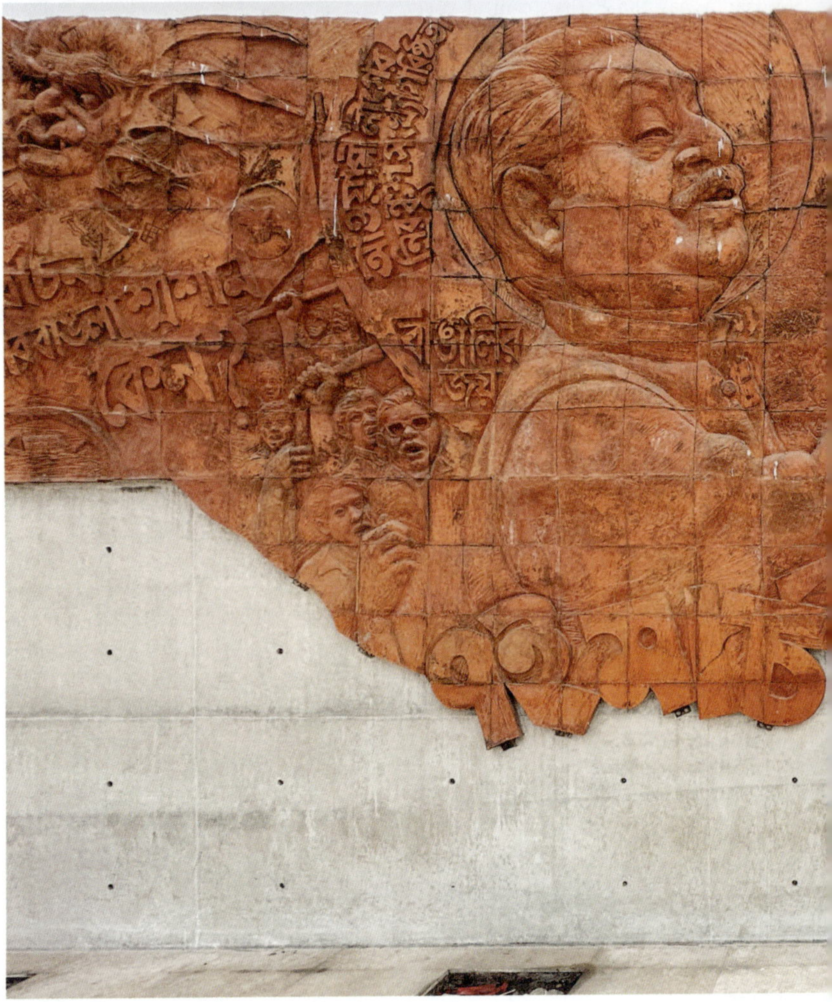

National Archives of Bangladesh

On the spot where the Pakistan Army surrendered, the Racecourse Field, Sheikh Mujibur Rahman gave his historical speech on 7 March 1971. Now an iconic motif in the history of Bangladesh, this picture has been mounted as a ceramic mural in Independence Park. The same applies to the scene of the Pakistan Army's surrender (see right).

A rare Gupta-era piece of metalwork from the 6th century AD: an architect's plummet, found in the Surma River (Sylhet region). Made of iron coated with bronze, the plummet is 11 inches high.

Buildings and Architects in Bangladesh

Sayed Ahmed

According to Indo-mythology, when the male River Brahmmaputra, which originates in China, and the holy Ganges, a female river which has its source in the Himalayas in north India, met at an auspicious spot, they gave birth to a bountiful offspring: the largest and most fertile delta in this world, Bengal. The *Mahābhārata*, the great Indian epic, talks of a forest land in the south – which may be Sundarbans, the largest mangrove forest in the world today – as home to a prolific port civilisation whose people are skilled in herbal medicine, but until recently no trace had been found. An excavation in 2018 at sites throughout Sundarbans turned up relics dating to 1200 years ago. Other important antiquities are the megalithic pillars (25 menhirs and 32 dolmens) erected by Khasia tribes in Jainta Hills in the Sylhet district of Bengal in the Iron Age (1500 BC–100 AD). The Western world first noticed our potential wealth, however, in the second century BC. The Macedonian conqueror Alexander the Great had to call off his campaign when confronted with 4000 war elephants belonging to the Nanda Dynasty, as recounted by Ptolemy in his *Geography*. Ptolemy describes this state as 'Gangaridai', a very prosperous kingdom with a trained elephant cavalry. Archaeologists identify this realm with today's Wari Bateshwar in the Narshingdi district of mid-Bangladesh; they think this well-developed civilisation existed here at least 2500 years ago. In fact, this sunken fort city from the Gupta period was known to other Indian kingdoms by the name of 'Sounagoura'. Pundranagar, another citadel dating to the third century BC, was an important urban centre in the Mauryan Empire and was inhabited until the sixteenth century. Thus, as an indispensable part of the broader ancient Indian civilisation stretching across the Ganges delta plain for more than 4000 years, this country is home to different architectural styles from various historical periods and subject to frequent political changes. This architectural history can roughly be divided into three segments. Here I would like to introduce an innovative 'three window' concept as a device with which to examine our architectural past. The first window still exists: an ever-changing parallel phenomenon, which varies depending upon topography, region, epoch, and ethnicity. Traces of this phenomenon were left by the early inhabitants of this region, such as the Vedda people from sixth century BC and the Austrics, who lived 5000 years ago, long before the Indo-Aryans arrived on the subcontinent. There can be no doubt that the early agricultural pastoralism of

Alexander the Great and the Wounded King Porus, Charles de Brun, 1673

Buddhist temple at Paharpur, 8th century

the Neolithic era, roughly from 8000 to 4000 BC, began with cattle domestication and rice cultivation on the scattered plains of the vast delta. The 13 proverbs of a little-known wise lady called 'Khona' (probably from the seventh century) tell us how the architecture of this agriculture-based society must have looked; her prescriptions are still followed in various rural parts of this country. My second window refers to the golden age of the Pala

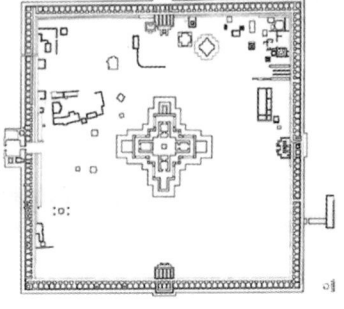

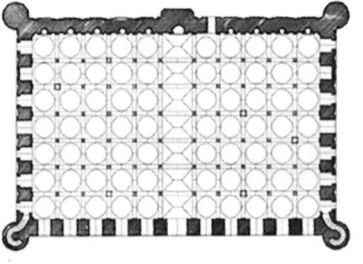

Dynasty, which reached its peak in the seventh century. Scholars believe that there were more than 50 Buddhist monasteries along the oblique course of the Ganges at this time. These institutions were so influential that they shaped the temples and monasteries of the Far East and Indo-China, possibly through trade and the exchange of knowledge along the maritime

Shat Gombuj Moshjid, 15th century

Kantaji Temple, Dinajpur, 1722

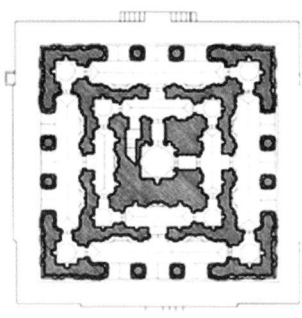

Silk Road. Ancient Bengal was at the centre of this trade route. The Bay of Bengal, the largest bay in the world, was its busiest hub. The best example of this architecture is the Buddhist university and citadel in Mahasthangarh in North Bengal. Dating to the third century BC, this is the largest such institution in Bangladesh and is now a UNESCO World Heritage site. Visiting Mahasthangarh in 638 AD, the Chinese traveller Hsuan Tsang found 3000 priests belonging to 20 different schools of Buddhist thought (*shanghrams*) as well as 100 Brahmin temples! The third window is more complicated and belongs to the Middle Ages, an era of confusion which started in the thirteenth century, when Turkish invaders advanced from the west and conquered Gaur in 1204. Islam might be Arabic, but Turco-Persian influences were predominant. The Middle Ages are regarded as a compromising era of 'Bengalisation' for this geographical area, but the same is true of the formation of Bengal's architecture, which has long been misunderstood. The architecture of this period includes all the medieval magnificent Hindu temples and Sultani mosques and their fusions of styles. This is a truly surprising story of how a 'weird' new Middle Eastern religion arrived and successfully adapted to the agriculture-based society, leading to the rapid spread of Islam. Jungles and marshland were cleared, and small mosques were built with local materials that were suitable to the climatic conditions. All this was made possible by the fact that these were tax-free lands with secure means of food production. The famous Moroccan traveller Ibn Battuta visited Bengal in 1346 and described such a scenario. These

Sir Patrick Geddes, (1854–1932)

A bungalow in Bandarban, 1860

A bungalow in Paksey, 1912

mosque-based settlements later acted as hubs for Sufi education, a maritime business centre for trade in agricultural products, and administrative lynchpins. Together, they formed a network of mosque cities in eastern Bengal. Shaitgombuj Mosque, a UNESCO World Heritage site in Bagerhat in the Sundarbans mangrove region, is the perfect example of such a mosque. Surprisingly perhaps, Muslim rulers patronised local culture and literature. The revival of the making of terracotta plaques created an architectural vocabulary with and without figurative expression; this has a distinctive character which goes beyond its religious background and yet remains attached to daily life. The magnificent sixteenth-century Kantajew Temple in Dinajpur with lavish terracotta decoration depicting the march of the Muslim emperor in North Bengal is a fine example. Terracotta façades spread rapidly. Exchange with the pre-existing Hindu-Buddhist culture influenced architecture and gave this country a distinctive language of its own. The Mughals conquered Bengal in 1676 but only established a stronghold here 40 years later.

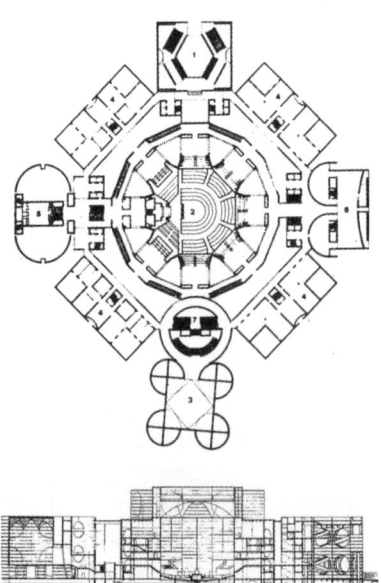

Construction workers, 1970s

Mymensing Agriculture University, designed by Paul Rudolph, 1961

Once Dhaka emerged as their capital, the Mughals attempted to introduce their own architecture. Stone is rare in Bengal, so façades of plaster attached to walls of brick were a useful deception to achieve the fashionable North Indian look. The Mughals achieved marvellous feats of engineering in construction of fortifications and roads. After 1617, political turmoil led to a decline in Bengal; the Mughals started to control the revenue through their representatives, called 'nawabs'. British colonisation began in the wealthiest part of the subcontinent, Bengal. The next two centuries of British colonial exploitation created a 'Dark Age' for our architectural culture. During the period of British rule from 23 June 1757 to 14 August 1947 European features were added and an architectural exchange took place between two contrasting cultures. The result was a bizarre amalgam: an exquisite, unrooted fantasy that was detached from its bold base. The Nobel laureate Rabindranath Tagore, who wrote Bangladesh's national anthem, criticised this 'confusion' and dreamed of a revolutionary nationalist architecture and eco-friendly planning in his

Lecture by Loius I. Kahn (1901–1974) at EPUET (today BUET)

University campus in Comilla, Division Chittagong, Doxiadis Associates, 1959

Richard Neutra (1892–1970)

Biswabharati University complex in West Bengal (India today). Some early and late colonial buildings are shown in this book to demonstrate the style and historic importance of this particular period. Perhaps the only positive result was a new type of building that was developed in this region by the British rulers in response to security needs: the 'bungalow.' This type subsequently spread all over the world, especially in the US during World War II. The bungalow offers protection and comfort, permeability, and a straightforward relation with one's surroundings; it is perfect pavilion architecture.

A first and a second independence

From 1947 to 1971, following the partition of British India along religious lines, Bangladesh was the east part of Pakistan. For these 23 years architects employed cheap Islamic clichés or the Mughal Revival style, echoing the manifesto of the emphatically military government of Pakistan. The result was the development of 'eclecticism' in our architecture. The New Market, Azimpur Housing Estate, and Rajarbagh Police barracks, designed by the British architect Edward Hicks, lacked respect for the new nation's context. Ronald McConnel, the chief architect of the Pakistan government, designed Holy Family Hospital, Vikarunnesa Girls School, and the nine-storey Secretariat Building; these were functional structures but not architecture. The most popular non-Bengali architect was Abdulhusein Thariani, one of the first formally trained architects in Pakistan. Thariani created a number of blots on the cityscape, including DIT, (RAJUK today) Baitul Mokarram National Mosque (1960–65), Shilpakala Academy (1963), the New High Court buildings, Government House, and Victoria Park Memorial. His Hotel Intercontinental, however, may be regarded as an example of efficient planning and neatly detailed Islamic

Constantinos Apostolos Doxiadis in his Athens studio (1913–1975)

design. In 1960 Berger Engineers, an architecture firm comprised of groups of foreign nationals, introduced a new dimension into our architecture. Berger Engineers designed a number of perfectly acceptable buildings in Dhaka. Specifically, the US architect Robert Boughey designed the Gymnasium Building, the Civil Engineering building, three hostels and a pavilion on the BUET campus (1963–67), Brothers' Hostel at Notre Dame College (1963), St. Joseph's School, and the Sisters' Hostel at Holy Family Hospital. His best work was Kamalapur Railway Station. Rolf Kaiser, though not an architect, designed Motijheel Co-operative Bank (1962–63) and the Insurance Building (1963–67). And Stanley Dukes, a British architect, designed studios for the Film Development Corporation (1962–65). All these projects may be described as 'ephemeral events' exemplifying respectable architectural practice. It was only in the late 1960s that architects started making their presence felt; this was the high tide of Modernism, following the establishment of the first technical university (today's BUET) in Dhaka in 1962. Foreign architects, such as Louis I. Kahn, Paul Rudolph, Stanley Tigermann, Constantinos Doxiadis, and Richard Neutra, started working in Bangladesh; some also taught here. This was a period when we were in quest of our own identity. A key figure was Muzharul Islam (1923–2012), father of modern architecture in Bangladesh. As a close companion of Bangabandhu Sheikh Mujibur Rahman, the founding father of today's Bangladesh, Muzharul Islam understood very well that as possessor of one of the richest cultures on the planet, Bangladesh should exploit this architectural heritage in its approach to Modernism. He looked to the country's luxuriant green horizon with watery plains prone to flash floods reflecting the blue skies. He found another texture too: the burnt brown of brick as an emblem of archaeological pride. The bricks in his projects are small, and the buildings themselves are likewise of no great size. They are rhythmically juxtaposed with the surrounding landscape, are climate-responsive, and are contextually deeply rooted in Bangladeshi culture. Having adopted and adapted all this, Muzharul Islam helped create a masterpiece, the Parliament Building, following in the footsteps of Louis Kahn, his teacher. Kahn's 'idiosyncratic approach' properly emphasised the horizontality of our culture and landscape. In this context it is worth recalling the famous architecture critic Kenneth Frampton, who introduced the idea of 'six critical points of resistance', so vital for

Muzharul Islam (1925–2012) with his followers, the Chetona Study Group

understanding Regional Modernism today. Frampton's six points are: site, programme, topography, climate, culture, and context. The Indian subcontinent is, I think, the perfect example of such an 'additive' inheritance. This regional school of thought includes masters such as Muzharul Islam from Bangladesh, Indian architects such as Charles Correa and V.B. Doshi (Pritzker Prize winner in 2018), and the Sri Lankan architect Geoffrey Bawa. The benchmark they have created is clearly more than perfection; it is also a guideline to show us which direction we should take in practising architecture in this part of the world – and perhaps elsewhere in the contemporary world as well. As an architect, Islam was rationalist and set out to create strictly geometrical architecture in his early works. This was probably a result of the inevitable influence exerted on him by Le Corbusier and Alvar Aalto. In the middle of his career, on returning from Yale University, he started exploring

Fazlur R. Khan contributed to the Hajj terminal at Jeddah International Airport, 1980

The iconic staircase at Dhaka University's Fine Arts Institute, Muzharul Islam, 1955

materiality. The result was cuboid volumes varying in formal appearance in accordance with the laws of subtraction and addition. Islam's later works, however, prioritised inlaid topographical patterns connected with climate and the building's programme. Bangladesh's independence made it possible for him to develop a layout based on a diagonal grid and dynamic formal expressions. This was a joyous creation of regional and substantial architecture. For his valuable contribution to

Bangladeshi culture, in 1999 Muzharul Islam was awarded the Independence Award, our country's highest civilian award. Another US-based structural engineer, Fazlur Rahman Khan (an honorary architect today), is a perfect example of professional success and working abroad. Known as 'the Einstein of structural engineering', Khan was the inventor of the tubular structural system, which enabled the construction of taller and lighter skyscrapers and is the system still in use today. His Sears Tower (today: Willis Tower) in Chicago was the tallest building in the world from 1973 to 1998. He also bagged the Aga Khan Award for designing the Hajj terminal of King Abdul-Aziz International Airport in Jeddah and the AIA award for his distinguished achievement as 'father of tubular design'; both marks of recognition came in 1983.

Import and export of architecture

Enriched by new ideas from abroad, Bangladesh's architecture has recently come to attention on various international stages and through monographs published by international publishers. The German architect Anna Heringer (with Eike Roswag-Klinge) has found her 'soul base' here and taken our vernacular architecture

Fazlur Rahman Khan (1929–1982)

Philipp Meuser

Marina Tabassum (born in 1968) in her Dhaka studio

to the next level with her use of mud, clay, and bamboo in the service of principles of sustainability. She was awarded the Aga Khan Award for her METI school project in 2007 and the Global Award for Sustainable Architecture in 2011. Eight other architects have won Aga Khan awards to date: Marina Tabassum (for Baitur Rauf Jame Mosque in 2016), Kashef Mahboob Chowdhury (for the Friendship Centre in 2016), Saiful Haque (for his Arcadia Education Project in 2019), Khondaker Hasibul Kabir, Suhailey Farzana (for Urban River Spaces in 2022), Rizvi Hassan, Khwaja Fatmi, and Saad Ben Mostafa (for Refugee Community Space in 2022). Marina Tabassum was recognised as one of the top 50 thinkers in the world by the British magazine *Prospect* in 2020; her mosque was selected as one of the 25 most influential buildings to have been erected after 1945. Recently, Kashef Mahboob

Right:
German architect Anna Heringer (centre) with women from the METI school in Rudrapur, Dinajpur. Architects: Anna Heringer, Eike Roswag-Klinge, 2006

Fouzia Jahan Suma

Mohammad Foyez Ullah (born in 1967)

Philipp Meuser

1 Andreas Ruby et al. (ed.),
*Bengal Stream: The Vibrant Architecture
Scene of Bangladesh* (Basel, 2017)

2 Marina Tabassum,
Architecture, My Journey.
(Berlin, 2023)

3 Oscar Riera Ojeda (ed.),
*Foyez Ullah: Dhaka's Tropical Expressive
Architecture (*Hong Kong, 2022)

4 *Meditations in Entropy.
The Work of Kashef Chowdhury /
URBANA in Bangladesh* (Zurich, 2023)

Chowdhury won the prestigious RIBA International Prize (2021). Moreover, Mohammad Foyez Ullah has won recognition as the principal of Volumezero Ltd., the largest architecture firm in the country. With 300 employees this firm has dramatically increased the architectural quality of investor-driven real estate development in Dhaka and its environs.

At this point, I could easily have introduced a fourth window. But I am afraid of unnecessarily constraining my representation of Bangladesh's diverse architecture, which is based on patriotism and guidance as well as the ideals of Muzharul Islam and his disciples. Or possibly this is not the right moment to introduce a fourth window; the next century will, I hope, see the formation of an architecture with a distinctive character in Bangladesh. The historical journey from citadels in Pundravardhana in the Buddhist era to the Modernist master plan for Sher-e-Bangla Nagar makes for an impressive motto but conceals great diversity in terms of creativity. Bangladesh's architecture is, I have to admit, still evolving as it strives to create a distinct language of its own. Propelled by our glorious architectural past, we must press on towards our dream of a 'Golden Bengal' (the aspiration sung in our national anthem). This book is an attempt to look back at our past, evaluate our present, and inspire our future. It adds another piece to the vibrant mosaic of architecture publishing in Bangladesh.

Rafiq Azam (born in 1963)

Kashef M. Chowdhury (born in 1970)

Binat Bibi Mosque

6 Narinda Road/
Shorat Gupta Road
1454

001 C

This is the earliest surviving mosque from ancient Dhaka. Surprisingly, its land and money were dedicated to a woman named Bakht Binat, the daughter of an Arabian merchant called Marhamat or Arkan Ali from the Persian Gulf coast or Yemen who settled here for business. Both father and daughter have their final resting places beside this mosque. A pre-Mughal basalt stone inscription found here praises the independent Sultan Nasiruddin Mahmud Shah (1435–1459). The mosque is a square praying chamber measuring 3.7 metres on each side. Its brickwork is one metre thick. Its single hemispherical dome is supported by arched squinches. Except on the west elevation, there are three arched entrances in the middle of each façade. The curved parapets and cornices, octagonal corner turrets, and simple arches are proof of Turkish-Afghan influence. There are niches in every wall of the mosque. Built to serve nearby markets, it is evidence that Dhaka was at this time already an important business centre in the Islamic world, long before the arrival of the Mughals and at least 200 years before it acquired the status of capital city. The mosque's plaster exterior is ornately decorated with white-coloured broken ceramics in the technique known as *chini tikri* (pieces of china). The later addition of a 21-metre-high new minaret and three storeys to the historical built form have endangered the mosque's structural and aesthetic stability.

Avijit Barman (all pictures)

1

Kazi Karar Naier (all pictures)

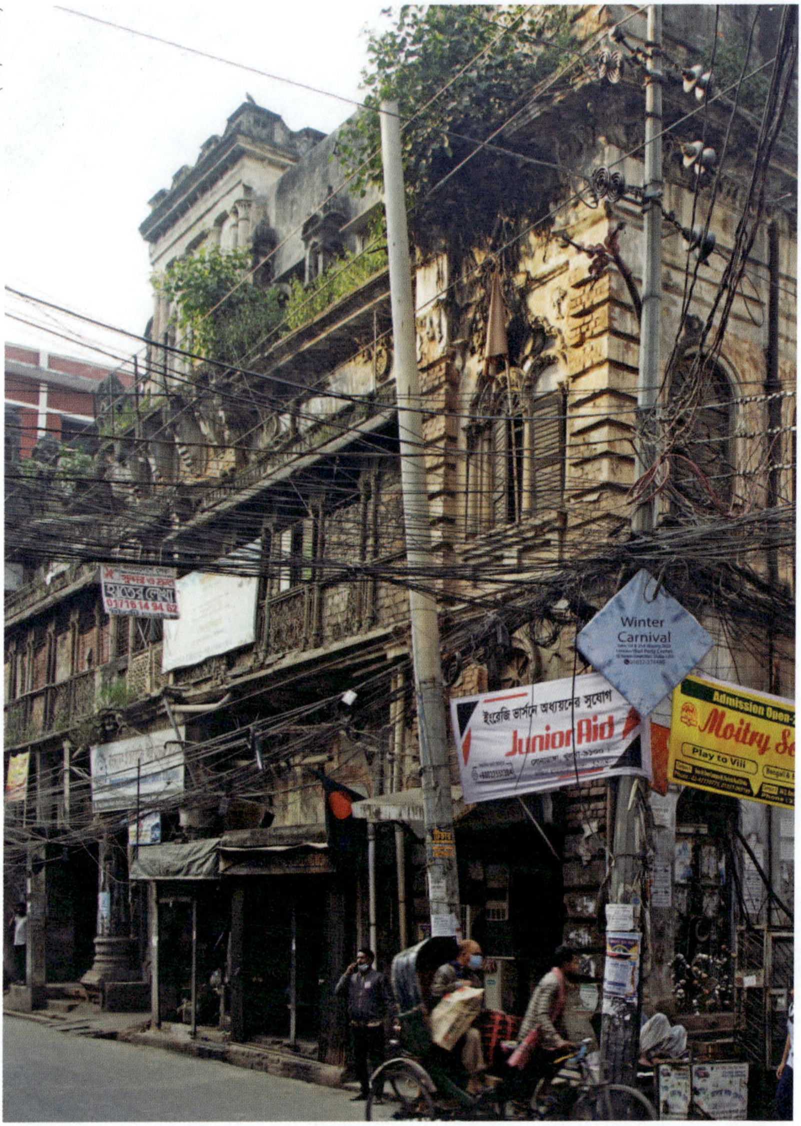

Shankhanidhi Nauch Ghar 002 C

38 Tipu Sultan Road, Wari

1926

At the beginning of the twentieth century three brothers from Dhaka were made immensely wealthy by their diverse business, enabling them to become *shankhanidhis* (conch bearers) as opposed to mere *boniks* (merchants). One of the brothers was Lalmohan Saha, who built this house for entertaining in 1921. On the east side of the building was a ballroom 15.24 metres wide with 7.62-metre ceilings, decorated in the manner of a Hindu temple. The ceiling had wooden decoration, and the walls were colourfully embellished. The house has a 1.52-high plinth oriented towards the south. This is a symmetrical building with two storeys and octagonal towers at either end. There are domes over the towers. The veranda is accessed via a 6.10-metre-wide platform. The façade is fronted by four slender Corinthian columns. The bay windows are formed by three multi-pointed arches, supported by four triangular and ornamented buttresses beneath. The house has five rooms of different shapes and sizes, of approximately 42 square metres each. In 1991 part of the ballroom was demolished to make space for a school.

Kazi Karar Naier (all pictures)

Sutrapur Jamindarbari/Palace 003 C
Reboti Mohan Das Road/
Keshob Benarjee Road,
Sutrapur
1905

This palace was built and owned by the head of Dhaka municipality, Sattendra Kumar Das. In 1947 the partition of India forced Das and his family to leave Dhaka and set sail for Kolkata. The palace is now housing for members of the fire service and the civil defence. It consists of two distinct buildings of the same height linked by a structure in the middle. The south wing is the older one. The north was erected as an exact copy of the south wing. The building has a total footprint of 4047 square metres. The four columns in the Corinthian order in the middle section are 15.43 metres high. On both façades the fenestration consists of semicircular lintels adorned with floral decoration and containing circles above double arches – a treatment which reflects Renaissance influences. In the middle is a 4.65-square-metre open courtyard surrounded on all sides by rooms. The building contains a total of 35 rooms of various sizes. The open ends of the two wings used to stand on the bank of the Dholai Canal, which has since been filled in. The parapets on the roof have small punched apertures by way of ornamentation.

Kazi Karar Naier (all pictures)

Baldha Garden

004 C

Narinda Road, Wari
1909

Narendra Narayan Roy Chowdhury, the landlord of the Baldha estate (today: Gazipur), who was also a naturalist, philanthropist, and famous poet, established this garden in 1909 following the partition of Bengal. It is one of the oldest and most historic privately owned botanical gardens in Bangladesh. Under the terms of Chowdhury's will, all expenditure required to maintain the museum and garden is to come from the revenue from his estate. The collection of plants here continued to increase until his death in 1943. The garden was laid out over 12,700 square metres of land in the most aristocratic part of Dhaka's Wari district.

Narendra Chowdhury invited famous curators from England. Nearly 800 different species of 15,000 native and exotic plants from 50 other countries of the world are cultivated here. Some are exceptionally rare. There are seven categories of flora: trees, aquatic plants, cacti, conservatory plants, roses, rockery and wall creepers, orchids, and miscellaneous. One example of the latter category is the so-called 'century plant', which blooms once in 100 years. Other notable attractions are: the *Adansonia digitata* tree, which was used to mummify the corpses of Egyptian pharaohs, and large wild nuts the size of tennis balls. Baldha Garden is currently a branch of the National Botanical Garden and has been part of the Department of Forestry since 1962. Its layout is based on the English garden. There are two beautifully named parts with walkways crisscrossing the nurseries in between them. The larger unit is named after the Greek goddess of nature or fertility, Cybele. This rectilinear piece of land has an obliquely cut north corner and is 136 metres long and 76 metres wide. It is home to a famous sundial, which gives the precise time, but only on sunny days. The collection of roses in this section is unique in the subcontinent. There is also a rest-house-cum-amphitheatre, called 'Joy House', beside a pond named 'Shankhanidi'. During his stay at the Joy House in 1926 the poet and Nobel Prize winner Rabindranath Tagore wrote a poem dedicated to the Japanese camelia flower. The second part of the garden is smaller – 100 metres long and 45 metres wide – and is named 'Psyche' (soul). This part is known for its aquatic plants and contains an enormous collection of water lilies, Bangladesh's national flower (*Nymphea pubescens*) in a pond known as 'Shapla House'. The Baldha Museum, a long rectangular structure comprising four halls, was established in 1925. All its collections have unfortunately been removed for display at the Bangladesh National Museum at Shahbag. After the country's Liberation War, two new greenhouses were added to display orchids, aroids, and conservatory plants all year round, and more modern civil amenities were added throughout the complex.

Kazi Karar Naier (all pictures)

Narinda Christian Cemetery
Narinda Road, Wari
1800

005 C

This cemetery was formally consecrated in 1828 to meet the burial needs of Europeans living in Dhaka. After the independence movement failed in 1858, however, the number of English settlers increased greatly. Most of the tombs here accordingly belong to clerks of the East India Company and their relatives. The oldest grave is of a British administrator of Kolkata, Reverend Joseph Paget, who died at the age of 26 during an official visit in 1721. Some other notable interments include the wealthy merchant and landlord Nicholas Pogose (buried here in 1876), who also established the famous Pogose School in old Dhaka, and Jane Rennell, a daughter of the father of oceanography and surveyor general of Bengal, James Rennell. She probably died sometime after 1773. Interestingly, Wilhelm Kerkmann and Wongsi Quan, a Dutchman and a Chinaman, were buried here in the same grave. The daredevil hot air balloon rider Jeanette Van Tessell is also buried here; she was American. The cemetery's original pattern of paths has faded, but there are still traces of the intersecting network with spaces for tombs in between. There are clusters of topsy-turvy graves falling over one another on the same spot of ground, making it difficult to distinguish individual tombstones. Various types of graves may be observed. Some are plain tombs with their tombstones laid flat on the ground. Others have a white Moorish archway with Ionic columns and a Gothic crypt. There are also pyramidal and diagonally progressive tombs. The latter are a combination of the western obelisk with Indian urns on top of a rectangular base. Similar graves are to be found in the all-European graveyards in Kolkata. The most attractive grave, however, is that of Colombo Saheb – a combination of three tombs which is a protected monument of archaeological interest. It has an octagonal base, Doric and Ionic columns on its eight edges, and fenestrations that reveal Mughal influences. Other tombs in the cemetery have a square base with sunken doorways in the middle of the four surfaces with engravings of human faces in relief. Sculptures of deities standing on the roofs of the tombs are common. Notable ornamentation includes carved daffodils, local flowers crafted

in geometric mosaic, and Renaissance-style worked stone. The painted mouth of a Hindu goddess and a Roman archway with an unusual V-shaped keystone indicate the transitional character of the colonial era. Although this cemetery is a showcase for the city's cosmopolitan history, all its graves have suffered vandalism; many are in a state of decay, and some have collapsed.

1

Rose Garden
Kamini Mohan Das Lane
1931

006 C

This mansion was built by the wealthy merchant Hrishikesh Das in 1931, following an insult. One day Hrishikesh Das was refused admission by Narendra Narayan Roy Chowdhury to an elite party at the Baldha Garden on grounds of inferiority of caste. This ignited in Das the determination to upstage Chowdhury: he built a palace with a beautiful lake and a vast rose garden with marble statues, a residence unparalleled in Dhaka. Today the eponymous rose garden no longer exists. Hrishikesh Das' life of luxury ended in bankruptcy just five years after he built his mansion; in 1936 he sold it to the owner of a publishing house, Moulavi Kazi Abdur Rashid, who renamed it 'Rashid Manzil'. In the 1940s politicians used to gather here for discussions and meetings. Kazi Muhammad Bashir was elected chairman of the Dhaka City Corporation from 1953 to 1958. As a result, the country's most powerful political party, Awami League, was formed here on 23 June 1949. Later, this party guided Bangladesh to liberation in 1971. In the 1960s the mansion was rented out to Bengal Studio and Motion Pictures Ltd,

1

a movies company; it turned the building into a hot spot for Pakistan's film industry. In 1966 Kazi Muhammad's brother Kazi Humayun Bashir purchased the house and rented it out for weddings and functions as a kind of community centre. The complex as a whole occupies an area of 25,438 square metres. Originally, there was a rose garden with rare species of roses, so fine that the mansion itself was known by this name. The building has a symmetrical plan with ten 10.36-metre-high Corinthian columns on its façade. Its architectural style is a blend of European Renaissance and Bengali architecture. The ground floor has a central hall; just above

it, there is a ballroom on the second floor. Around these two halls, three living rooms are arranged on each floor. There are five cantilevered verandas – three at the front of the house and two at the sides. The east entrance has a triple-arched porch leading to the grand staircase. There are two pediments at the tops of the south and north sides; in the middle of the building an ornamented tower draws the gaze. The gorgeous windows are decorated with complex geometrical patterns, including wooden fringes depicting various vegetation and contours of animals and coloured iron frames containing colourful Belgian glass. The ballroom has a ceiling with a greenish mirror with a floral pattern. An intricate spiral staircase connects the ballroom with the roof. The cascades, high crystal chandeliers, and luscious landscape with a fountain at the front of the building create a regal appearance. The building is almost 14 metres high and has a footprint of 650 square metres. Its façade is a pinkish white colour. The Rose Garden was listed as a national monument on 21 December 1989. The heirs of the Kazi family were awarded the rights to the building by the High Court in 1993 – making this the only private property in Bangladesh to have national heritage status. On 9 August 2018, the government acquired the Rose Garden and turned it into a museum.

Banga Bhaban, Presidential Palace

Dilkusha Presidential Complex
1905

007 C

This area was a spot used for meditation by the Sufi preacher Shahjalal Dokhini. A hillock from that time remains inside the palace complex to this day. In the 1660s this site contained the residence of Mir Mukim, a supervisory official appointed by the governor, Mir Jumla. A wealthy Armenian rich merchant, Manuk, bought the land and erected a garden house beside a vast body of water called 'Motijheel'. The house was subsequently purchased by Nawab Abdul Gani, who named it 'Dilkusha' (garden house). After Bengal was partitioned in 1905, the government of British India acquired a part of this house and used it as the residence of the governor general of East Bengal. It subsequently became the official residence of the governor appointed by the Pakistan government. In the period leading up to 1964 it underwent substantial refurbishment. The property was twice devastated: a tornado struck it in 1961, and it was bombed by the Indian Air Force during the Liberation War of 1971. On 12 January 1972 it was declared the official residence of the president of Bangladesh and renamed 'Bangavaban', which means 'the edifice of Bengal'. The house has three floors and a total floor area of 6700 square metres. In the north-eastern corner is the president's private apartment with two grand suites and five lavish bedrooms. The ground floor contains the presidential office, the office of the Defence Ministry, the cabinet room, an enormous banqueting hall, the state dining hall, a mini auditorium, and a room for visitors. The building's main attraction is the Darbar Hall, where the cabinet ministers take their oath of office after each election. The second floor contains control rooms and a studio. The third floor has four suites for visiting heads of state. The north part of the property is a 190,202-square-metre park. The main gate includes a post office, a bank, a security post, a mosque, and barracks.

1

Ishtiaque Ahmed

Naira Al Husain

People's Insurance Bhavan

008 C

36 Dilkusha C/A,
Motijheel
M. K. Palash,
Mohammad Foyez Ullah
2005

This 89-metre-high building has 22 sto-reys and a total floor area of 20,000 square metres. It represents a formal expression of rational and responsive massing that reflects the shape of the site on which it stands. The architect took the outline of a circle and interlocked it with a rectilinear form. The building's two major achieve-ments are responsiveness to climatic con-siderations and efficient use of space. The design concentrates on energy saving and maximising natural light in the interior. Flexibility and comfort are also impor-tant concerns. The horizontal bands gir-dling the building become heavier, with deep recesses, on the side facing from east to west. This is where most of the ser-vices are located, minimising exposure to the western sun. The building's north side has a curtain of glazing, allowing diffused light to penetrate the workspaces. The fa-çade is an interplay of reflective glass and bands of unworked concrete. Its paral-lel bands suggest the basic form of a cyl-inder. Shading devices, such as rotated T profiles, have been installed with two dif-ferent orientations: vertically oriented on the west side and horizontally oriented on the cooler north and east façades. The double-height entrance hall wrapped in a frameless suspended-glass system makes for clear and easy interaction between in-side and outside. The ground floor con-tains public offices. To reduce pressure on the elevators, a separate staircase pro-vides access to the mezzanine level. This high-rise building won the Berger Award for Excellence in 2007. It has defined the language of contemporary high-rise building at the heart of the CTD (Central Trade District).

1

F. M. Faruque Abdullah Shawon, H. M. Fozla Rabby Apurbo (all pictures)

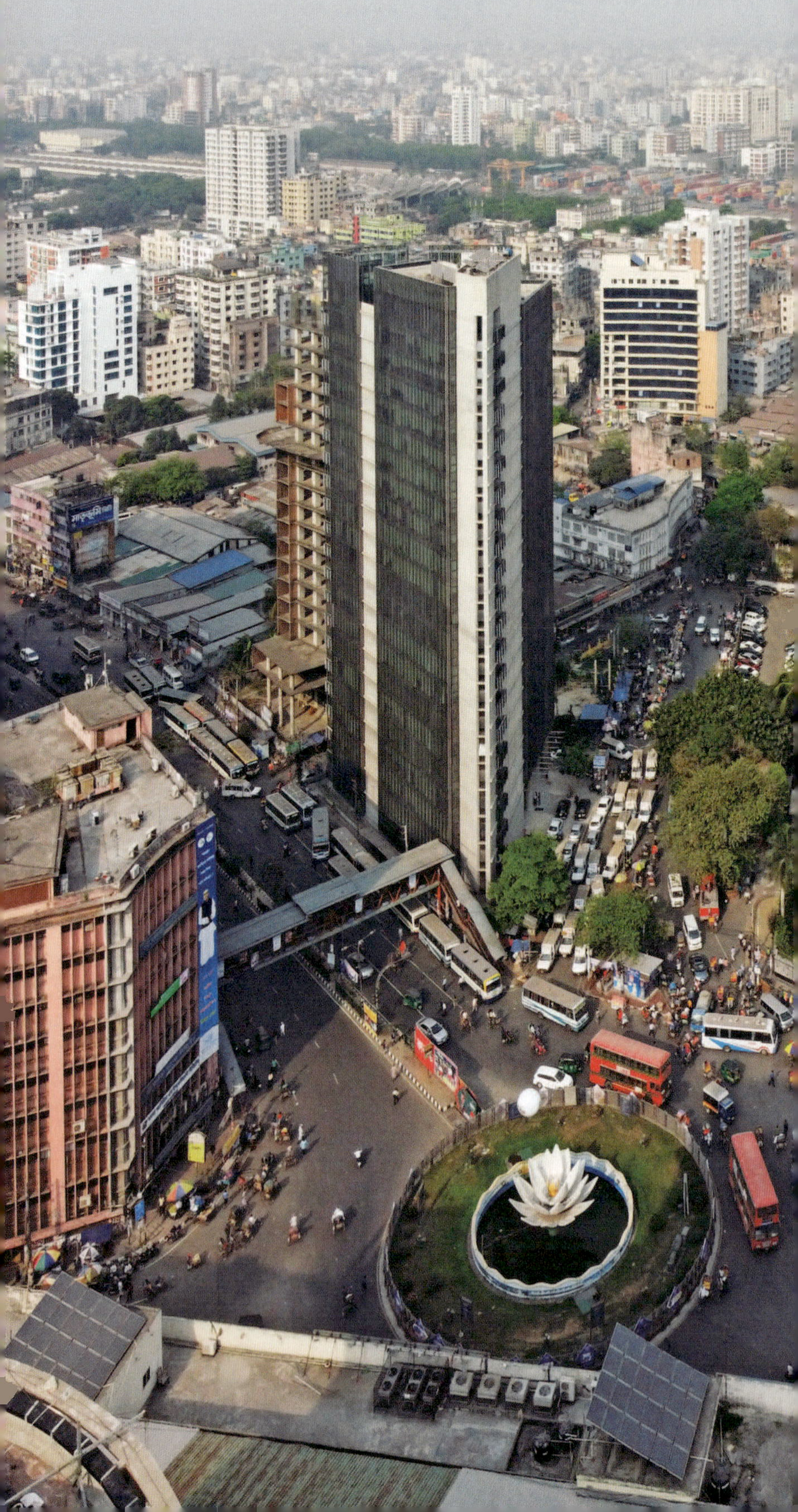

1

Kamalapur Railway Station

Outer Circular Road
Daniel Dunham,
Robert Boughey
1961

009 C

This building has a unique silhouette that symbolises the 'golden age of modernisation' during the 1960s as the dictator Ayub Khan strove to keep East Pakistan calm with architectural gimmicks. With eight 1.65-metre-high 'through' platforms, this is the largest railway station in the country. Prior to this, Dhaka's main station – from 1885 forwards – had been Fulbaria. Fulbaria Station had hampered the north-south flow of traffic in the city by crossing roads at various points, which became a growing problem as traffic was rapidly motorised after partition in 1947. The station was demolished and a site on agricultural land at Kamlapur was chosen for a new central station. The train line was diverted from Tejgoan to Khilgaon and then to Kamlapur by removing the east-west barrier. The governor general of East Pakistan invited Berger Consultancy of New Jersey (USA) to design the new station. Stanley Jewkes was appointed as advisor due to his experience in building concrete structures. Daniel Dunham, the principal architect for this project, was a Harvard graduate practising here in Dhaka. The challenge was to create a wide-span structure that would combine Modernism with suitability to the tropical climate and provide sufficient daylight and cross ventilation. Dunham's expertise was in using thin-shell concrete structures to cover large spans. He was asked to use features taken from Mughal architecture, specifically the pointed arch. He proposed an umbrella-like repetitive form which, when seen from the front, conveys the impression of an arch and at the same time spans a large space. Dunham subsequently left the project to teach architecture at BUET (EPEUT at that time). Another American, Robert Boughey, took over; he prepared all the architectural drawings and structural-engineering documents. The vaulted domes and parabolic roof were cast *in situ* using reusable wooden formwork. The shell-like canopies encourage interconnected series of activities and create an urban atmosphere. The gently pointed roof is a kind of umbrella providing shelter from the monsoon rain; it gives the station a resemblance to a Mughal pavilion with deeply recessed spatial volumes.

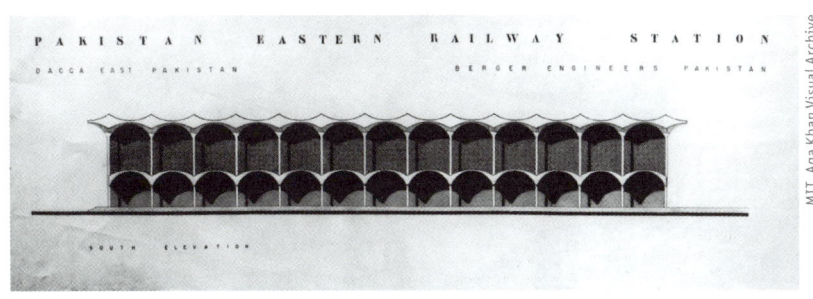

PAKISTAN EASTERN RAILWAY STATION

DACCA EAST PAKISTAN

BERGER ENGINEERS PAKISTAN

SOUTH ELEVATION

MIT, Aga Khan Visual Archive

Liberation War Museum

F11/A & F11/B,
Shere Bangla Nagar
Civic Centre, Agargoan
Tanzim Hasan Salim
Naheed Farzana
2017

This building is the outcome of civic participation. In 1996 the Liberation War Museum trustee board started collecting personal items from victims who had suffered in the 1971 war. The trust organised fund-raising campaigns throughout Bangladesh to finance construction. Finally, it acquired 4047 square metres of land in Dhaka's Agargaon district from the Government of Bangladesh. The design for the building was selected from 70 entries in a competition. It has 3500 square metres of gallery space in four galleries containing a collection of 21,000 items. An additional 500-square-metre space is for temporary exhibitions. The museum building also houses two institutes: the Institute of Liberation War Studies and the Centre for Genocide and Justice Studies. There are three seminar rooms (the largest with seating for 50 people). Other functions include an amphitheatre for school programmes, an extensive archive, a data storage area, a collection of rare documents, a processing lab, a kiosk, and a canteen. The 260-seat auditorium is equipped with the latest sound and lighting systems. Both covered and open spaces here may be used as backup space for the auditorium for gatherings and conferences and are equipped with large screens and projectors. The building's design did not follow the principles of green architecture directly, but some eco-friendly features have since been added, including rainwater harvesting, LED lamps, and solar panels. The building is of striking appearance; the pinned horizontal or vertical posts over fair-faced concrete convey the nation's will to resist. The dark, gloomy interior evokes the suffering of the Liberation War. The raised entrance lobby has a black tiled staircase. From here, the building's surroundings are visible. The long ramps adorned with natural light against the roughly textured concrete serve to prepare visitors psychologically. In the lobby an eternal flame rises above a circular pool. Above it a conical atrium stretching nearly the height of three floors and open to the sky above reinforces the visual tension, its height rhyming with the leaping flame.

Avijit Barman

1

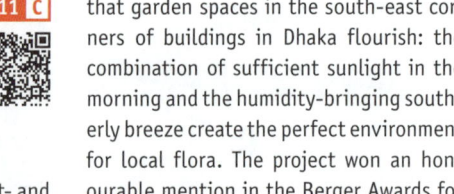

Shatabdi Factory

73/4 First Lane, Malibagh
Sabbir Ahmed,
Sania Akter
2016

011 C

This factory is an achievement in cost- and time-saving, two objectives which came together in the design process. Cheap materials, such as brick masonry for the load-bearing walls and corrugated sheets for the roofing, were chosen so as to complete construction within four months and reduce construction costs. Another aspect of the project was the use of microclimate analysis to ensure sufficiency of both natural light and ventilation – particularly important given that this small two-storey building stands in a suffocating urban area, surrounded by much taller multi-storey structures in the heart of disorderly Dhaka. The project also revealed that garden spaces in the south-east corners of buildings in Dhaka flourish: the combination of sufficient sunlight in the morning and the humidity-bringing southerly breeze create the perfect environment for local flora. The project won an honourable mention in the Berger Awards for Excellence in Architecture in 2017.

Md. Mohaimin Ali Khan (all pictures)

Mohila Samity Complex

1 Bailey Road, Dayaganj
Ehsan Khan,
EK Architects
2016

`012` `C`

This building belongs to the largest voluntary organisation for women's development in the country, Bangladesh Mohila Samity, whose motto is 'A better tomorrow'. The location is a cultural corridor well known for its vibrancy. A famous auditorium here used to serve as a kind of gathering place for prominent theatre groups – which is why the adjacent road is called 'Theatre Avenue'. Mohila Samity is the birthplace of the country's cultural movement. Its four-storey, 14.63-metre-high new building includes two theatres – one with 250 seats, the other with 100. Other facilities include a conference room, offices, training centres, and a primary school. The inviting walkway at the entrance is an extension of the pavement. Decks at different levels and bridges and ramps connecting the sequences of spaces make for interesting circulation illuminated with diffuse daylight. The combination of brick masonry, fair-faced concrete, and brise-soleils on the façade draws the gaze of passers-by. The front elevation has a light appearance – with vertical fins (concrete panels) and curtain walls placed at uneven intervals. A heavy masonry wall defines functional spaces, while light concrete indicates semi-outdoor areas. The left edge of the façade has an expanse of blue glazing. There is a rooftop garden. The Mohita Samity building won the Commonwealth Association of Architects' Public Amenity Buildings Award in the institutional category in 2018.

National Museum

Shahbagh Road/
Kazi Nazrul Islam Avenue
Robert C Boughy
1983

013 C

This museum was originally opened by Thomas Gibson-Carmichael, the first governor of Bengal, as the Dhaka Museum in 1913. In 1915 its collection was transferred to Naib e Nazim of Dhaka, who housed it in his Nimtoli Palace. The museum was declared 'the National Museum of Bangladesh' in 1975. Construction of a building for the collection of more than 86,000 pieces was completed in 1983 on a 34,924-square-metre site. The grounds contain old cannons from the times of the Mughal governor Shah Suja and the pre-Mughal ruler Isha Khan, but also sculptures by the artist Novera Ahmed. The building's ground floor has office wings on both sides and a grand staircase ascending from the entrance lobby. Behind the lobby is an exhibition hall named after the museum's first notable curator, Nalini Kanta Bhattashali. The second floor has 22 rooms arranged along an open courtyard. The third floor contains two libraries; the fourth is devoted to international art. Altogether, there are three auditoriums, two exhibition halls, and 44 galleries. The first ten galleries are dedicated to natural history. The next 11 display classical art, and the 16 that follow are devoted to ethnography. The remaining seven are for decorative art, contemporary art, and world civilisation. The Modernist building is four storeys high with a total floor area of 18,777 square metres. Its exterior has exposed-concrete columns up to the third storey; the upper two floors have a solid-wall façade topped with 13 circular windows with hemispherical hoods, providing the galleries on the top floor with natural illumination. The building's corners interrupt the continuity of the façades; the towers contain staircases and

National Museum

services. The highlights of the museum's collection include delicate ivory handiwork, ancient manuscripts inscribed on palm leaves, swords owned by Tipu Sultan, the carpet of Nawab Shiraj Uddaula, famous sketches of the 1943 famine by Zainul Abedin, paintings by S.M. Sultan and Potua Quamrul Hassan, world-famous sculptures, terracotta from the Pala dynasty (dating from the seventh century to the 'golden age' in the eleventh century), and items commemorating the Liberation War.

Sayed Ahmed

Sayed Ahmed

Kazi Karar Naïer (all pictures)

Fine Arts Institute, Charu Kola, DU

014 C

Kazi Nazrul Islam Avenue
Muzharul Islam
1955

An art school was established in 1948 by pioneering master artists, including Zainul Abedin and Qamrul Hassan. It moved to its present location in 1956, before becoming an art college in 1963 and then a fully fledged faculty of Dhaka University in 2008. The building which houses it is the first masterpiece by Muzharul Islam, the founding father of Bangladeshi Modernism. By moving beyond the stigmatised colonial style and hybridised dogma, this building defined the Modernist vocabulary for the first time. The site at Shahbag had scattered trees; the architect decided to keep the original topography. While responsive to the climate, his design follows Le Corbusier's strategy of the free plan. It reflects the indoor/outdoor quality of Bangladesh's traditional vernacular architecture. Full of sensorial cues, the campus is ideal for contemplation and learning art. The lattices and perforated screens create thresholds while also connecting spaces in series. The use of a post-and-slab structural system allows the ground and second floors to have differing free-plan layouts. Two circles comprise the exhibition galleries on ground floor. A wonderful, iconic sculptural staircase capitalises on daylight and the presence of an artistic tree. The courtyard is full of activities and has visual connections with the corridors and classrooms. A long colonnaded corridor ends in the Lotus Pond, a circle of water surrounded by paving. The building is 7.32 metres high and has two floors. The exposed wooden panels, shading devices, and pergolas are varnished in brown. The bricks used in the building were custom designed and recall the country's rich tradition of terracotta plaques. The building houses eight departments with 43 teachers and 720 students. Mangal Shovayatra, a mass procession that takes place on the first day of the Bengali New Year, has since the 1960s been organised by the faculty's teachers and students to protest against cultural suppression by Pakistan.

Kazi Nazrul Islam Tomb

Kazi Nazrul Islam Avenue
Vitti Sthapati Brindo Ltd.
2008 (renovated)

015 C

The architect Muzharul Islam drew the idea for this tomb as a sketch on a map; Vitti architects were responsible for realising it. The entrance has a gate of raw-textured concrete and glass boxes on either side; the vertical wooden slats in front of the boxes are spaced 40.64 centimetres apart. Nearby are a public library, Dhaka University, and the university's central mosque. Kazi Nazrul Islam, the national poet of Bangladesh, died in 1976. He had wanted to be buried beside a mosque so as to hear the calls to prayer after his death. The poet's tomb has seven steps of exposed brick and is 1.22 metres high. His grave is marked with white marble among the green of the grass. Martyrs who died on the dark night of 25 March 1973, when the government of Pakistan attacked East Pakistan, are also buried here, as are the master artisan Zainul Abedin and the artist Patua Qaium Chowdhury. This is a calm spot. Visitors will find interesting texts from the poetry of Nazrul and Tagore in parts of the monument.

Anik Sarker

Madhu's Canteen, DU
Kazi Nazrul Islam Avenue
1876

016 C

Originally the *darbar hall* (court building) of the nawabs of Dhaka, this was built in the north-east part of what is today the Arts Faculty compound as a music room for the nawabs' Israt Manzil (Garden House) Palace. Meetings both formal and informal were held here. In 1906 a conference called by Nawab Khwaja Salimullah led to the founding of the All-India Muslim League. The *darbar* was converted to a dining hall for university students in 1921, when the university was established. Madhu started this canteen with his father at the age of 15. It is still an important social epicentre for student politics and various independence movements – and offers delicious food besides. The floor and spacious surrounding area are paved with marble. The circular room on the west side was built as a pavilion containing a skating rink with an attached ballroom. The building has a colonnaded veranda covered with corrugated sheeting in the traditional *chauchala* (four-pitched) roofing style. The cylindrical pavilions have paired columns at regular intervals with arches connecting the bases of each pair. The building is nearly six metres high; there is a perforated parapet. It is famous for its owner, Madhusudan (Madhu) Dey, who was brutally killed, together with many students at Dhaka University, by the Pakistan Army in a massacre on the black night of 25 March 1971, in the events known as 'Operation Searchlight'. A bust of Madhu was erected in front of the main entrance in 1995. Today, the canteen is hidden from view between the tall buildings of the Arts Faculty and the Institute of Business Administration.

Kazi Karar Najer (all pictures)

Ragib Hasan

Gurdwara Nanak Shahi
Nilkhet Road
1628

017 **C**

Situated in the Dhaka University area, this is the principal *gurdwara* (Sikh place of worship) among Bangladesh's nine Sikh temples. Its previous name was 'Sujatpur Sikh Sangat' since it was in the Sujatpur *mouza* (tax district) in Mughal times. A Sikh priest named Almast was sent by the sixth Sikh guru Hargovind Singh in the early 1600s to preach Sikhism here. Other scholars believe that the ninth Sikh guru Teg Bahadur Singh himself built this temple or that a priest named Bhai Nathaji built it to commemorate the visit of Teg Bahadur after being commanded to do so in a dream by Guru Nanak. In 1883 the *gurdwara* was renovated, and in 1915 a residence was attached to its east side for the *granthi* (Sikh priest). After the partition of India in 1947, the temple was abandoned – to be renovated only after the liberation of Bangladesh in 1988. Facing south onto a ditch and a graveyard, the temple is entered from the north; to its west is a pond with a stepped deck. The main façade has three doors flanked by two *jali* (lattice-work) windows. A single onion dome with flutes rise above its roof. The building's height from the ground to the highest point of its curved roof is seven metres. The main temple has rooms for devotees and a square plinth. A 1.5-metre-wide *parkarma* veranda or circumambulation path, built around the main prayer two-storey hall known as 'Darbar Shahib' under Sardar Harban Singh, provides an opportunity to imbibe energy. The hall has doors from four directions leading into four rooms. At its northern edge the *Granth Shahib* (holy book of hymns) – 45.72 centimetres by 30.48 centimetres with 1336 *angs* (limbs) or pages – rests on a wooden platform. A pair of wooden sandals belonging to Teg Bahadur Singh is preserved under the book in a glass box. The building's interior and exterior are white. The interior has a floor of red carpet. Free food known as *langar* is served on Fridays.

Dipanjan Das

Shomaj Biggyan Chattar Landscaping, Faculty of Social Sciences

Dhaka University Campus
Sthanik Consultants,
Saiqa Iqbal Meghna,
Suvro Sovon Chowdhury
2016

018 C

This site was once an unattractive wasteland, a dumping zone for construction waste that was for many years used as a shortcut. The objective of the landscape design was to create a place where students could pause and contemplate amidst the landmarks of the university campus. To ensure maintenance and liveliness, there is a semi-open food kiosk. To explain the idea of a 'non-place', the architects used metaphors and literature instead of concepts and drawings. They were inspired by the French anthropologist Marc Auge, who identified the 'non-place' as a transient space which is not significant enough to become a 'place' and where people are anonymous. This approach incorporates the 'pits and mounds' of traditional landscaping; the terrain on the site fluctuates from 0.91 metres below the existing normal ground level to 0.91 metres above it. The design conserves existing trees and extends the functions of the campus programmes in a kind of 'choreographed encounter' of spaces of different shapes and sizes. So, here we find a reading area that is an extension of the reading rooms in the central library, a gathering place that is adjacent to the university's central mosque, and a forum for discussion that is additional to Madhur's Canteen. This archive of spaces is a multisensory experience. A hijol tree planted at its centre is an allusion to the village pond – an opportunity for students from every corner of the country to review their childhood memories and a stage for ever-changing, contrasting phenomena, such as light/shadow, blue sky/cloud, and reflection/reality. The paving of perforated brick allows the grass to grow through its porous body. Red oxide-coated metals and turquoise coloured cement texture were chosen because they do not clash with nature. The hanging bridge emphasises the route towards the node linking the campus's central mosque and library and the faculty building. In the early morning, visitors are greeted by yellow konokchura flowers covering the paths. The vegetation predominantly consists of other local fauna, including rain tree, mango, jackfruit, mahogany, neem, kadam, bakul, rare figs, dalim, kamini, radha chura, and joba. This has helped maintain biodiversity: birds chirp in every branch; squirrels and mongooses run over the ground; and even rare birds such as the boshontobouri are to be found here after the change of landscape.

Md. Mohaimin Ali Khan

Dhaka University Library

Kazi Nazrul Islam Avenue
Muzharul Islam
1970

019 **C**

With 680,000 books and 30,000 rare manuscripts, Dhaka University Library is the largest library in the country. It was also the first masterpiece by the architect Muzharul Islam, distinctive for its exposed brickwork, wide windows, and spacious interior. The complex consists of several parts: an administrative unit, the main library, the science library, and an extension. The total floor area is 14,000 square metres. The three-storey building is 10.97 metres high. There are four sciences reading rooms on the second floor; here 400 students can read at a time. Seven horizontally projecting vaulted arches cover the roofline. Slender brick panels filled with square glass blocks from top to bottom are evenly distributed at intervals of two metres over the entire west façade. The main entrance is on the east side. This entire elevation with its rhythm of vertical and horizontal mullions and in-between voids offers both transparency and fine *jali* work (latticework)– a perfect blend of Modernism and traditional permeability. The projecting part of the building's roof is a waffle construction supported by a row of exposed white slender columns against the red-brick wall. Light and shadow always conveys a strong Modernist vocabulary. In the interior the beautiful ramp with its wooden frame gives pleasure to its users. The influence of Le Corbusier is clearly to be seen here in the post-and-lintel structural system, white colour, and plan with free-flowing spaces.

1

Kazi Karar Naier

ঢাকা বিশ্ববিদ্যালয় গ্রন্থাগার

NO MASK NO ENTRY
NO MASK NO SERVICE

ঢাকা বিশ্ববিদ্যালয় গ্রন্থাগার Dhaka University Library

Teacher Student Center, DU
Secratariate Road
Constantinos A. Doxiadis
1961

020 C

There is only one teacher-student centre for all of Bangladesh's universities. Designed as a campus community and cultural hub for the city of Dhaka, it contains cafeterias, bookshop lounges, dining rooms, a library, a reading room, an art and music room, a multipurpose hall, a games room, and venues for international seminars and symposiums. Numerous student organisations use the complex for meetings, functions, exhibitions, concerts, and publishing journals and bulletins. It also serves as a public square where wide screens are set up for viewing cricket matches. At least 20 plays are staged here yearly, and this venue has also witnessed the birth of stars such as the late singer Shanjib Chowdhury. Many red-letter days in Bangladesh's glorious national history were germinated from this spot, including movements such as the mass uprising in 1969 and the fall of the autocrat General Hussain Muhammad Ershad in 1990. The design by the legendary Greek architect and town planner Constantinos Apostolou Doxiadis reveals a well-judged Modernist approach which takes into account indigenous culture, climate, and spatial arrangements. The site chosen for the building includes land that once belonged to the Sujatpur Palace. Funding came from the Ford Foundation as well as the government. A semi-cylindrical canopy sweeps down to the ground on each side of one block to keep the interior cool; another block has a butterfly roof. The complex is arranged around a courtyard; the courtyard corridors have low roofs supported by round metal columns. There is an unknown Greek tomb dating from 1915 on the west edge of the green lawn – the only evidence of a Greek presence in Bangladesh. The swimming-pool enclosure contains two small Shiva temples. A sculpture by the famous artist Hamiduzzaman Khan stands at the entrance. The open promenade with its leafy canopy is thronged with tea stalls.

Kazi Karar Naier

1

Salimullah Muslim Hall

Zahir Raihan Road/
Pilkhana Road/Fuller Road
Engineer: Gwyther
1931

021 C

Named after Sir Khwaja Salimullah Bahadur, the fourth nawab of Dhaka, this residential hall for Dhaka University derives from a decision taken by the Nathan Committee under the British government in 1912 to investigate the possibility of a residence-based university and from Calcutta University Commission's recommendation that there should be separate halls for students from different religions. This is the most famous of Dhaka University's three student halls. Two separate halls were proposed: Salimullah for Muslims and Jagannath for Hindus and Buddhists. The annual dinners that took place here during the 1920s and 1930s involved 800 guests and set a great example of communal harmony. The student residence, housing 75 students, was in fact on the second floor of the original building; the ground floor was occupied by the East Bengal Secretariat. The largest room on the ground floor was divided into a dining room, a kitchen, a common area, and a library. The remaining 61 rooms were used by the secretariat. In 1927 the number of Muslim students increased to 127, causing a housing shortage. On 22 August 1929 Lord Stanley Jackson laid the keystone for a new building and an English architect named Gwyther from the department of public works was appointed to design it.

The work was supervised by civil engineers including D.J. Blomfield and H. Harrison. The student hall has a symmetrical plan with a two-storey entrance gateway in the south and two courtyards, one on either side of a central path extending from the main door of the mosque in the north of the site. The gateway has three pointed arches flanked by square-based towers with bulbous yellow-tiled domes, an interesting take on Saracen architecture. Centred around the activity hub of the courtyard, wide verandas run along the inner façades, establishing an optical connection with the open space in the middle. Wood logs support the verandas' thick roofs, which are made of lime mortar mixed with brick chips. The building's projecting eaves and railings show Mughal influences. The plinth is one metre high, and the building has a total height of eight metres. The side towers are 12 metres high without their domes. The fenestration features two pointed semicircular arches. The student hall complex occupies a vast piece of land – nearly 52,300 square metres, while the garden in the courtyard has an area of 6968 square metres, which is typical of the Mughal Charbagh garden. The garden's rectangular layout reproduces the plan of the Mughal fort of Lalbagh, where the west and east wings are shorter than the south and north wings. Its beauty on a moonlit night is incomparable. Salimullah Muslim Hall has been called one of the best three buildings in Dhaka (the other two being Curzon Hall and the High Court building). Today it houses almost 800 students.

Dhaka University

BUET Architecture Building

022 C

Asian Highway/Shahid Sarani,
M.K. Palashi
Richard Edwin Vrooman
1968

This flagship building is the cradle of architectural education on Bangladesh's most prestigious engineering campus, BUET. The university was originally 'the Dhaka Survey School', founded at Nagola in 1876. Just a short distance from the present-day architecture department stands a red-and-white colonial building with *jalis* (pierced screens) on its railings. This was used by Lord Curzon as the government press office when Bengal was partitioned in 1905. Later, in 1912, it was acquired by the Ahsanullah School of Engineering, together with a vast 311,000-square-metre plot of land. Definitely an interesting spot to visit, this site is currently used by the university for its administrative building. In 1948 the school was promoted to college of engineering. By 1966 the college had four American teachers and 68 students. At the same time, six Bengali lecturers came back from Texas, where they had completed their further studies, to join as faculty members. During his stay in Dhaka from 1961 to 1968, the American architect and faculty member of Texas A & M University Richard Edwin Vrooman started teaching here as part of a USAID cold-war project. His team was joined by Daniel Dunham, Jack Yardly, James Walden, and Samuel Lanford. In 1962 the East Pakistan government wanted to upgrade the existing Ahsanullah Engineering College to make it a fully fledged university under the name 'EPUET'. The objective was to train local architects and establish a school that would help the tyrant Ayub Khan carry out his burgeoning construction programme. Vrooman was asked to design the academic building; the engineer Saber Jafar from IIT (the Indian Institute of Engineering Science and Technology) in Shibpur, West Bengal, worked with him as local architect. The building was completed in 1968 on a wedge-shaped site on the north-west side of the BUET campus. The foundations are precast concrete pylons driven into the unstable soil. Daniel Dunham had the idea of incorporating the main library, auditorium, cafeteria, and teachers' club in the academic building. Vrooman's wish was to create a holistic temple of academe similar to Gropius's Bauhaus building. The BUET Architecture Building consists of a four-storey academic block, a rectangle of 60.96 metres by 24.38 metres, flanked by a two-storey administrative block, forming an L shape. The cafeteria building and central library form well-proportioned courtyards adorned with lush greenery, establishing a visual and sensory connection with the recessed corridors. The administrative block has a convex wall supporting a porch for use by vehicles. The two blocks are connected by a bridge at the level of the second floor. The academic block has a diagonal beam structural system with a rhythmic, perforated envelope. The envelope consists of precast concrete louvre panels which also

Sahabi Mahmud Aunonto

serve as railings. Each panel is 1.07 metres wide and 2.44 metres long and has nine angled louvres. Four panels form a group; after a short interval consisting of adjoining beams, the pattern is repeated. This treatment, obviously influenced by Le Corbusier's brise soleils, consciously blurs the boundary between indoors and outdoors. The way this building is raised on exposed heavy piers may cause some to see it as an example of Brutalism. The block's east-west orientation allows cross ventilation from the south. The studios on the upper floors have open-plan layouts to reinforce a sense of community. The end walls are of curved concrete. At their centre are protruding spouts that collect and discharge rainwater. The staircases are rationally positioned between the box-like mass and the curved walls at either end of the block. The climatic and cultural intermingling is here emphatic. The building's courtyard turns into a celebration plaza during the first day of the Bangla calendar. Bangladesh's Modernist architecture would never have had got off to such a good start without this magnificent womb.

Kazi Karar Naier

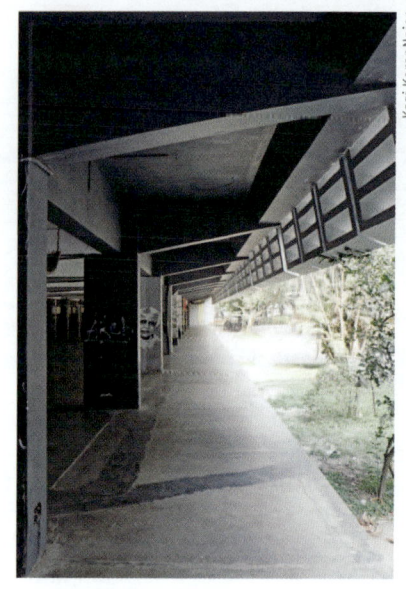

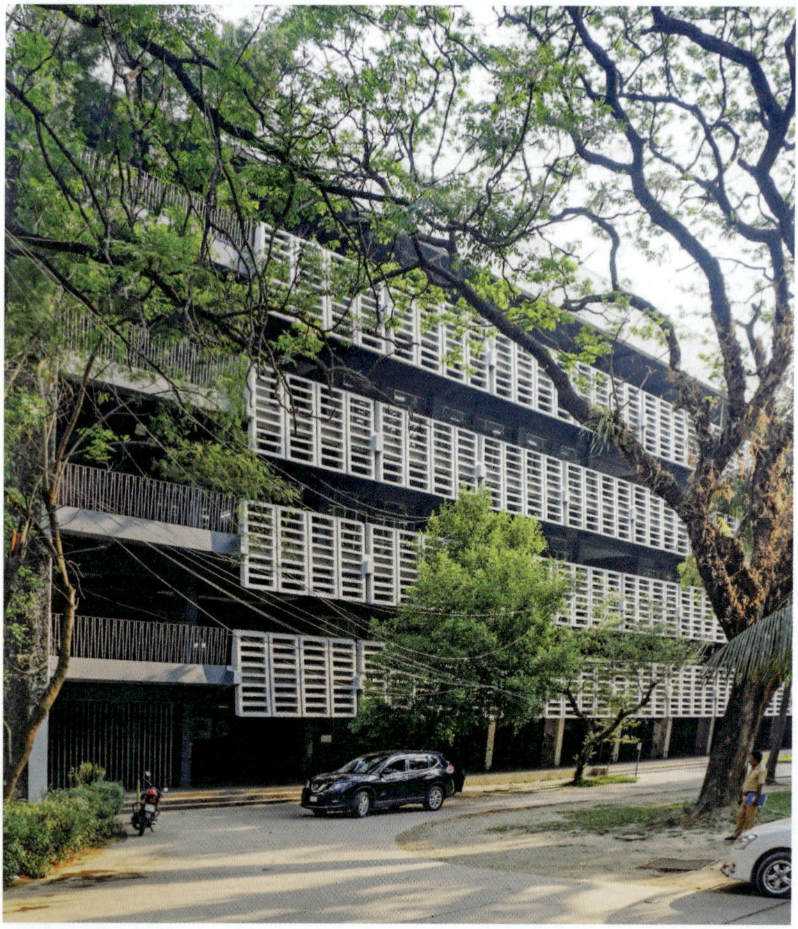

Kazi Karar Naier

Shahid Minar

Secretariate Road
Hamidur Rahman,
Novera Ahmed
1963

023 C

This monument to martyrs for the Bengali language has a central structure which is 14 metres high. It marks the exact spot where in 1952 police fired on a procession of students and people from all strata of society who demanded acknowledgment of their mother tongue. After Bengali was recognised as the state language in 1956, work started on building the memorial. Its construction was delayed due to the introduction of martial law; several times the structure was knocked down by Pakistanis, and on the black night of 25 March 1971, it was demolished completely. Following the country's liberation, the monument was rebuilt under the supervision of Abul Bashar, the chief architect of DOA, SHM. The memorial complex was expanded, and the structures were rebuilt to the original design. Unfortunately, much authenticity and integrity was lost in the process.

The design is a semicircular arrangement of five pillars symbolising 'a caring mother (the central structure) with her fallen offspring on either side'. The vertical structures are of marble. The steps leading down towards the road have dividing lines marked in white originating from the main dais, like the rays of the sun radiating from the dazzling source in the centre. The marble floors were designed to enhance the impact of moving shadows at different times of day. The basement contains a 140-square-metre area with a fresco depicting the history of the language movement. This monument is today an emblem of UNESCO's International Mother Language Day, which is celebrated all over the world on 21 February every year. Its motto is to promote linguistic diversity and avert the extinction of languages. Throngs of people walk barefoot, sing patriotic songs, and dedicate flower banquets to pay homage to the martyrs. From the civic point of view, this is the epicentre for epoch-making protests and the venue for public funerals at which last respects are paid to leaders, artistes, and intellectuals.

1

Avijit Barman

Bangla Academy

3 Kazi Nazrul Islam Avenue/
Secretariat Road
Dhaka University area, Ramna
1911
Rabiul Hossain, 2010 (restoration)
Tanya Karim and NR Khan Assoc., 2012

024 **C**

After the annulment of the partition of Bengal in 1911, three enormous residences were built for the members of the executive council appointed by the governor of Bengal. They included this house, which was owned by the king of Bardhaman in West Bengal. The complex stretched all the way to a Shiva temple at the rear, where the king used to worship during his visits. After Dhaka University was established in 1921, the building provided a home for many famous professors, including the scientist Kazi Motahar Hossain and the historian Ramesh Chandra Majumdar. The national poet Kazi Nazrul Islam was also invited to stay here as a guest in 1926. The house was the official residence of the prime minister of East Pakistan from 1947 forwards. This was where the state conspiracy against the Bangla language started, which is why this historic house was subsequently given to Bangla Academy – in exactment of sweet revenge and in fulfilment of the one of the 21 promises in the election manifesto of the Bengali leaders of the United Front in the 1954 provincial election. Bangla Academy was established in 1955 to research and promote the Bangla language and culture. The brainchild of the famous Bengali intellectual and linguist Muhammad Shahidullah, the academy is moulded after the Académie Française. Every year in February, the famous month-long Ekushey Book Fair is held in the courtyard here and in the adjacent park in order to pay testimony to the language martyrs of 1952. The architect Rabiul Hossain restored the building. The ground floor was converted to a museum documenting prominent writers and the language movement; the museum has been home to valuable documents

and a rich collection of photographs and rare manuscripts since 2010. A folk heritage museum was also established here in 2018; this has nearly 500 artefacts. The old building is three-storey and has a simple archway colonnade with keystones on each side. Its entrance portico is two-storeyed with contrasting Renaissance elements. The plan is asymmetrical and rectangular. An open semi-circular terrace on the second floor is supported by Tuscan columns standing on a circular stepped base on the ground floor on the west side. The decorative balustrades are smaller than usual. A new seven-storey building has been erected on the west side of the historical building; this was completed in 2012. Earlier, in 2005, a specialist jury at IAB (the Institute of Architects) held a competition, which was won by Tanya Karim and NR Khan Associates. The contemporary building has a total floor area of 1195.48 square metres (390.33 square metres per storey). Its ground floor has a car park, an auditorium for 500 persons named after the singer Shah Abdul Karim (ornate with selected verses from Bangla literature on its façade), and a seminar room with capacity for 100 persons. From the fourth to eighth floors there are workstations for 250 people and various offices. The new building is naturally ventilated and illuminated – a first for Bangladesh and a source of substantial savings to the government. The only air-conditioned parts of the building are the library and reading room on the second and third floors, where valuable manuscripts have to be protected. Around the pond, the architects built two *ghats* (traditional decks).

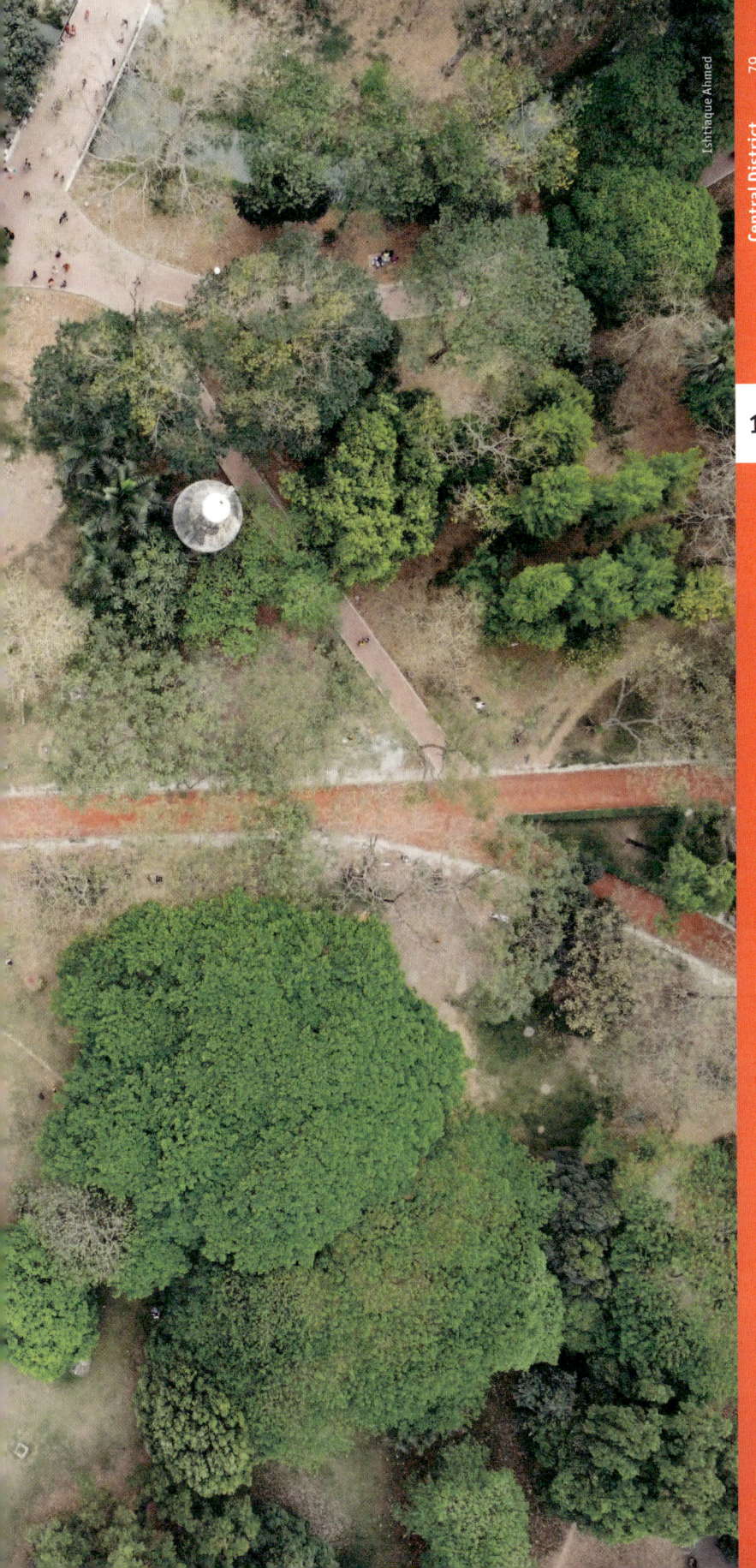

1

Medical College, DU

Secretariat Road,
Zahir Raihan Road/
Shahid Minar Road
James Ransome
1904–1921

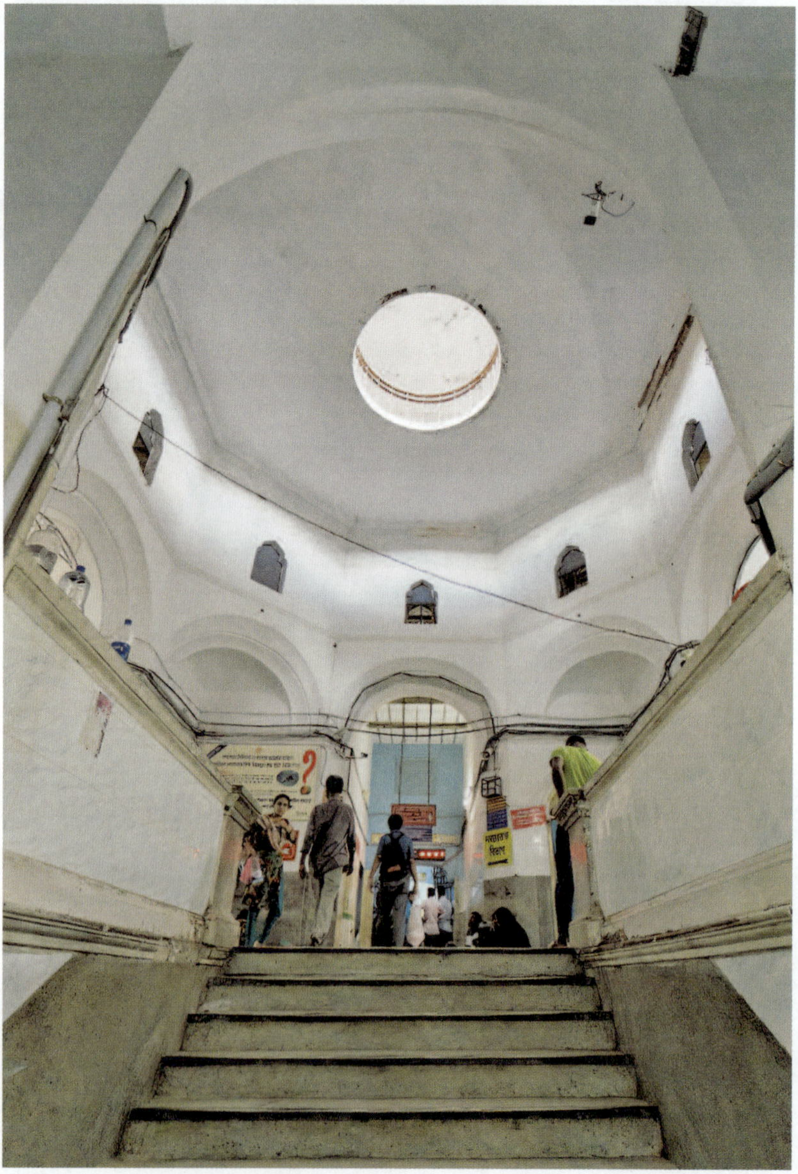

This building is located at the point where old and new Dhaka meet. Over time it has been used for four types of function. In 1904 it housed the secretariat of the newly formed province of East Bengal and Assam. In 1921 it became Dhaka University's medical centre: one wing was a student dormitory; another housed the faculty of arts. During World War II, from 1941 to 1945, there was an American military base here. The building's final incarnation, since February 1946, has been as Dhaka Medical College and Hospital. Surprisingly, the building has adapted to all these purposes without any major changes to its plan or façades. Its architectural style is the British late-colonial style of the '*zamindar* (landlord) bungalow' compound. Conspicuous colonial features include the dome, portico, porch, kiosk, parapet, three columned entrances, the high raised plinth, the oblong plan, the series of courtyards, and the symmetrical elevation. Its load-bearing wall is 46 centimetres thick on the ground floor and 23 centimetres thick on the upper

floors. The bricks are bonded using *surkhi* (brick dust) and lime mortar. Limestone was sealed in the central structure to support the dome's structural stability. Brick chips mixed with lime mortar were used to construct horizontal elements such as the projective eaves, cornices, and diagonal buttresses, and were also, as was typical for colonial buildings, cast as floors beneath and in-between the beams. Burmese teak (*Tectona grandis*) was used for the wooden beams, frames, doors, and window friezes. Longitudinal planks of teak were placed over the beams. The building is naturally ventilated. The first-time visitor might see this as an ordinary hospital with a colonial legacy, but its astonishing appeal lies in something else: this building is regarded as the beating heart of the Bengali language movement. At 4 pm on 21 February 21 1952, students decided to defy Section 144 from a historic mango tree, the Aam-tola (the tree is no longer more; the hospital's emergency gate stands in its place), so as to uphold the claim of their mother tongue to the status of state language of Pakistan; many were martyred. To mark this event, 21 February was declared International Mother Language Day by UNESCO in 1999.

Shohrawardy Park and Independence Pillar

Ramna Green, Suhrawary Udyan
Marina Tabassum
Kashef Mahboob Chowdhury
1997–2013

026 C

In 1997 a national architectural competition was held to design the Museum of Independence. Participating architects were faced with the difficult task of designing a building that would reflect the country's difficult history and its struggle for independence. The competition was won by the architecture firm URBANA, whose lead architects are Marina Tabassum and Kashef Mahboob Chowdhury. However, partly due to changes of government, the construction process took more than a decade. The tower, the final component in the project, could not be erected until 2013. The site of the memorial has had a wide variety of functions over time. Once a Mughal garden, this piece of land was converted into a horse racing track under British colonial rule and then served as a meeting place for the urban population when Bangladesh was part of Pakistan. It was here that Sheikh Mujibur Rahman,

Kazi Karar Naier

regarded as the nation's father, declared Bangladesh's independence in front of a million people in March 1971. It was therefore important for URBANA to preserve the green space for the city's residents; this meant building the museum with its exhibition area and ancillary functions underground. Above ground, the Independence Monument stands in a specially designed public square. Clad in glass, the slender tower is essentially a tower of light. Below ground, a water column set in a circular space is a memorial to the martyrs of the war.

Shahbaz Khan Mosque

Badshahi Mosque Road
1676

027 C

During the reign of Governor Prince Mohammad Azam, a rich merchant called Haji Khwaja Shahbaz Khan migrated from Kashmir and built this mosque, listed as heritage by the Department of Archaeology in 1950. Built in the Shaista Khan style, the mosque has three domes with octagonal minarets at its four corners. Other features, no longer extant, were fortified walls, a *diwan* compartment on two floors, a bath-house or *hammam*, and scattered bastions. The mosque has three bays formed by two lateral cusped arches spanning the entire prayer hall. This was the first use of such arches in Bengal and was probably influenced by Mughal practice. Stone piers are embedded in the east and west walls to support the arches, making for an elegant interior. The *mihrab* (niche indicating the direction of the Kaaba in Mecca) is adorned with cypress-filled *kanjuras* (*kanjura*: a merlon or undulating decorative pattern), terracotta reliefs on spandrels, a cusped arch, and colonettes on bulbous bases with a floral motif. The mosque's symmetrical plan has an east façade with three arched entrances punctuated by four slender columns – a deviation from typical Mughal architecture. All the entrances are flanked by rows of sunken niches. The base of the exterior walls is lined with imported black basalt. This stonework has engraved decoration and also forms thresholds for the doors. The water-supply system fashioned from terracotta pipes is considered unique and advanced for its time. Next to the mosque is the grave of Shahbaz Khan; this was converted into a *mazar* (prayer tomb). This single-domed, small, square tomb is known as 'Dargah Sharif'; its design reproduces that of the mosque. The veranda on its south side is covered by a traditional *dauchala* (double-folded pitched roof); the roof is supported by engaged and ribbed corner turrets. Scholars believe that this tomb is a prototype of the tomb of Anwar Shaheed in Bardhaman in West Bengal.

Mausoleum of Three Leaders

Shuhrawardy Park Road
Saif Ul Haque,
Shah Alam Zahiruddin
1963

028 C

A. K. Fazlul Haque, Huseyn Shaheed Suhrawardy, and Khwaja Nazimuddin served as prime ministers of united Bengal in British India and had great influence on our national history. They died in 1962, 1963, and 1964 respectively. This is their resting place. Fazlul Haque was a pioneering advocate of the creation of a separate land for Indian Muslims. He presented the Lahore Resolution in 1940, for which he was given the title 'Sher e Bangla' (Tiger of Bengal). Suhrawardy was the prime minister of Pakistan in 1956 to 1957. Nazimuddin was the second prime minister of Pakistan from 1951 to 1953. History tells us that these three leaders were political rivals, but now they forever rest together in the same spot. The mausoleum is a Modernist take on the gorgeous shrine architecture of the Islamic tradition. The architects' intention was to make the shell structure visible from the adjacent road, and they have certainly succeeded: the hyperbolic paraboloid arches make the mausoleum a true landmark. There are two entrances. The actual graves of the three men are beneath, surrounded by small, decorative arched pillars. Above ground, replicas mark the exact locations of the tombs below.

Kazi Karar Naier

Kazi Karar Naier

Kazi Karar Naier

Pinu Rahman

Akram Khan/dreamstime

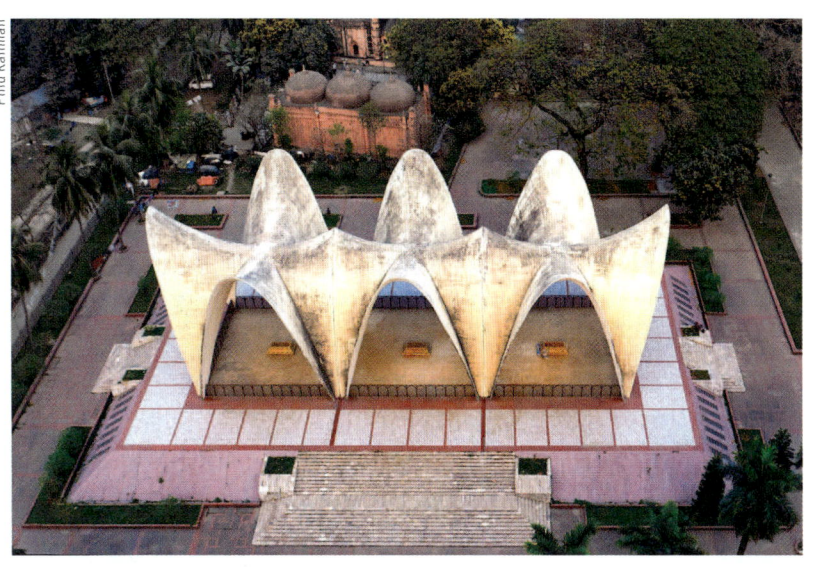

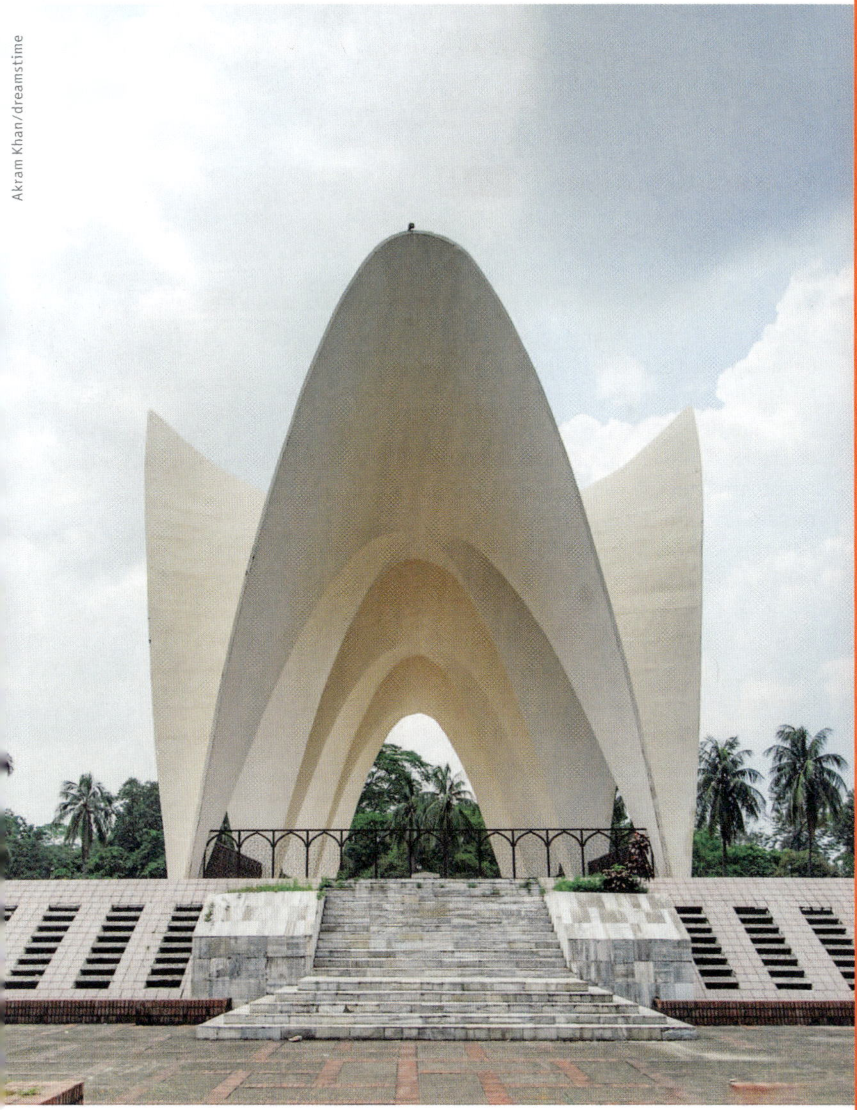

Kazi Karar Naier

Mir Jumla Gate/Dhaka Gate

Shuhrawardy Park Road
Ramna Green
1663

029 C

Mir Jumla II, the Mughal governor of Bengal, wanted to secure Dhaka from raids by Portuguese and Arakanese Magh pirates and slave traders. With the consent of Emperor Aurangzeb, he established a post controlling entry to the city here. In the seventeenth and eighteenth centuries, this gateway was the northern point of entry to the city's core on the bank of the River Buriganga. Other entry points were Jafarabad in the west, Postagola in the east, and Tongi Bridge in the north. Outside the gate was a vast garden called 'Bag e Badshahi' (Emperor's Garden). Known as 'Sujatpur' and 'Chishtia', this area contained scattered settlements that were used by the aristocrats as residences and for the purpose of amusement. In the nineteenth century the British rulers laid out a racecourse here. In 1825 the gate was rebuilt by the magistrate Charles Dowse, but in the European style. It is a simple structure with two sloping walls incorporating supporting pillars and, in the centre of the two walls, a tall pillar (4.57 metres high). The two pillars on

Babul Abdul Malek

each side diminish in size; the lowest are 2.14 metres high. The column capitals have cornices and spherical ornamentation. The original structure suffered considerable damage when the nearby road was widened in the late 1950s. The upper parts of the thick walls have semicircular decorative shapes perforated with square holes.

Kazi Karar Naier

Musa Khan Mosque

Suhrawardi Uddan Road,
Curzon Hall
1623

`030` `C`

Less than a half kilometre from Khwaja Shabaz Khan Mosque is another tomb-based mosque. Musa Khan was a son of Isha Khan who was a Muslim Rajput commander and the last leader among the 12 landlords or *bhuyans* of Bengal to resist the Mughal conquest. Musa died in 1623, and this mosque was subsequently built behind Curzon Hall by his grandson, Diwan Munwar Khan, in the sixteenth century. It has three shouldered domes resting on octagonal drums and four octagonal minarets and stands on a raised vaulted platform which is 3.05 metres above ground level. The mosque contained a series of rooms that are not accessible today. As in the case of Chawk Mosque (1676), the reason why it was built on a high terrace was to accommodate a madrasa beneath; this was a 'madrasa mosque'. The walls of the vaulted space of the madrasa contained niches fitted with bookshelves. The mosque's central dome is larger than its two counterparts and has four smaller half-domed squinches on the upper corners; the other two domes have triangular pendentives. All domes are crowned with lotus and pot finials. Inside, the apices of the domes are ornately decorated with large painted medallions. The mosque's length is 17.68 metres from north to south; its width, 14 metres from east to west. There is an extended staircase in the south-west corner. The main prayer hall is on the west side. The exterior dimensions of the prayer hall are 14.94 metres by 7.62 metres. Three archways open under the half-domed vaults and have two rows of doors. Each entrance is divided into two halves by a north-south horizontal arch. The central arch is larger and decorated with a projecting pediment and turrets. There are four centred archways on each side on the south and north walls. The three *mihrabs* (niches indicating the direction of the Kaaba in Mecca) are semi-octagonal arches; the larger central *mihrab* is flanked by ornamental turrets. The central bay is wider and is a 4.88-by-4.88-metre square. The side bays are rectangular with dimensions of 4.88 by 3.05 metres.

Kazi Karar Naier

Curzon Hall

Curzon Hall Road,
Dhaka University Campus
1908

031 C

This building currently houses the Faculty of Sciences of Dhaka University. Originally built as the town hall for the newly formed province of Assam and East Bengal, it was named after the viceroy, Lord Curzon, who laid its foundation stone in 1904. Half of the budget for its construction was provided by a member of the *zamindar* (landlord) Bhawal family, Raja Ronendranarayan. After the partition of Bengal was revoked in 1911, the two Bengals were reunited, but Dhaka lost its capital status and Curzon Hall was repurposed as the library of Dhaka College. In 1921 it was chosen as the site for the inauguration of Dhaka University and subsequently became the university's physics department – the cradle of a revolutionary development in scientific knowledge, the Bose-Einstein theory in quantum physics. This building is also notable for its connection with the Bengali language movement. When Muhammad Ali Jinnah, the founder of Pakistan, delivered his speech imposing Urdu as the sole state language of Pakistan on 24 March 1948, the first protest broke out here instantly among the students. This two-storey building has an enormous central hall. The projecting north façade incorporates both horseshoe and cusped arches; this wing contains 18 rooms. The transverse wings are oriented east to west. The entire building is wrapped in continuous verandas. The tracery work, deep projecting eaves, *chhatris* (arched and domed terrace pavilions), and red brickwork resembling red sandstone are, especially in the middle section, a clear allusion to the sixteenth-century Diwan I Khas (Red Fort) in Agra. The British government, however, preferred the Mughal Emperor Akbar the Great's citadel of Fatehpur Sikri in Rajasthan; they believed that of all the past rulers of India, Akbar followed an ideology which was uniquely wise, tolerant, and respectful to others. An artist and architect from Rajasthan was hired to execute the façade ornamentation. The treatment of the fenestration, which combines Mughal and Rajput features, and the Anglo-Indian fusion of bay windows and *jalis* (latticework) could be seen as a meticulous and enthusiastic assimilation of the best features from the Indian subcontinent. The surrounding garden is the largest, most spacious, and best-maintained botanical garden in the country and is known for its botanical gems and rare herbs.

Sajid Muhaimin Choudhury

Belayet Hasan Limon

Nimtoli Deuri, Asiatic Society

College Road/Phoenix Road
1765

032 C

Archibald Swinton, an administrator lieutenant at the East India Company, took over the Lalbag Fort and turned it into his Dhaka office after the company obtained the right to collect taxes, probably shortly after 1765. This meant that an alternative residential complex had to be built for the *naib e nazim* (deputy governor), Jaserat Khan. The Nimtali Palace is where he and his family moved to. The building had a façade which fused Mughal and early British colonial architecture. In 1843 the post of *naib e nazim* was abolished, and the palace went into decline. According to Bishop Heber, who visited it in 1824, the complex had open galleries for performances, inner courtyards, private residences, a mosque, water reservoirs, a soldier's barracks, and gardens – all typical of Mughal palatial architecture. There was also an octagonal hall supported by Gothic arches; the surrounding verandas had tall Gothic windows. Another hall was called 'Baroduari'; this had 12 doors, which were used as the individual entrances of the 12 leaders from the *mahallas* (townships) of Dhaka. A narrow canal ran through the north of the complex to connect with a body of water in the east, the now extinct Kamalapur River. The main gate on the west side is the only part of the palace that survives today. It is two storeys high and has a polygonal plan. Its east façade measures 15.20 metres; its west façade, 8.13 metres. In its middle a massive archway spans a five-metre-wide passage. The arch has pointed decoration around its border. The comparatively large hall on the second floor measures 13.75 by 8.30 metres. On the front side of the hall is an open veranda with three arches, whose dimensions are 3.68 by 1.70 metres. On either side of the veranda are bay windows capped by small domes. The ground floor contains three rooms and a staircase on the south side. The flat roof rests on wooden rafters. The bay windows have louvre shutters resembling Venetian blinds. The careful restoration used plaster made from brick dust mixed with lime. The building was previously used by Dhaka University and Dhaka Museum. Since 1952 it has housed the Asiatic Society of Bangladesh.

Old High Court, National Eidgagh and Supreme Court complex

033 C

Kazi Nazrul Islam Avenue/
High Court Street
1911

The two-storey Old High Court build-ing was originally designed as the res-idence of the governor of Bengal and Assam in 1905. However, it was regarded as too unsuitable to ever be inhabited by any official. The British governors pre-ferred to stay at Dilkusha Lodge. In 1908 Dhaka College moved into the building. In 1947 the edifice was converted for use as the High Court of what was then East Pakistan. It now houses various govern-ment offices belonging to the Ministry of

Law. The complex consists of four wings arranged around a vast quadrangular cen-tral courtyard. The four oblong blocks ac-commodate nearly 50 compartments of different sizes on two floors. The residen-tial quarters were on the west side. The function of the rooms varies with their size. There are: drawing rooms (7.62 by 10.36 metres), dining rooms (7.62 by 4.88 metres), bedrooms, dressing rooms, lamp rooms, etc. The building's entrance hall is square with sides of 8.53 metres. A con-tinuous covered veranda (2.95 metres wide) runs along the entire length of the façade, from north to south. The east wing contains a large ballroom (18.30 by 16.76 metres) with a floor of polished teak. The triangular pediment, columns of the Corinthian order, emphatic rustication on the façade, and the approach through a formal garden are all features of the European Renaissance Style. While the lantern dome supported by a ring of slender piers clearly derives from English architecture, the recessed arches beneath it could be described as 'Saracen fusion'. The bifurcated central staircase of marble and two subsidiary spiral stairs in the inner corners of the quadrilateral blocks are points of interest. The entire ground floor has a floor of white marble. To the north of the Old High Court, a massive new court building, designed by Thariani and Sons, was completed in 1967 to accommodate the Supreme Court. The arcade on the first floor follows the Mughal Revival style, but the ground-floor corridor has arbitrarily been given a look of solidity with rough *jali* (latticework) windows. Four columns front the ground-floor entrance. None of the eight columns on the second floor is aligned with its counterpart on the ground floor. Such an unsophisticated hotchpotch of architectural details is a misleading representation of Bangladesh's culture with respect to materials, climate, and context. The slender naive porch is an imitation of the porches of the palaces of the nawabs. In between the two buildings is an enormous expanse of green lawn; this is the National Eidgah, where congregational prayers are held at two festivals. At every *Eid* (feast) around 100,000 Muslims join in special prayers. The president, members of the cabinet, other politicians, and diplomats come together to pray. This piece of land is also the site of a number of unidentified tombs. Another tomb is thought to be that of Hazrat Sharfuddin Chisti (RA), the second son of the great Sufi Hazrat Khwaja Mainuddin Chisti (RA) of Ajmer and a companion of Hazrat Shahjalal (RA) of Sylhet. Hazrat Sharfuddin Chisti entered the jungle in the vicinity of today's Ramna district to preach Islam in 1306. His tomb is now a famous place of prayer.

Azizur Rahman

Samia Binte Azhar (all pictures of this object)

Chummery House, CIRDAP

034 C

17 Topkhana Road
Robert Luis Proudolk
1920

Chummery House was built in 1920 as accommodation for unmarried British officials. It was converted to the women's dormitory of Dhaka University in 1938. Later, in the 1950s, it became the headquarters of a public-service commission and then, in 1985, home to the head office of CIRDAP in Bangladesh. Untypically for a building on the plains, its architecture alludes to the English cottage style. This building was an integral part of the unique set up that was colonial Dhaka. The entire Ramna area was elegantly planned, following the English garden city model, by Patrick Geddes in 1917 as a civil station for Europeans. It is said that the British architect Robert Luis Proudolk designed other buildings here and may also have designed this one, but there is no historical proof of this. The red tiles of the pitched roof (which have now turned a clay colour), the expanse of open lawn, and the green backyard are all attributes of the English country house. When the building was renovated in 2005, many original features, both exterior and interior, were altered. A tower with a conical roof over a hexagonal base was attached to the left part of the main block. There is a projecting bay with three windows on the right-hand part of the façade. The building has only two storeys but is comparatively tall – at nearly 12.5 metres. The balustrades reproduce the half-timbered character of European vernacular architecture. In 1995 a six-storey extension was proposed; only two floors have been built to date. This has disturbed the original character of the building, and especially the sprightly Englishness of the front garden.

Md. Mohaimin Ali Khan (all pictures of this object)

Osmani Memorial Convention Hall

Zero point, Poltan/
Abdul Gani Road
Shah Alam Zahiruddin,
M A Muktadir, 1981
Paradigm Architects and Engineers
2019 (refurbishment)

035 C

1

This building is protected by the Public Works Department and Department of Archaeology. It consists of an auditorium with an RCC framed structure; from the ground floor up there are clear spaces with spans of 30 metres. There are four storeys above ground and four additional storeys for car parking in the basement. The influence of Le Corbusier is clearly to be seen in the post-and-lintel structural system, the use of the colour white, and the free-flowing spaces that characterise the plan. This is a very safe, quiet area and close to the administrative hub of the Secretariat Building – which explains why Osmani Hall has been a popular venue for cultural and political events over the last four decades and is still the venue of choice for national and political events organised by the prime minister and president. It has a footprint of 9664 square metres. The acoustic design is by a company from Singapore. Accessibility for the disabled was the main concern when the building was refurbished in 2019. Elevators capable of accommodating wheelchairs were added. The number of seats in the auditorium was increased to 720. An ultrasound system, LED screens, audio equipment, cableless media connections, a well-furnished VIP lounge, two conference rooms, security units, and an attractive interior-lighting system were installed in order to meet international standards. There is a garden in front of the building. The façade is decorated with a magnificent mural by the well-known artist Kayum Chowdhury.

Dhaka Nagar Bhaban

036 C

Fulbaria, Pheonix Road/
Banga Bazar Circle
A. Imamuddin,
Lailun Nahar Ekram
1995

The municipality of Dhaka was created in 1864, when the city became the seat of the divisional headquarters of East Bengal. In 1983 the municipality was transformed into Dhaka City Corporation. As the seat of the city's mayor, the location for this headquarters building was chosen carefully; it marks the point where the two Dhakas – old and new – meet. The 15-storey city hall contains offices, conference rooms, a bank, a museum, a prayer hall, and public terraces. Its rhythmic, repetitive façade is dominated by gigantic columns flanking arches. An enormous portico contains an inviting arched entrance. The lift core and services are at the east and west ends of the façade, where expanses of solid wall emphasise the edges of this enormous structure. The first two storeys have a double-height colonnade with a waffle roof above the corridor. The building's design is very symmetrical. At the top of its central part is a bastion-like mass containing gigantic clocks over the south and north façades. The building's polished texture gives it a timeless appearance. The garden in front helps preserve normality of scale and at the same time reinforces this building's status as a landmark. In 2011 the city of Dhaka was divided into two halves; this building is now home to Dhaka South City Corporation.

Md. Mohaimin Ali Khan

Akram Khan/dreamstime

Baitul Mokarram Mosque

037 C

GPO Road/Baitul Mokarram
Road/Bangabandhu Avenue
Abul Husein M. Thariani
1968

The proprietor of the Bawany jute mill, Haji Abdul Latif Ibrahim Bawany, owned a large pond in Paltan, on the border between the old and new Dhaka. In 1960 he filled in the pond and donated this land to the Pakistan government. Shortly afterwards, the mosque built here was declared the national mosque of Bangladesh and passed under the control of the Ministry of Religious Affairs. Its name means 'the holy house'. This was the first dome-less Modernist mosque yet remains faithful to the principles of traditional Mughal architecture. The large, cube-shaped central structure is eight storeys (30 metres) high and resembles Islam's holiest structure, the Kaaba in Mecca. The platform on which the mosque stands is nearly three metres high; beneath it are shops for rent. The mosque's main entrance is on its east side. The vast, 2700-square-metre sahn (courtyard) is modelled on that of the great Umayyad Mosque in Damascus, Syria. The absence of the central dome is partly compensated for by the shallow domes above the porticos of the south and north entrances, where there are ablution facilities. Two patios ensure sufficient light and air for the interiors. The main prayer space has an area of 2500 square metres; there is a mezzanine floor of 171 square metres in the eastern part. This hall is surrounded by verandas on three sides. The *mihrab* (prayer niche) is rectangular. Ornamentation on floors and walls has here been kept to a minimum; blue is the predominant colour. There used to be a garden in front of the mosque, but during the renovation in 2008 this was converted into an open space on top with lavatories and services at the bottom. Two high minarets were also added, together with an enormous gate on the east side (the original design by Thariani included a detached *minar* (tower) on the south side). The extension work was carried out with the help of a subsidy granted by the Saudi Arabian government in recognition of its friendly relationship with Bangladesh. The entire complex occupies an area of 33,560 square metres and includes 22 warehouses and 350 shops in an arcade that runs north–south. The complex also includes the offices of an Islamic foundation, an assembly hall, libraries, and parking areas. The mosque has a maximum capacity of 40,000 persons for Friday and Eid prayers.

Md. Maruf Hassan/iStock

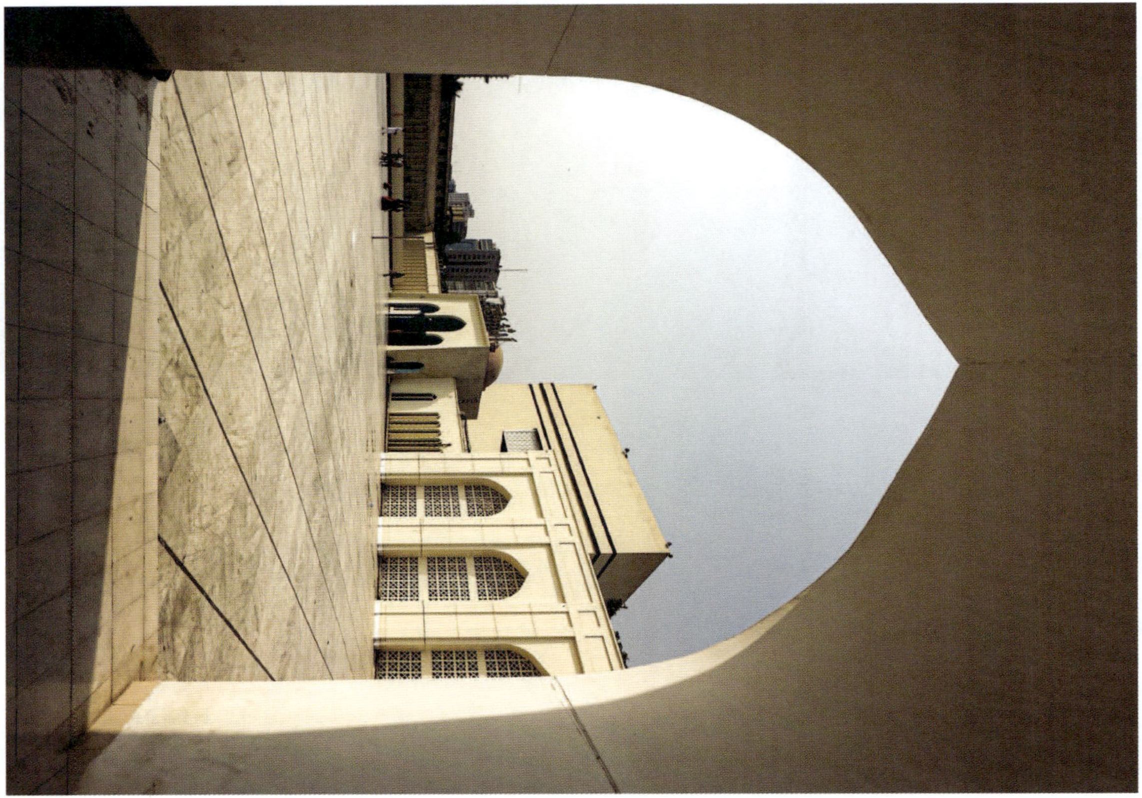

Sukanta Kumar/iStock

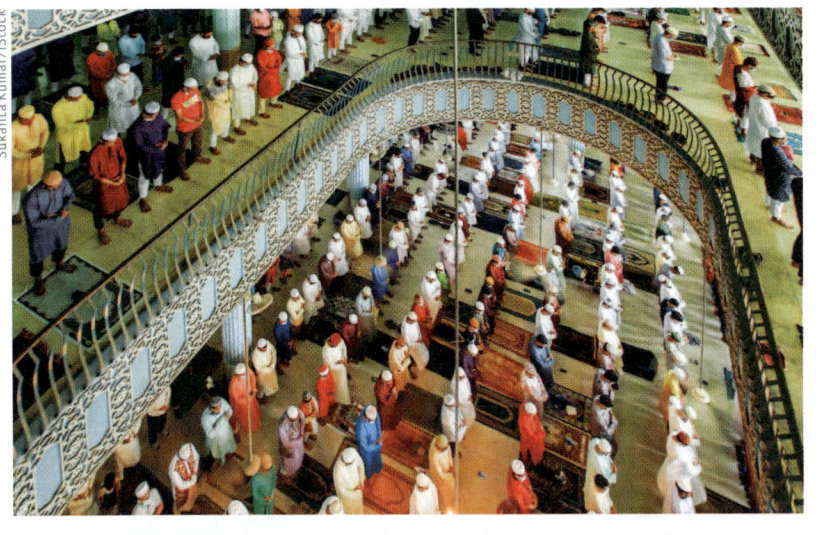

Jiban Bima Tower

DIT Avenue/Toyenbee Road
Muzharul Islam
1971

038 C

Jiban Bima Tower is in the city's central business district, Motijheel. This 21-storey building has a floor area of 16722.55 square metres, is 84.62 metres high, and was the tallest building in the country from 1971 to 1983. It is the headquarters of Jivban Bima Corporation, a premier government-owned company headed by Khuda Buksh, the man known as 'the wizard of insurance', and today the largest life-insurance company in Bangladesh. Octagonal in shape, the tower stands on a seven-storey podium shaped like a horseshoe. Muzharul Islam, the author of the project, realised that a sudden and dramatic increase in height from street level would make it impossible to maintain a human scale. The first three storeys of the podium have accordingly been recessed; the resulting triple-height colonnade takes account of adjacent traffic and pedestrian movement. The top floor of the octagonal tower has a band of fenestration framed by folded arches. The tower's eighth and ninth floors are compressed to emphasise the point where the tower and the podium meet. Here Muzharul Islam, the pioneer of modern architecture, demonstrated how to fit a high-rise to the scale of our city.

Md. Mohaimin Ali Khan

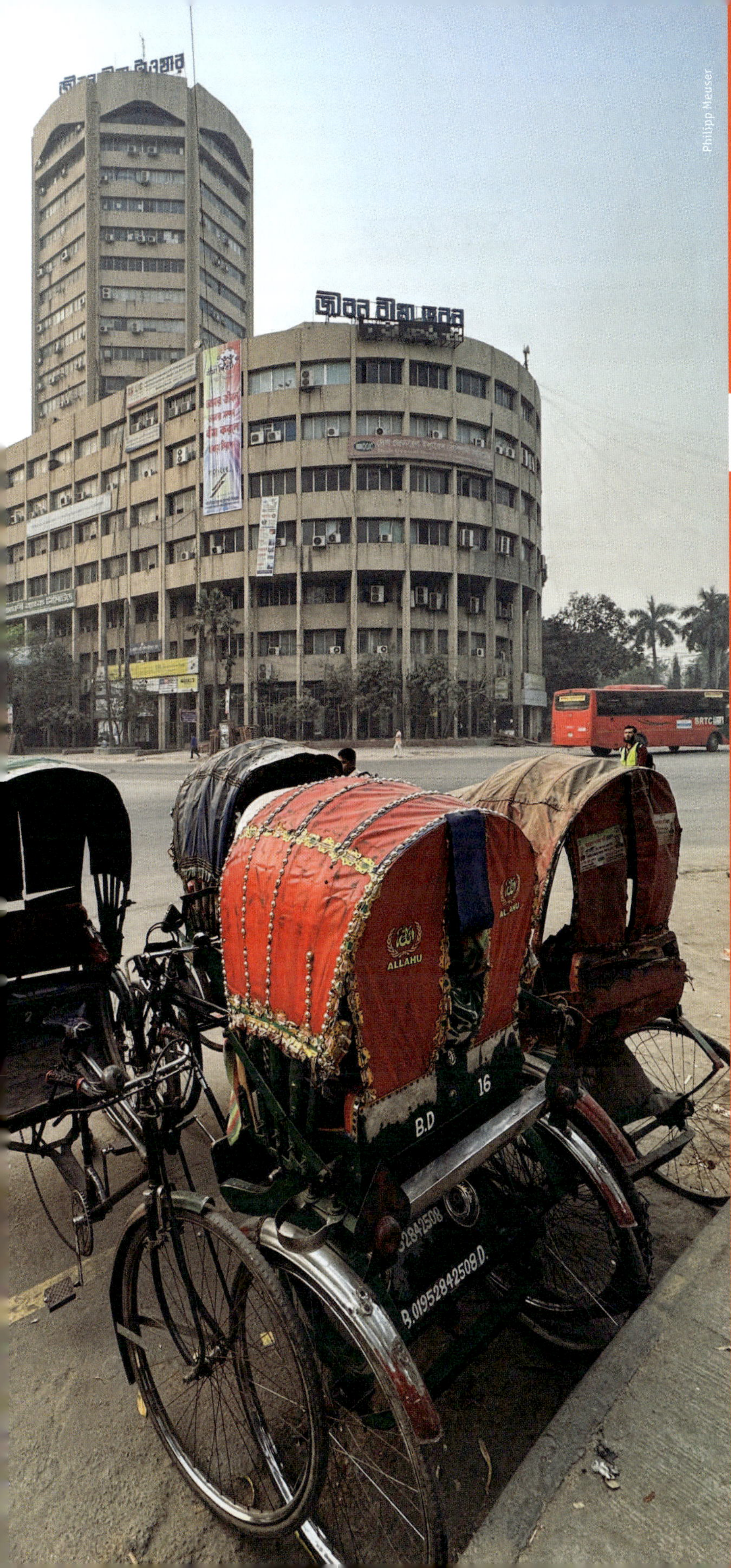

Philipp Meuser

Philipp Meuser

Ruplal House

039 **C**

Ahsanullah Road/B. K. Das Road
Martin Company
1825/1850

Situated in Farashganj beside the Buckland Dam, this house was first known as 'Aratun House' after its original owner, Stephen Aratun, an Armenian. In 1840 the house was bought by two merchant brothers, Ruplal and Raghunath Das. The Das family however, left this property in 1947, following the partition of India. In 1962 a rich Muslim businessman, Siddiq Jamal, acquired it. Lord Dufferin, Viceroy of Indian, stayed here during his visit to Dhaka in 1886. At that time there was only one mansion in Dhaka that could compete with Aratun House: Ahsan Manzil (the Pink Palace). Ruplal House is now protected heritage, although in a very poor condition and currently occupied by a spice market. It is in the Renaissance style with decoration mostly in the Greek Doric order. The complex comprises four unequal blocks of the same height arranged in an E shape. Its two storeys are nearly 11.6 metres high. The façade facing the river stretches to a length of almost 91 metres. The east side had a garden with a pool (no longer extant). There was a huge

clock at the top of the building; this fell victim to the 1987 earthquake. The house has 50 rooms of different sizes. There is a continuous veranda running from east to west and on the south and north façades, despite the fact that on the ground floor the building's various blocks are detached from one another. The verandas were supported by brick pillars with trefoil arches. The building's structure consists of 0.64-metre-thick brickwork bonded using lime mortar. The entire complex stands on a 0.61-metre-high plinth. The west wing, known as 'the Ruplal Block', has a floor area of 2322 square metres and Neoclassical decoration, including a grand portico with gigantic fluted Corinthian columns supporting a triangular pediment. This block is square in plan with rooms arranged around a central square courtyard. The service blocks are lower in height and slightly detached from the main layout. Steel I-beams of various sizes were used instead of wooden beams. On top of these beams are 0.28-metre-thick floors made from a mixture of red oxide, brick chips, and lime mortar. The floors were then finished with marble and terrazzo tiles grooved with tinted glass. The east block, known as 'the Raghunath Block', is the newest;

its comparatively ordinary features are typical of mid-nineteenth-century colonial architecture. This wing of the house has a floor area of 1114 square metres. Its circular columns have capitals featuring Indian elements. There are two rectangular courtyards; the rooms are elongated in shape. The Raghunath Block has wooden beams. The wooden staircases are supported by a wooden cross-beam system and have iron joists at either end. Brick tiles were used to form all the cornices and projecting eaves. The house's central block is comparatively large, nearly 183 metres long, and 6.70 metres high, with a floor area of 836 square metres. This wing includes a ballroom and a music room on the upper floor. It is connected to the neighbouring blocks by archways. Its walls are nearly 0.76 metres thick, and its roof is supported by wooden rafters. The floors and ceilings are extensively decorated with geometric and floral patterns, with mirrors in between.

Avijit Barman

Avijit Barman

Northbrook Hall

Farashganj Road,
Oaiseghat
1880

In 1850 the British parliament passed a library act allowing the governors of its colonies to establish libraries. A consequence was this building in Dhaka, which was both town hall and the city's first public library and whose name commemorates the visits of Lord Northbrook, Viceroy of India, in 1874 and 1876. Funding for the building came from prominent landlords and aristocrats, most notably Raja Rai Bahadur, who donated ten thousand taka. The district commissioner of Dhaka, W.A. Larminie, inaugurated the building in 1879. In 1882 a public library with 1000 books was added on the south-east side, together with a club house known as 'Johnson Hall'. In 1905 Nawab Salimullah launched the Muhammadan Provincial Union, a union for Muslims. During his visit to Dhaka University, the poet Rabindranath Tagore was honoured here by the Dhaka Municipality Student Forum and the Citizens' Association on 7 February 1926. In 1952 the building was converted for use as a telegram office. Later, in 1956, it became home to a women's college. During the Liberation War of 1971, Northbrook Hall was burnt down by the Pakistan Army. In 2009 Northbrook Hall was declared protected heritage but, ironically, the library was then closed due to its poor structural

Philipp Meuser

condition in 2017. The main entrance, on the north side, is flanked by five horseshoe arches. This two-storey entrance porch facing south towards the River Buriganga is 10 metres wide and is a fusion of Mughal and Renaissance architecture. Four octagonal minarets on the north part of the building stand out for their pinnacles, ornamental parapet, and domes. The delicate Mughal features, such as *jalis* (latticework screens) and onion domes with budding finials, are an expression of Islamic style. By contrast, the windows and doors display allude to the European Renaissance. The verandas are three metres wide. The library has a 3.96-metre ceiling and dimensions of 7 by 4.57 metres. Its 15 enormous bookshelves contain 15,000 books, including

rare volumes some of which are over 200 years old. The distinctive exterior and interior plasterwork and paint are responsible for the building's nickname – *lalkuthi*, which means 'red house'. The deep red of the façades with its roofs on different levels used to present a magnificent sight when seen from the riverfront; today, however, this view is obscured by the city's haphazard urbanisation.

1

Avijit Barman

Avijit Barman

Avijit Barman

Bahadur Shah Park

041 C

Johnson Road
Laxsmibazar/Sadarghat
1800
Rafiq Azam
2020 (renovation)

In the eighteenth century Armenians prospered and established themselves on the north bank of the River Buriganga in Dhaka in a settlement of 42 houses with its own clubhouse. The locals ridiculed their billiard ball as an *'anta'* (egg) and nicknamed this clubhouse *'antaghor'* or 'egg house'. Later, in the first half of 1800, the British demolished the club in order to lay out an urban park as a circular promenade for St. Thomas' Church. The park had 250 species of local trees. In 1857, during the Sepoy mutiny, British soldiers publicly executed the mutineers, including one woman, hanging them on trees in the park; the corpses were left to hang for several days. In 1858 Mr. Peacock, the district commissioner of Dhaka, announced in front of a large crowd that the Indian Empire was to be taken under the direct rule of Queen Victoria. Khwaja Abdul Ghani, the Nawab of Dhaka, rebuilt the park in 1875, when the British government gave him the honorific title of *nawab bahadur* for his support during the revolt. To commemorate this honour and convey gratitude to Queen Victoria, Khwaja Abdul Ghani renamed the park 'Victoria Park'. The park contains two obelisks. One,

Avijit Barman (all pictures)

erected in 1885, commemorates Khwaja Hafijullah, the grandson of Khwaja Abdul Ghani. The other obelisk is a smaller iron obelisk representing the throne of Queen Victoria. In 1957, exactly 100 years after the subcontinent's first independence movement, the park was renamed after Bahadur Shah Zafar, the last Mughal emperor. In 1960 a cenotaph was erected by the Dhaka Improvement Trust (DIT) to perpetuate the sacrifice of the patriots. In 1962 a monumental memorial structure nearly five storeys high was built on the eastern edge of the park. This has a one-metre-high square plinth with continuous steps on all sides and huge identical arches. The park is the best urban green space for the inhabitants of old Dhaka to relax in. Oval-shaped, it has two entrances and an area of nearly 27,114 square metres. Also here are four cannons belonging to the British Army, placed here after the 1858 mutiny. The park was renovated by Bangladesh's famous architecture firm Shatotto in 2018 as part of 'Dhaka in Water and Greenery', a development scheme by Dhaka City Corporation (South).

Kabi Nazrul Government College

1 Municipality Street/
Lakshimibazar Street
*Major Mann, Vivian Scott,
Rakhal Das Chatterjee*
1880

042 C

The first Islamic education centre in East Bengal, this started life as Mohsania Madrasa in 1874 with help from the mighty fund set up by the philanthropist Haji Mohammad Mohsin. In 1915 this institution became Dhaka Madrasa. After Dhaka University was established in 1921, it was transformed into an intermediate college. Today Kabi Nazrul Government College has approximately 30,000 students and occupies a site with a total area of 8093.71 square metres. This three-storey building could be described as colonial architecture with an Indo-Saracen twist. The red-plastered façade is dominated by multi-cusped arches in front of white walls. Instead of keystones, the arches, framed in rectangles, have floral motifs resembling betel leaves on their sides. On the external surface of the lower part of each pier is a square depression. The bases of the pillars and the meeting points of the arches are decorated with interweaved bands of merlons. Originally, the building had a symmetrical plan with small domes on the corner pillars at each side. There are wooden balustrades and railings and louvred doors and windows, all painted deep green – a typical choice for the colonial period. The floors are supported by steel beams on the ground floor; the upper floors have beams of teakwood. The slabs of each floor project 50 centimetres metres from the exterior walls, creating horizontal bands on the façade. The library contains 40,000 books. There is a large playground in the middle of the courtyard.

Tanima Nasrin

M A Zubair

St. Thomas Church

043 C

Nawabpur Road/Johnson Road
1821

Fritz Kapp

1

This small church used to be surrounded by luxuriant greenery, and to this day it has the green expanses of Victoria Park to its south. Its architectural style could be described as 'Eastern Gothic'. The originally Anglican church was inaugurated by Reginald Heber, Bishop of Kolkata, during a visit to Dhaka in 1824. Convicts from Dacca Prison were employed in the church's construction. It has a square clock tower with arched windows with two segments. The tower's top is capped with fortress-like battlements. The roof has wooden battens fastened to iron joists. The verandas have sloping wooden beams, allowing rainwater to run off easily. The delicate stone- and brickwork and white plaster exert an attraction which has not faded over two centuries. A perpendicular-Gothic porch with four columns marks the main entrance to the building . The nave is rectangular; its west end has two non-load-bearing, grooved columns. Two columns at the back of the nave flank an arch leading to a rectangular pulpit with a brass cross. The wooden altar at the east end of the church has a brass cross on top of it. The walls are studded with stone plaques commemorating deceased members of the church. The curved chairs of thick teak for the congregation,

stone font, and marble baptismal font are all in a good state of preservation. Later, the open colonnades on two sides of the nave were filled in to create solid wall – a pity from the point of view of aesthetics. The church was given the status of cathedral in 1951. The religious body it belongs to has been known as 'the Church of Bangladesh' since Anglicans, Presbyterians, Congregationalists, and various Methodist and Baptist bodies came together in the 1970s. In 1975 the Church of Bangladesh became a member of the World Council of Churches.

Mahmud Hasan

Mahmud Hasan

Mahmud Hasan

Jagannath University

Jagannath University
Chattarangan Avenue
1884

044 C

Jagannath University is located on a 44,515-square-metre site near the bank of the River Buriganga. The site was initially, from 1858 forwards, home to Dhaka Brahma School, a primary school. In 1872 Kishorilal Chowdhury, a landlord from Baliati in the Tangail district, bought the school and named it after his father. The school was upgraded to second-class college in 1884 and further upgraded to first-class college in 1908. In 1910 the college was affiliated to Pramoth Manmoth College in Tangail and became the best equipped private college in Dacca. In 1968 it was taken over by the government. In 2005 it became a public university. The administrative building of Jagannath University is a perfect blend of Renaissance and colonial architecture. The pediment has an emphatically projecting cornice with dentils. Two pairs of Corinthian columns support a double-height portico. The ground floor is distinguished by a rusticated arcade. The second floor has arches with keystones – a feature typical of British colonial residential architecture. The roof parapet echoes the balustrade between the columns of the second-floor colonnade; the pillars of the parapet are capped with urns. At each corner of the building are square rooms with a floor area of 100 square metres. Except on its west side, this listed heritage building has been surrounded by new buildings which have tried to copy its ornamentation. To its south and north are two courtyards filled with greenery and new sculptures dedicated to the language movement and the Liberation War. The university currently has 36 departments, 960 teachers, and 17,134 students.

Avijit Barman (all pictures of this project)

Brahmo Mandir
Loyal Street, Potuatuli
1869

After coming into contact with European philosophy, educated Indians started reforming Bengali socio-cultural beliefs, first in Kolkata and then in the rest of Bengal. The religious beliefs of Brahmins now concentrated on 'incorporeal God'; the worship of idols was prohibited. This so-called 'monotheistic reformation' was initiated by Raja Ram Mohan Roy, the first modern Indian and philanthropist, in 1828. Debendranath Tagore, the grandfather of Bangladesh's national poet, Rabindranath Tagore, was the next key figure in this movement. In 1846 Braja Sundar Mitra founded the first Brahma Samaj temple in Dhaka at his home in Shakharibazar. The academy moved to its current location in 1869, and a library was added in 1871 at the right side of the building. The first library in Dacca, it was called 'the Raja Ram Mohan Roy Reading Room'. It contained approximately 30,000 books and was visited by Rabindranath Tagore in 1926. The building burned down during the Liberation War in 1971. Today this is still a learning centre for creative and progressive minds from all faiths. The red and white façade of the two-storey colonial building has six Doric columns punctuating five hemispherical archways. The keystones of the arches have a motif based on local flora and white rope-like bands at the edges. The middle arch is used as a gateway; the other arches have simple balustrades blocking access. The roof parapet echoes the Dutch Renaissance with motifs taken from local ornamentation. The columns are capped with flat and square capitals. The interior is more like a church: there is an 'Om' sign, a dais at the corner of the hall room for *acharyas* (preachers), and long benches in the centre for the singing of devotional songs.

Biswarup Ganguly

Saeed Ahmed

Philipp Meuser

Ahsan Manzil

2/3 Islampur Road, Kumartoli
1872
Gobinda Chandra Roy,
1888 (renovation)
Abu H Imamuddin,
1992 (conservation)

046 C

After Lord Curzon's long-awaited visit to Dhaka on 18–19 February 1904, it became obvious that a separate Muslim state would be created in India. The Ahsan Manzil (Pink Palace) witnessed the creation of a state named 'Pakistan' as a home for Indian Muslims. This was the cradle of Muslim political awareness: the All-India Muslim League was launched here in 1905 under the leadership of Nawab Khwaja Salimullah. The building's origin remains obscure. During the Mughal era, Sheikh Enayet Ullah, the landlord of Jamalpur district, built Rongmohol, a garden house for dances, parties, and entertainment and accommodation for his harem. Later, his son Sheikh Moti Ullah sold the property to French merchants who established a *kuthi* (trade post) here in 1740, during the reign of Nawab Alibardi Khan. The French dug a pool called 'Les Jalla' as a source of drinking water; it still exists today. After the Battle of Plassey in 1757, as allies of the defeated ruler, Nawab Shiraj Ud Doula, the French were expelled from Dhaka by the British East India Company. In 1827, under the Paris agreement of 1814, France laid claim

to all its previous possessions in India. Eventually, this building was given back to them, but the French were never able to re-establish their trading rights; the monopoly belonged to the British. In 1830 the French sold the building to a native landlord, Khwaja Alimullah, and left Dhaka forever. The nawab renovated the house and added stables and a family mosque. His son Khwaja Abdul Ghani named it 'Ahsan Manzil' after his own beloved son Khwaja Ahsanullah. He extended the palace, adding a new wing on the east side. The old wing (Andormohol) was converted for use as private quarters; the new wing (Rongmohol) became a public venue for parties and dancing. On the west side are a number of small living rooms, a massive dining hall, a ballroom, and the Hindustani Room. In the middle of these rooms on the ground floor is a secret vault in which treasures can be stored. The east side comprises a large drawing room, a cards room, a library, a state room, and two other guest rooms. The house's front, which faces the river, has a grand set of steps leading directly to the vast second-floor terrace and a projecting triple-arched portico. There used to be a fountain in the garden in front of the steps; it no longer exists. The two-storey palace has load-bearing brick walls that are 0.78 metres thick. As was common practice, it was built on a one-metre-high platform to keep it out of the reach of flash floods. Its footprint measures 125.4 by 28.75 metres. The ground

floor is five metres high; the second storey, 5.8 metres high. The porticos on the north and south sides are five metres high. Wooden beams support the roof, which is made from brick chips and lime mortar. The building's unique architectural style is known as 'Indo-Saracenic Revival'. The vaulted wooden ceilings in the drawing room and the *jalsaghar* (music room) were decorated with lavish Islamic geometric designs. The floors of the dining room, chest room, and *darbar* (assembly) halls are ornately paved with ceramic tiles in yellow, white, and green. The floors of the spacious verandas and bedrooms are lined with marble, which was also used for parts of the top floor. The doorways are in the form of semicircular arches; all the interior doors have panels of colourful glass. The gorgeous wooden staircases with iron balusters are decorated with patterns of vine leaves. On 7 April 1888 a devastating tornado smashed into Ahsan Manzil. Both the old and the new wings had to be reconstructed. The original French style of the Rongmohol (the east wing) was restored. A wooden bridge was built to connect the second floors of the two wings, and a high octagonal dome was constructed over the central round room. The top of this dome is 27.13 metres above ground level. The square room on the ground floor was converted to an octagonal shape by the addition of brickwork to its corners and of squinches to the corners of the ceiling. The eight corners of the octagon were then slanted gradually to give the dome a resemblance to the bud of a lotus. In 1897 the palace was again devastated, this time by an earthquake. When Nawab Khwaja Ahsanullah died in 1901, there was no heir to take an interest in maintaining the palace. Tenants damaged its original aesthetic. In 1952 the East Pakistan Government acquired the property under the East Bengal Estate Acquisition Act. After independence, the successors of the nawab called an auction, but this was cancelled by Bangabandhu Sheikh Mujibur Rahman on 2 November 1974; he wanted to establish a museum and tourism centre here. In 1985 the National Museum was given authority over the building and its contents, and conservation work began under the Directorate of Public Works and Architecture in 1986. The government acquired the 22,864-square-metre site, but it was eventually possible to develop a museum complex on 20,072 square metres of land, including the palace. On 20 September 1992 Ahsan Manzil was reopened to the public. This was the first successful conservation project in Bangladesh.

Kazi Karar Naier

Nawab Bari Mosque

10 DIT Avenue, Dilkusha
1670

047 C

This typical three-dome Mughal mosque is formally known as 'Shahjalal Dakhini Mosque'. Shahjalal Dakhini was a Sufi from Gujarat who arrived in Bengal during the reign of Sultan Shamsuddin Yusuf Shah (1474–81). He established a settlement in the Motijheel area. When he became a threat to the ruler, Yusuf Shah killed him and all his followers and buried them nearby. Two hundred years later, a mosque was erected during the time of another Sufi, Niamutullah, whose tomb also lies in this complex. Today the site is called 'Nawab Bari Mosque'. The mosque was renovated by Nawab Ahsanullah in the 1900s and became a favourite burial place for the family of the nawab. This is less ornamental than other Mughal mosques. The octagonal corner towers have five regularly spaced horizontal bands. The middle space is a square with a large dome above, while the side spaces are elongated rectangles with smaller domes above each. The parapets are decorated with blind merlons; the roof is flat.

1

Najmul Farhad (all pictures)

Gol Talab Pond

Islampur Road
Excavated in 1880s

048 C

Got Talab means 'circular tank', although this pond's shape is in fact oval. Locals also know it as 'Nawabbari Pond' since it is near the north-east corner of Ahsan Manjil. The site was listed by Dhaka City Corporation as a heritage site in 2009 and is regularly maintained under the National Water Management Plan. The pond has a surface area of 2.2 acres; its maximum depth is seven metres. Its banks are lined with trees such as coconuts, mangos, neems, and jackfruits. There is an abundance of local aquatic fauna as well. In the north-west part of the pond is a deck used for bathing.

Ishtiaque Ahmed

Kazi Karar Naier (all pictures of this project)

Amiruddin Daroga Mosque   `049` `C`

Sadarghat-Gabtoli Road
1840

Also known as 'Ghat Mosque', this mosque has three domes. The middle dome is the largest; its companions on each side are smaller. The mosque's patron was a police officer called Amiruddin, whose house was attached to the mosque. The house no longer exists, but Amiruddin himself is commemorated by a small tomb with Mughal features and an ornamental dome. The mosque was erected on the bank of the Buriganga; today it is suffocated by the surrounding tall buildings. The domes rest on octagonal drums decorated with blind merlons. From the middle of each octagon a vertical band rises to the top of the lotus finials. At the points where the bays of the mosque adjoin each other are turrets capped with smaller domes. The mosque's western wall has high, perforation-like windows.

Qassabtuli/Koshaituli Mosque 050 C
PK Ghosh Road
1919

Known locally as 'the Butchers' Mosque', this is one of the most decorative and exquisitely colourful mosques in Dhaka. Founded by two community leaders, Abdul Bari Bepari and Qamruddin Sardar, who were followers of Saint Moulana Keramat, it was extended in 1945 and renovated in 1971. It reintroduces pre-Mughal features but continues the Mughal practice of building mosques on a high plinth. Its three-flute domes are decorated with *chini tikri* (broken china); the middle dome is the largest. There is a balcony on the north side. On the west side are two towers with turrets and domes. The *mihrab* (prayer niche) on the west side is a concave depression with a spherical onion-shaped dome overhead; it is decorated with floral motifs, branches, a crescent, stars, and vases of flowers. It is said that local women with embroidery skills took part in creating the motifs, star-shaped inscriptions in Arabic, calligraphy, and geometrical designs around the inner hall. Even the doors are studded with colourful floral decorations. The use of glazed tiles shows Persian influences. The prayer chamber can accommodate 120 devotees at a time; the outer enclosure has capacity for an additional 1000.

2

Avijit Barman (all pictures)

Milosk50/dreamstime

Aviiit Barman

Armenian Church
Armenian Street, Armanitola
1781

051 C

The Ottoman and Persian quest for dominance over Armenia led to many Christian and Jewish Armenians being deported from the Julfa region in eastern Armenia. In 1605 they were forcibly resettled in the 'new Julfa' area of Ispahan in Iran during the rule of Shah Abbas I of the Safavid dynasty. Later, the 40 Armenian tribes spread all over the world, following the East India Company, with whom they had reached an agreement in 1688 guaranteeing them religious freedom and low customs rates for maritime trade. Nearly 100 Julfan Armenians settled in Dhaka. They became rich through the role they played in the jute and leather trades, especially from a trade post in the neighbouring Narayanganj district. The area in which they gathered in Dhaka became a thriving trade centre called Armanitola. This church complex was initially a graveyard with a small chapel. Agaminus Catachik, a businessman, donated the land for construction of an apostolic church. The graveyard contains 350 mostly nameless tombs. An iconic statue in the praying position was erected beside the grave of Catachik Avatik Thomas, portraying his wife; this was sculpted in and imported from Kolkata. The church is 230 metres long with a 4.32-metre-wide nave, four doors, and a total of 27 windows. The ground floor is divided into three sections: a pulpit with railings, behind which is a 0.75-metre-deep baptismal font; the nave with two folding doors at its entrance; and a separate praying area, where seats are enclosed by a wooden railing. Two paintings by the English painter Charles Port, who was also head of Pogose School, have recently been renovated. Other notable features are a spiral staircase and a watch tower beside the central nave. The tower was built by Johans Paru Piyete Sarkis. A clock tower was added at the western edge in 1830; its bell could be heard six kilometres away, and the people of Dhaka used to synchronise their clocks with its strikes. In 1880 the clock stopped, and an earthquake in 1897 caused both towers to collapse. A third tower still stands; this has a square base and is known as a *shankhanil minar*, a sign of a North Indian influence. In 1996 Mother Teresa stayed in the church compound during her visit to the city. The church was given national heritage status after documentaries by the BBC and AFP emphasised its significance. After 1947 and the events of 1971, most of the city's Armenian population emigrated to Canada and Australia. The last remaining Armenian to take care of the church was Michael Joseph Martin, who left Bangladesh in 2014.

Shaista Khan Mosque
Mitford Hospital complex
1678

It is believed that the palace compound of the Mughal *subader* (governor) was in this area, which used to be known as Katra Pakurtali. The mosque has a typical oblong plan measuring 14.13 by 7.62 metres. It has three naves; the middle nave is square and larger since it accommodates the larger, central, dome. There are four octagonal towers topped by kiosks terminating in *kalasha* (pot) finials. There are five arched gateways – three in the east wall and one each in the north and south façades, which is rare in Mughal architecture. The central archway is larger and set within a projecting fronton, flanked by ornamental turrets. All the east archways serve as main entrances and consist of two successive arches, the outer one of which is a half-domed vault. The *mihrab* (prayer niche) in the centre of the west wall is semi-octagonal; its ornamental turrets are no longer extant. Like other mosques from the Mughal era, this has domes resting on octagonal drums and crowned with lotus and pitcher finials. The parapets and drums below the domes have ornate merlon friezes. An inscription in Persian on the main door indicates the reign of Shaista Khan. This mosque is distinctive for its style, the 'Shaista Khan style'. Here for the first time the corner towers do not protrude but fit within the thickness of the walls. Only three other mosques in this style survive today: Bibi Marium Mosque (1670) in Narayanganj, Bakshi Hamid Mosque (1692) in Chittagong, and Azimpur Mosque (1746) in Dhaka.

2

Sazzadur Rasheed (all photos of this project)

Tara Mosque

Abul Khairat Road,
Armanitola
1800–1850

053 C

The precise date of the construction of this mosque is unknown. What is certain is that it was built by a local chief called Mirza Golam Pir, who died in 1860. This makes it likely that it was built in the first half of the nineteenth century as an ordinary Mughal mosque. In 1926 its refurbishment was funded by Ali Jan Bepari, a rich businessman. He imported tiles from Japan, China, and England to add a touch of luxury in the decoration. At the same time a veranda as wide as the original mosque was added; this has five arches punctuated by four pillars in a typical symmetrical plan. In 1987 an extension supervised by the Department of Architecture added four more arches to the east façade, making a total of nine. The entrance is from the east side, where there is a star-shaped fountain for the pre-prayer ablution ritual. The courtyard is entirely paved with the same marble as covers the façade. There are small towers at the four corners of the mosque. The core of the prayer hall originally had only three doorways and measured ten by 3.35 metres. The total length of the building is now 21.34 metres; its exterior width is 7.98 metres. Tara Mosque is a rare example of *chini tikri* (broken china), a decorative technique which is now almost extinct. The dominance of the stars as a decorative theme was responsible for the mosque coming to be known as 'Tara (star) Mosque'. The mosaic of shards of china and porcelain in the interior and on the exterior of this cosy small mosque is eye-catching. In fact, the mosque shows two different uses of *chini tikri*. One method is cutting coloured clay tiles to fit a pattern and attaching the tiles to a white plastered façade. The other involves forming patterns by carefully positioning pieces of white marble on coloured walls. In the interior, floral and vase patterns cover the pendentives; the three *mihrabs* (prayer niches) are decorated with assorted glazed tiles. On the outer wall a mountain motif on glazed tiles was used to decorate the spaces in between the doors. The upper part of the façade displays common repetitive patterns involving a crescent and a star. The two larger domes form a row with the three smaller domes; all the domes are adorned with blue stars on a background of white marble.

2

Avijit Barman

Avijit Barman

Kazi Karar Najer (aL.pictures)

Kartalab Khan Mosque

Begum Bazar Road
Diwan Murshid Kuli Khan,
alias Kartalab Khan
1704

054 C

Kartalab Khan Mosque is an exceptional Mughal mosque with a structure that echoes Satgambuj and Lalbagfort mosques. Its dimensions are 39.62 by 13.41 metres, and it stretches lengthwise from north to south and widthways from east to west. Its non-symmetrical raised platform has an apse-like shape on its north side containing the tomb and sarcophagus of the mosque's first imam. Below the raised platform is a series of square and rectangular rooms, initially built to accommodate students of the madrasa but now rented to shopkeepers. The east façade has five arched doors providing access to the mosque. Each of these doorways leads to a space covered with a half dome and is flanked by slender octagonal turrets that rise above the parapet. The north and south walls have only one central door each. The vaulted terrace was originally open but is now enclosed by a wall. The corner towers have an octagonal base and are capped by solid kiosks with cupolas with flanking slender turrets. On the east side an arched gateway with a flight of steps leads to the main prayer hall, which is a large oblong measuring 25.60 by 5.18 metres. The overall built structure with its towers measures 28.65 by 8.23 metres. Four transverse arches divide the hall into five bays on the inside. The central bay, the largest, is square. All the bays have a dome resting on an octagonal drum and are decorated with lotus motifs on the inside and *kalasa* (pot) finials on the outside. The west façade contains five semi-octagonal *mihrabs* (prayer niches). On the outer wall these niches protrude and are bordered by turrets. The central niche is the largest; a three-stepped masonry pulpit is attached to its right side. The mosque's delightful ornamentation includes arched doorways, parapets, octagonal drums, and framed *mihrabs* crowned with merlons, basal leaf patterns on the interior surface of the dome, medallions with a rosette motif in the central portion of the dome, and *muqarnas* (decorative vaulting) in stucco on the east entrance. A unique feature is a *dauchala* (double-pitched roof) annex with curved eaves on its north part, covering an area of 6.10 by 2.13 metres. This articulated mass has two doors, on its east and south sides. It was, and still is, the imam's residence. Its interior wall is distinguished by rectangular and square alcoves that function as bookshelves. The east part of the complex includes a stepped well called a *baoli*, where devotees draw water for their ablutions. This is the only one of its kind in Bengal; the idea for it came from the Deccan, whence Kartalab Khan migrated to Dhaka.

Chhoto (Small) Katra

Hakim Habibur Rahman Lane
1671

055 C

Approximately 185 metres to the east of Boro Katra stands another *katra* (caravan-serai, inn) that was built during the reign of Governor Shaista Khan to accommodate the growing number of officers and their families in Dhaka. It follows a similar pattern to Boro Katra but is slightly smaller in size, which explains its name: *chhoto* means 'small'. Chhoto Katra contained luxurious residential enclaves with unusual names, such as 'Maya', 'Mukim', 'Nawab', and so on – a rare practice for any dwelling in greater Bengal. The *katra* is 101.20 metres long and 92.05 metres wide. The dimensions of its inner courtyard are 81.07 by 69.19 metres. The load-bearing walls are approximately one metre thick; the bastions, however, have much thicker walls, nearly 1.22 metres. Like Boro Katra, Chhoto Katra has two gateways, and the south gate is its main point of entry. At the corners of the south façade are two octagonal towers. During British colonial times the first English middle school in Dhaka was established here by Leonardo, a priest, in 1816. Later, the building was used as a storage space for coal and lime under the nawabs of Dhaka. The main entrance here is the same height as at Boro Katra but has less decoration. Some European features, such as the triple windows on the second floor and the tall turrets at the four corners on the roof, were added later. Inside, there is a nameless tomb which some believe to be the tomb of Champabibi, a local Hindu concubine of Shaista Khan; this has a multifoil saucer dome with sylph-like crooked spandrels. The Chhoto Katra complex is today in a lamentable state: a madrasa has illegally occupied part of the property, and its original configuration has been lost, with what remains constantly being erased by informal developments, which include shops and residences. The authenticity and integrity of the Mughal era have been destroyed; the building's structural stability is threatened.

Avijit Barman (all pictures of this project)

Boro (Large) Katra

Kazi Alauddin Road/
Nazimuddin Road
Diwan Mir Abul Qasim
1646

On the north bank of the River Buriganga and south of Chowk Bazaar, this *katra* was probably originally built as an official residence for Prince Shah Shuja, the second son of Mughal Emperor Shah Jahan of Delhi and governor of the newly conquered Bengal province. The word *katra* derives from Arabic, meaning a colonnaded building with a function similar to that of a caravanserai. This was a cellular dormitory with an oblong courtyard at its centre – a Persian tradition introduced to north India by the Mughals. What distinguished this from other *katras*, however, was its palatial quality. As indicated by an inscription over the north gateway, Boro Katra served as a charitable foundation: rent from its 22 shops was to be used to provide free accommodation to the needy. The building's plan shows the typical layout of central Asia: a quadrangular courtyard surrounded by shops and living units. The south block is a two-storey structure stretching 67.97 metres along the riverbank, its two corners marked by slender octagonal towers. It contained five vaulted rooms on the ground floor on each side of a central gateway. Above, the living rooms were arranged with a corridor facing the inner court. The east and west wings were nearly 70.10 metres long and were single-storey, containing shops and living quarters. There was also a gateway in the north block, but not so ornate as in the south block; it was obviously a less important rear entrance. The gateway in the middle of the south façade is the main entrance: a three-storey archway framed in a projecting rectangular bay. Its alcove is adorned with delicate plasterwork. The exterior wall around the spandrels has panels of plaster containing reliefs of various

Avijit Barman

Kazi Karar Naier

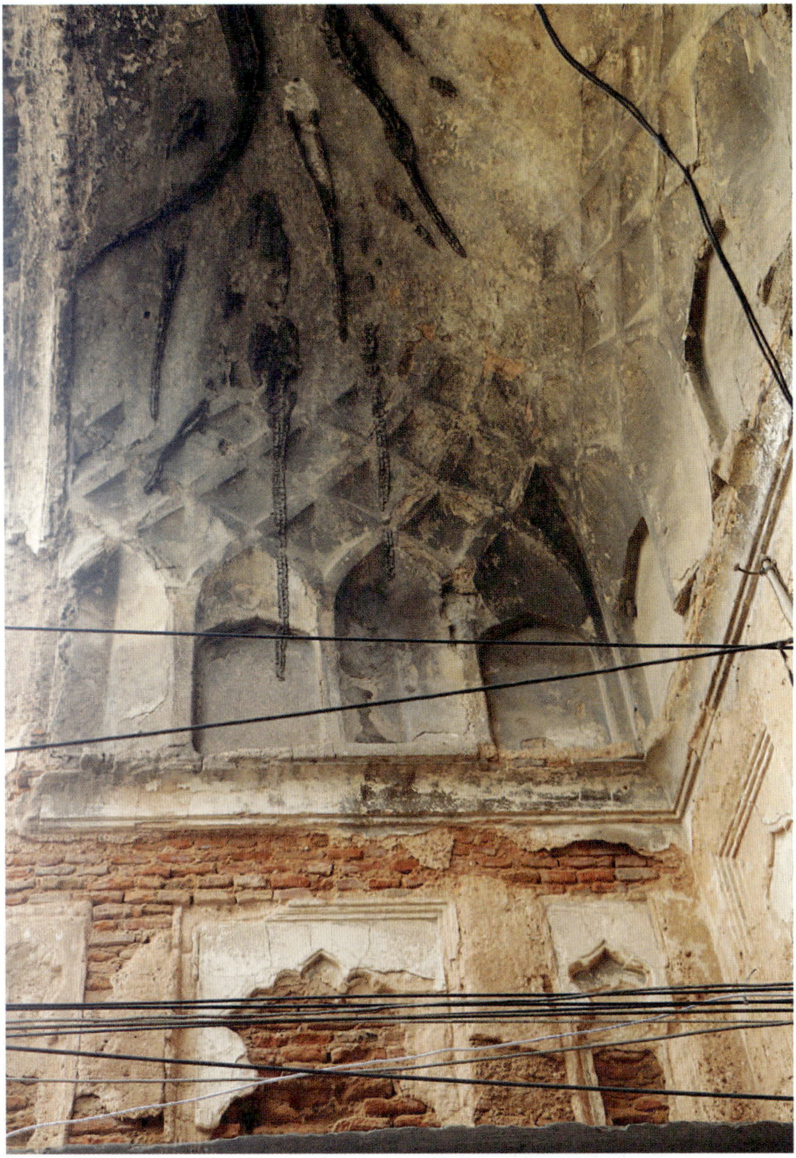

shapes, including four-centred, cusped, horseshoe, and flat arches. The gateway leads to a guardroom and, behind it, a hall with an octagonal dome overhead. The ceiling of the dome is plastered with a net pattern and foliage decoration. This hall provides access to the central courtyard. During a visit to Dhaka in the nineteenth century, the Orientalist James Atkinson described this building as 'a stupendous pile of grand architecture'. Today, however, the *katra* lies in ruins, more than half of it destroyed. The Department of Archaeology has failed to wrest control of this historical site from its present users.

Kazi Karar Naier

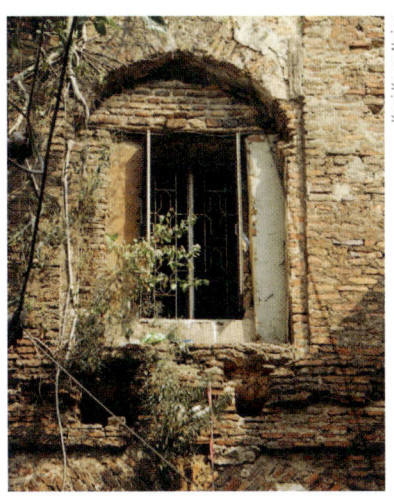

Central Jail of Dhaka
Nazimuddin Road
1788

057 C

July 2016 the prison was moved permanently to Keraniganj since the number of inmates at the time was triple the building's capacity and prisoners were having to take turns to stand, sit, and sleep. There are plans to establish two museums, an amusement park, a playground, and a mall on this site.

This is the oldest and largest prison in eastern Bengal. The Mughal governor Ibrahim Khan originally built a fort in the Chawkbazar area of the city. To this a residence was added for Naib Nazim in the seventeenth century. In 1788 an enclosure was built by the East India Company to hold 800 captives. After 1790 the entire fort was converted into a prison and extended; it now occupied 148,762 square metres of land. Of this, 71,022 square metres were enclosed by a perimeter wall; the remaining 77,740 square metres were outside the wall. Until 1836 Kotwali police station was also attached to the prison. The Sepoy mutineers were hanged here, and their bodies left to rot to induce fear in Dhaka's citizens during the 1860s. This building is of very simple colonial architecture. Its yellowish façade is decorated with white arches without keystones. There are 48 divisions and 12 cell buildings with 233 cells with a minimum floor area of 3.34 square metres, as well as other functions such as kitchens, working and training sheds, a bakery, a daycare centre, a hospital, a mosque, a small library, a visitor centre, and offices for 783 employees. The prison can hold a maximum of 2682 prisoners. There are a gallows and scaffolds for executing prisoners on death row (not open to visitors). The prison's Dewani cell was converted into a museum called 'the Memorial Museum of Bangabandhu' in 2010. Bangabandhu Sheikh Mujib Rahman was imprisoned here following his political protest in the 1960s; he planted two trees in the prison compound. Other notable inmates have included some of the nation's fathers: four national leaders were imprisoned and brutally killed here by army officers on 3 November in 1975; the army's coup plunged the country into prolonged military rule until 1991. Dhaka's central jail was also where Islamist leaders were hanged in 2013–2016 for their crimes against humanity and collaboration with the Pakistan Army during Bangladesh's Liberation War in 1971. In

2

ঢাকা কেন্দ্রীয় কারাগার

Lalbagh Fort

Lalbagh Road/
Shaishta Khan Road, Old Dhaka
1679

This fort complex on the western edge of Dhaka is a powerful emblem of the Mughal era. Once an important administrative centre, it is now an enclosure of green space amidst the haphazard cityscape. This was the principal and largest river fort of all the Mughal forts in the province of Bengal, built to protect the Mughals' new capital city, Dhaka. The fort was erected on the bank of the River Buriganga and had irrigation facilities typical of the Middle East. A water channel with fountains at regular intervals connected three buildings from east to west and north to south. Over the course of time, however, the river shifted further to the south; the fortress is now threatened by the advancing concrete jungle all around it. Constructed by the Mughal Prince Muhammad Azam Khan and later expanded by Viceroy Shaista Khan, the fortress complex is mainly a combination of four buildings: the Tomb of Iran Dukht, the Diwan-i-Aam, a hammam, and a small mosque. All were designed in the Mughal architectural style and built with local brick and a *surkhi* mortar consisting of lime and brick dust. The only imported material was basalt from Rajmahal in India, used to build the plinth to protect the fortress from flooding. The complex was surrounded by a three-metre-high fortified wall with two gateways and crowned by machicolated merlons. This wall is partly damaged. The fortress that we see today is only half of the intended design: the other, eastern, half (Girde Qilla), which probably had an administrative purpose, was either never built or has been lost. The southeast gate (adjacent to Lalbagh Shahi Masjid) was the fort's central and most imposing gate. Its high arched gateway is contained in a rectangular frame; both sides are decorated with plastered panels; the gateway is flanked by four incomplete corner bastions.

Kazi Kara Naier

Azim Khan Ronnie

Kazi Karar Naier

Kazi Karar Naier

Kazi Karar Naier

Dhakeshwari National Temple 059 C

Dhakeswari Road
10th to 12th centuries

Dhakeshwari Temple is a symbol of Dhaka itself since its name means 'protector goddess of Dhaka'. It was constructed in the twelfth century by King Ballal Sen of the Sena dynasty, who is thought to have been born nearby; it was presumably his intention to glorify his birthplace. Others believe that Ballal Sen found a sculpture of a deity – the goddess to which the temple is dedicated – buried underground in what was then dark jungle. However, no traces of any architectural style from the Sena period have ever been found, perhaps due to the fact that the building's façades have changed continually over time. The original 800-year-old, 45.72-centimetre high, ten-armed deity, Katyani Mahishasurmardini Durga (the goddess of the fort who killed a buffalo demon), has been kept in the Temple of Kumartuli in Kolkata since the partition of Bengal in 1947. A replica idol has been installed here. At the front of the temple is a *natamandir* (stage for performances), around which is a row of compounds, a large pond, and the Nahobottola Gate, a tall gate erected at the edge of the entrance area to allow elephants to pass through during the Janmashthami procession (marking the birth of Krishna). On the east side are tombs of unknown saints. Outside the temple complex are five conical tomb buildings (*moths*). In the middle of each tomb is a single object called 'the penis of the deity Shiva' (*Shiv linga*). Two styles of Bengal architecture are in evidence here: the ancient main temple is in the traditional five-jewel style (*pancharatna*), while the other structures demonstrate a fusion of the Bangla four-pitched-roof style (*chauchala*) and the 'mountain style' (*shikara*). Some

scholars believe that this temple could be a tenth-century Buddhist temple subsequently converted for use by Hindus. During the Liberation War of 1971 the temple was damaged by merciless raids by the Pakistan Army in which more than half of buildings in the complex were ruined, mobs grabbed land from adjacent properties, and the cella (the main room for worship) was converted to an ammunition store! The temple complex was declared 'National Temple' in 1996. In 2018 the government was able to recapture some of the lost land and give it back to the temple, making this the largest Hindu temple complex in Dhaka. Durga Puja, the most important festival for Bengali Hindus, is held here every year. The festival takes five days and is traditionally attended by prime ministers and presidents.

Avijit Barman

Hosaini Dalan
Nizamuddin Road
Sayyid Mir Murad
1642

060 C

This example of Indo-Iranian architecture is the main *imambara* (shrine) of Shia Muslims in Bangladesh and the starting point of the largest annual mourning procession on the tenth day of Muharram in the Arabic calendar commemorating the martyrdom of imam Hussain, a grandson of the holy prophet. The shrine's congregation consists of believers in the Twelve Imams, members of the largest branch of Shia Islam. Surprisingly, the shrine's patron was Prince Shah Shuja, a Sunni ruler. The building was renovated in 1807–1810. The *naib e nazim* (revenue officer) Nusrat Jung extended the complex to its present size of 1376.95 square metres in 1823. After the earthquake of 1897, Nawab Ahsanullah made the roof flat and added a second veranda on the south side, which is today the main façade abutting a large pond. A flight of steps on the east side connects the ground level with the main hall. The building is symmetrical in plan and stands on an elevated rectangular platform containing a number of graves. There are two polygonal structures at the corners of the pond; small minarets capped by domes rise from the four corners. The south façade is clearly influenced by western architecture: it has four Doric columns supporting its veranda.

A marquee attached to the north side has arched windows and *kanjura* (rows of decorative merlons) on its roof; this is probably an addition influenced by the Mughals. The building's core consists of two large back-to-back halls called 'Shirni' and 'Khutba'. Shirni Hall faces south and is coloured black to represent deep sorrow. Khutba Hall, on the other hand, is colourful and decorative; it contains a *mihrab* (prayer

Avijit Barman

niche) with seven steps. For women, these two halls have subsidiary double-height rooms at each side. A series of three rooms stretching east to west connects the entire ground floor; there are galleries on the second floor. The rooms in the north part of the building have no galleries; all the pillars of this façade are decorated with blue calligraphic tiles. The complex also includes two entrance gates, a *naobat khana* (a drum house where drums are beaten), graveyards on either side of the road, and the tomb of an unknown person called Gaziuddin. A silver filigree model of how the shrine originally looked is kept in the National Museum. The government of Iran sometimes subsidises renovation measures and helps pay the cost of maintaining the building as a mark of its friendly relationship with Bangladesh.

2

Kazi Karar Naier

Avijit Barman

Avijit Barman

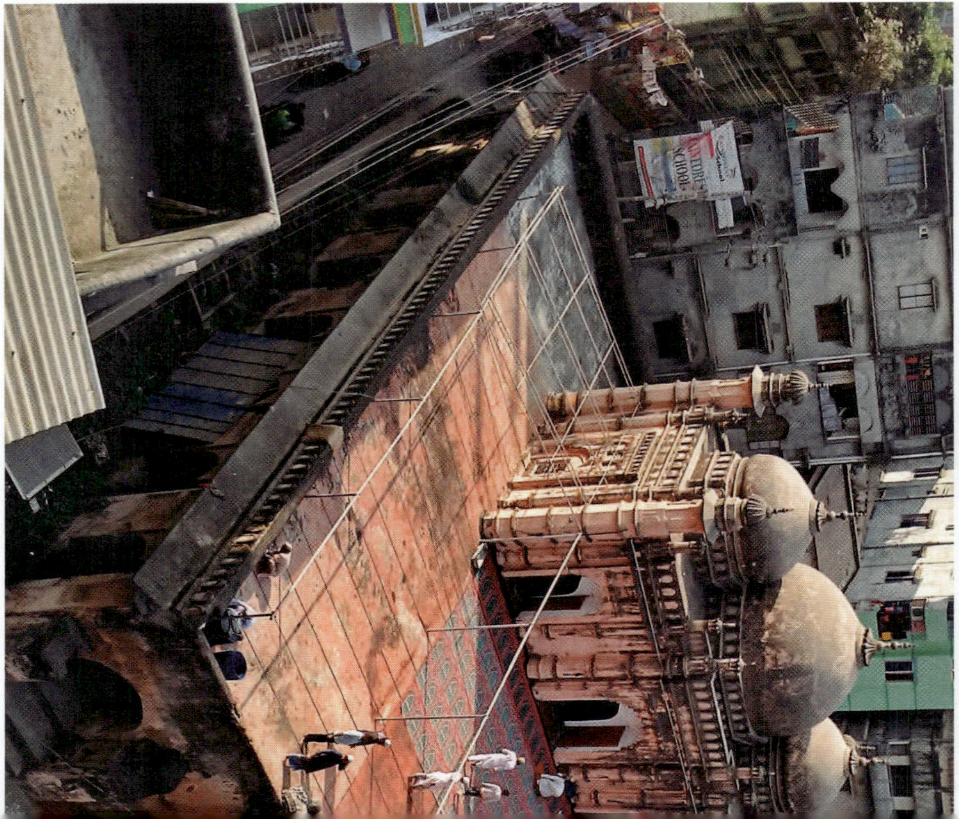

Avijit Earman

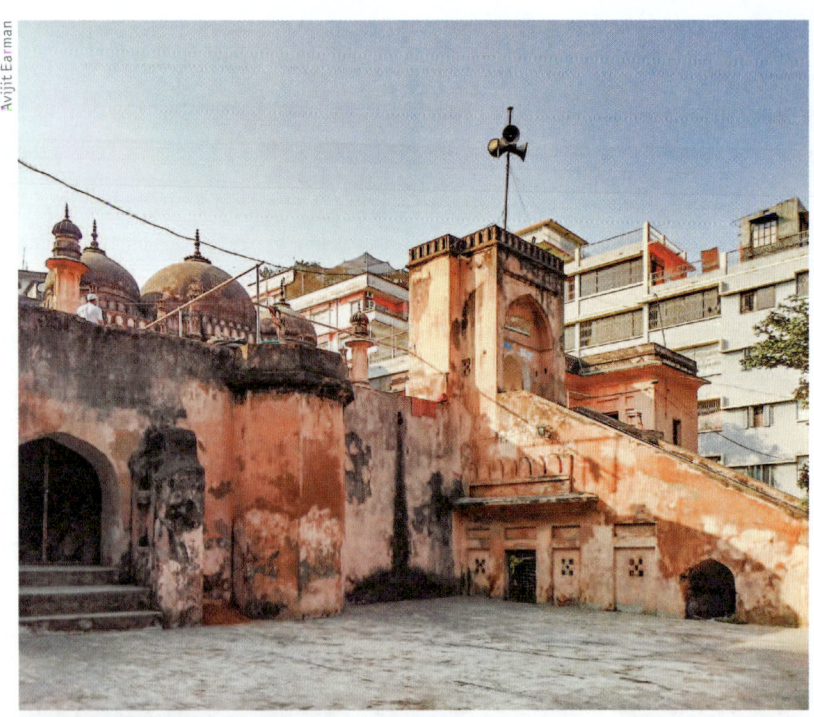

Khan Mohammad Mridha Mosque

Lalag Road
Khan Mohammad Mirza
1705

061 C

The mosque of Khan Mohammad Mridha was listed as a historical monument in 1913. Situated less than 500 metres from Lalbagh Fort, it still functions as a mosque. It was built during the reign of the deputy governor Farrukh Siyar by a *qazi* (judge) called Ibadullah, as we learn from two inscriptions in Persian – one over the prayer niche, the other in the central archway. The plinth stands nearly five metres above its surroundings; this contains *tahkhana*, underground vaulted rooms accommodating students. Its roof forms a spacious platform used for open-air prayers. Thus elevated, the main prayer hall, which is inside the mosque, remains cool with air flowing from all directions. Khan Mohammad Mridha Mosque has three domes; as was typical practice in the sixteenth century, the central dome is the largest. The three domes are supported by pendentives. From the garden on the east side a flight of 25 steps leads to the main prayer hall, which measures 14.63 by 7.32 metres. The towers at its corners are short and slender with ribbed cupolas. The ornate parapets contain merlons. The front façade is decorated with a square depression and rectangular panels. The east entrance is framed by multicusped arches and engaged columns. The prayer hall is divided into three bays by two lateral arches. Each bay has a *mihrab* (prayer niche) inset in the west wall. These niches have multi-cusped arches and rectangular panels. In the garden to the north is an abandoned well that was used for ablution rituals. On the east side is a nameless tomb.

Azimpur Dayera Sharif Khanqah

Pilkhana Road/Azimpur Road
1776

062 C

This area was developed by Shah Syed Muhammad Dayem, a Sufi who migrated here from Bihar in 1766. *Dayera* means 'circle' or 'work area'. It is thought that Shah Syed Muhammad Dayem was a descendant of the great thirteenth-century Sufi Bayezid Mahisawar, who reached the Chittagong coast from Baghdad by hitching a ride on a huge fish. The complex comprises a mosque, a tomb (*mazar*), and a graveyard. In 1891 Nawab Ahsahullah built an enormous two-storey gateway with a side staircase, a clear sign of a Turkish influence. The gate's multicusped arches are the only Indian elements here. Renovation carried out in 1908 included work on the three domes and the *mazar*; at the same time, octagonal towers capped with cupolas were added to the corners of the tomb and the floors were paved in marble. The small mosque is rectangular; its east wall contains three arches placed within half domes. The west wall has only one *mihrab* (prayer niche). The domes are supported by squinches and rest on octagonal drums ornamented with blind merlons. The veranda was added to the mosque's east wall in a later period. There are six graves inside the *mazar*. Two rectangular rooms were later attached to its south side. The entrances to the *mazar* are set in a projecting wall. In both the *mazar* and the mosque the central dome is the largest, as is characteristic of Mughal architecture. Nearby is Azimpur Mosque, a two-storey mosque built in 1746 by Faizullah. This has a similar layout to Khan Muhammad Mridha Mosque but with the difference that here large flanking half-dome vaults are attached to a single dome in the centre – a clear sign of Turkish influence, probably brought to Bengal by Armenians. Only two other mosques are to be found with this layout today: Atarou Mosque in Shatkhira (1680) and Mograpara Mosque in Narayanganj (1701).

Mayor Mohammad Hanif Jame Mosque

063 C

Azimpur Graveyard
Rafiq Azam, SHATOTTO
2018

With a floor area of 1533 square metres and two storeys accommodating 14,000 people, Mayor Mohammad Hanif Jame Mosque is a distinctive contemporary take on Azam Shah Mosque in the Mughal-era Lalbagh Fort. The *sahn* (open-air courtyard) adjacent to the main prayer hall is a dramatic space that serves as a social hub for 500 people: a philosophical termination point or, as the architect has put it, a realm of illusion, given that the busy road to the south represents the terrestrial world, while the graveyard on the opposite side represents the celestial world. The prayer hall's cement-textured, trunk-like columns have expanded canopies giving the impression of an indoor forest holding the beam-free flat slab above. The north and east walls do not touch the ceiling; the resulting gap is a vibrant source of daylight. A display of perforated brick masonry on the south wall filters out light and noise from outside. Grooves of ambient light in the floor demarcate lines for the prayer rows and create a religious atmosphere. Inside, the mosque has no *mihrab* (prayer niche) for the imam to stand in while praying; instead, there is a glass *minbar* (pulpit) in the centre to signify the imam's importance. When collective prayers are not taking place, this glass structure can accommodate shelves of holy books and benches allowing people to enjoy the intimacy of the diffused sky light coming from above.

Md. Mohaimin Ali Khan (all pictures)

A bridge made of glass and steel provides a contrast with the surrounding brick texture, connects the upper floors, and frames the graveyard behind it, forming a vista. The bridge's frosted glass is inscribed with holy verses from the Qur'an on its south side; its north side is open to the graveyard. The mosque's east wing is a prayer space for women; its ground floor includes a space for ablutions offering both faucets and pools. Part of this space has been left open to connect the rain and light of the sky with the water in the pool. The minaret (prayer tower) is actually an elevator shaft for physically challenged devotees. The combination of red brick, *jalis* (latticework), and voids on the mosque's façade is a distinctive take on Bengal's brick architecture and sets up a beautiful interplay of light and shadow.

2

Dhanmondi Shahi Eidgah

Dhanmondi 6/A
Diwan Mir Abul Qasim
1640

064 B

Built in 1640, this Mughal landmark is Dhaka's oldest surviving Mughal monument, as we know from the inscription in Persian found in the semi-octagonal, multi-cusped central *mihrab* (prayer niche) on the west façade. This is a very unusual niche in Mughal architecture, unequalled in features and forms. The walled enclosure was designed by Diwan Mir Abul Qa'asim, the trusted architect of Prince and Governor Shah Shuja who also designed Boro Katra. Dhanmondi Shahi Eidgah was built on the outskirts of the city's corner on a branch of the River Buriganga so as to preserve a connection with Saat Gombuj Mosque. This enclave-like space was used for open-air prayers on only two *eid* (feast) occasions each year. When prayers were over, the participants would form a procession involving every aristocrat in Dhaka. Dhanmondi Shahi Eidgah is a 4046.86-square-metre piece of vibrant green land surrounded by a high wall that forms an elegant red mural decorating the cityscape. The west wall was of beautiful red brickwork. The complex also included a small Mughal mosque. The wall was demolished, and the original mosque was replaced with a new six-storey mosque. In 1981 the *eidgah* complex was declared a site of archaeological interest. The enclosure is situated 1.22 to 1.83 metres above the existing road level; thus the Mughals protected the prayer ground from flash flooding. The construction technique involved building a shallow pile foundation by driving wooden piles into the ground and erecting a masonry substructure on top. The site has an oblong plan measuring 45.11 by 41.76 metres. The east side is open to facilitate entry and exit. The *mihrab* (prayer niche) in the centre of the west wall is 1.52 metres high and flanked by three subsidiary sunken niches on either side. The walls have battlements and corner towers decorated with horizontal bands and small onion domes in imitation of the Mughal system of fortification. The piers inside the walls serve both structural and aesthetic purposes.

Mamunur Rashid (all pictures of this project)

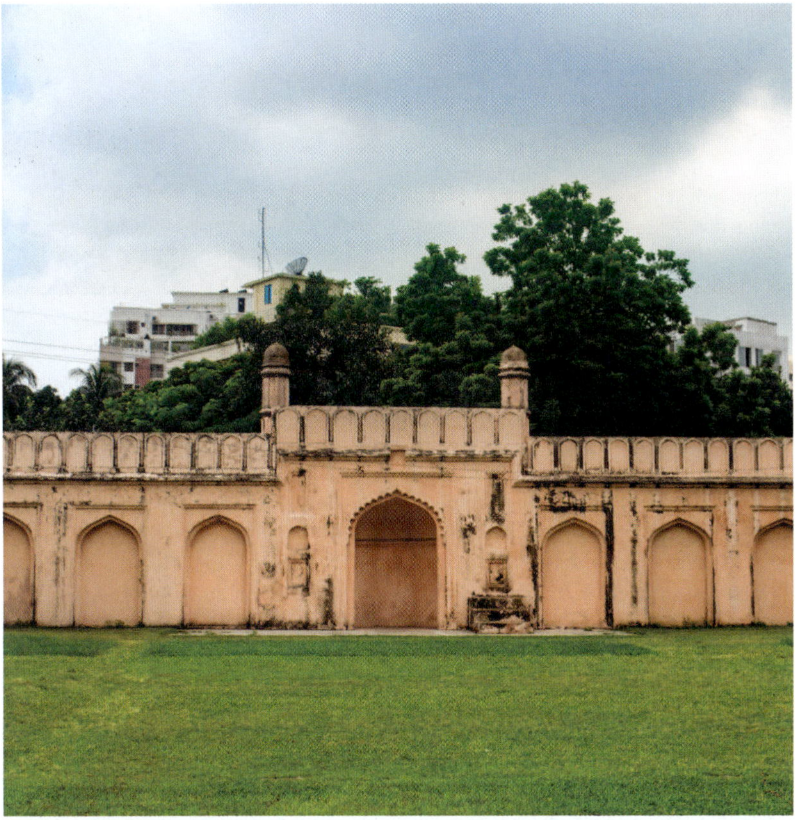

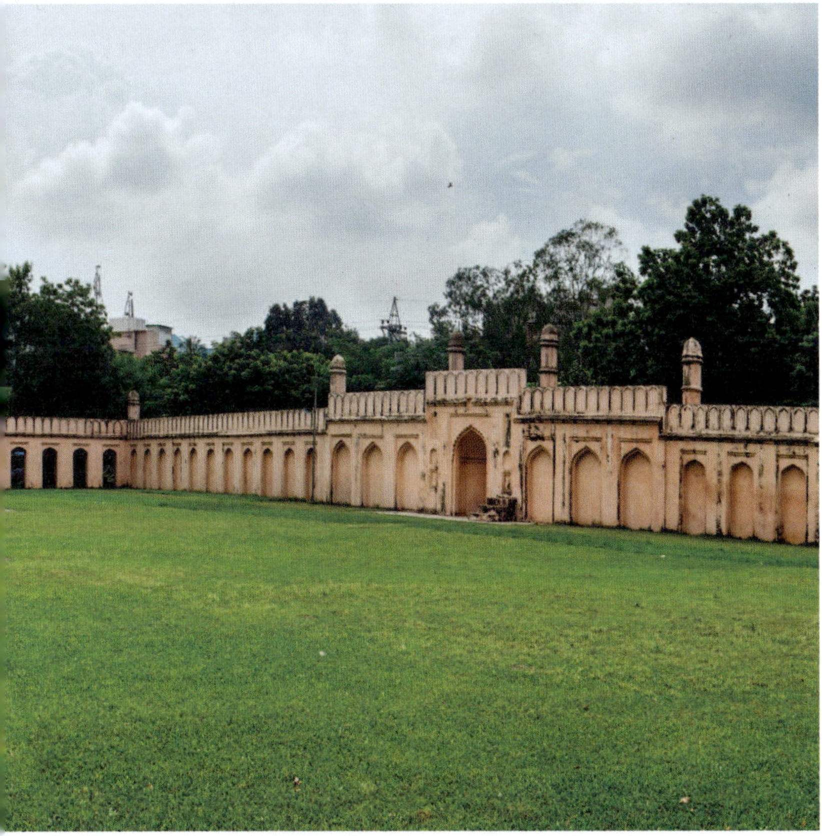

Dhanmondi Lake

Dhanmondi
Developed by
Vitti Sthapati Brindo Ltd.
2000

Jubair Bin Iqba

Dhanmondi Lake was originally part of the Pandu River, the now extinct river that used to connect with the River Buriganga near Satgambuj Mosque. There was a traditional *haat* (large weekly marketplace) here, as well as a Mughal bridge. The word *dhan* means 'rice', so Dhanmondi could well have been a place for storing rice or a wholesale rice market as well. Even in the 1950s this area was under-developed; the East Pakistan government then turned it into a residential area for the nobility. In 2000 the existing lake was excavated, and 98 acres of adjacent land were redeveloped. The lake's two segregated bodies of water were reunited to form a total length of three kilometres. With an average width of between 35 and 100 metres, the lake covers 16% of the neighbourhood, nearly 37 hectares in all. The redevelopment programme focused on three things: stewardship, restoration, and management. Light structures, such as food courts, decks, several astonishing pedestrian bridges, a swimming club, a boat club, and an open-air amphitheatre, were carefully interwoven with nature. The walkways protect the banks of the lake from further encroachment and pollution. The theatre is a successful public gathering and breathing space when no performance is being held. For the Dhanmondi area as a whole, the lake development has proved an important civic centre. The landscape design was awarded an IAB Design Award in 2002.

Jubair Bin Iqba

2

Mahmudul Anwar Riyaad and Md. Rajiv

Mahmudul Anwar Riyaad and Md. Rajiv

Junior Laboratory School `066` `B`

House 38, road no. 10/A,
Dhanmondi
Mahmudul Anwar Riyaad,
Mamnoon Murshed Chowdhury,
Ashik Vaskor
2004

This seven-storey building houses a well-known school. The lower four storeys are clad with brick. The monolithic form of the front elevation is a stepped mass that negotiates well with the scale of its surroundings. The large entrance is subtracted from a form which reveals layers of top-lit spaces. The building's monumentality is carefully diminished by upward spatial movements through a void placed at its centre. Its inverted form compels users to look inwards. The architectural massing transmits the building's presence through the residential fabric of the Dhanmondi area. The classrooms and circulation spaces pivot around the naturally ventilated, top-lit atrium. The raised podium of the atrium has cascading steps at its bottom that lead directly to the front yard; it serves as a kind of central stage for various occasions. The upper floors are for girls. The top floor is a residence for the school's principal. There is a basketball ground in the centre of the complex. The project won an IAB design award commendation in 2004 and an award in the 16th JK AYA awards in the Young Architects category in 2008. The rooftop garden is of particular interest to visitors.

Philipp Meuser

![Junior Laboratory School exterior]

Chayanat Cultural Building

067 B

72, Raod 15/A, Dhanmondi R/A
Bashirul Haq
2002

Chayanat Cultural Centre was set up in 1961 to celebrate the 100th birthday of Rabindranath Tagore, Bangladesh's national poet, and to protect against the cultural aggression directed by the Pakistani junta against Tagore, the country's central cultural figure. Since 1967 the centre has organised events marking the first day of the Bengali calendar (April 14) in Ramna under the famous banyan tree. During the Liberation War artists from the centre were involved in fundraising programmes to help people affected by the war. In 2001 the Ministry of Housing and Public Works gave the centre this 1337.8-square-metre site on which to construct a permanent home. The building is a centre for performing arts, including music, art, and dance. Lessons and training sessions are held in a single built structure with classes arranged on different floors according to age. Other amenities are a library on the fourth floor, a research centre, and a 350-seat auditorium. The semi-basement floor is a car park. In the middle of the beginning is a top-lit courtyard; this connects all the various facilities, defines the spaces, and takes care of circulation. It also contains a tree. The building's entrance is well defined and emphasises the indoor-outdoor relationship; its recessed fenestration sets up an interplay between light and shadow. As in his other projects, Bashirul Haq, the architect, exercised great care in selecting materials for this building; they include red brick, wooden panels, louvred windows, and perforated concrete balustrades. The result is a truly harmonious façade. The rooftop garden is a special feature.

2

Md. Mohaimin Ali Khan

Sayed Ahmed

Sayed Ahmed

F.M. Faruque Abdullah Shawon, H.M. Fozia Rabby Apurbo (all pictures)

Akij Uttaridhikar

House 64/A, Road 15/A,
Dhanmondi R/A
Volumezero Ltd.
Mohammad Foyez Ullah
2016

068 B

Akij Uttaridhikar is an eight-storey luxury residence and a manifestation of the ideas and strength of a cohesive family of individuals. Its architecture is an intimate layer of concrete enclosing layers of brick and wood. The detailing of the brick bonding and the planes of concrete evinces both the environmental and the aesthetic values of this building. The outermost layer evolves into a skin and then into a shell that is responsive to the elements. The spacious ground floor and mezzanine level contain most of the amenities, including a swimming pool on the ground floor and an open terrace garden at mezzanine level for the enjoyment of all residents of the house. The lavish second-floor dining space for 40 people is ideal for family gatherings. The manicured roof garden and the green landscapes on the ground and seventh floors enliven the overall ambience.

Martyred Intellectuals' Memorial

069 B

Rayer Bazar
Jami Al Shafi,
Farid Uddin Ahmed
1999

Bangladesh lost its best intellectuals on the eve of its victory on 16 December 1971. Just before its shameful defeat, the Pakistan Army made a cowardly attempt to rip out the nation's intellectual heart. The army's local Islamist allies killed 991 teachers and professors, 49 doctors, 42 lawyers, 13 journalists, and 16 others such as engineers, scientists, poets, artists, and writers. The victims were subjected to cruelty and blindfolded and then executed in torture cells. In 1991 an organisation of families of the martyred intellectuals laid the foundation stone for a memorial on the spot where their corpses were dumped. On 14 December every year, Bangladesh mourns the victims. The Martyred Intellectuals' Memorial is the result of a design competition organised by the Institute of Architects Bangladesh (IAB) and the Ministry of Public Works in 1993. From 22 entries the jurors selected this design, which is simple but bears eloquent testimony to the sacrifice made by Bangladesh's intellectuals. The design involved keeping an existing approximately 18-metre-high curved wall (0.9 metres thick and 115.8 metres long) on the grounds that it had been a witness to the massacre. The wall was broken at both its ends in a gesture of mourning and sorrow.

Pinu Rahman

Its raw-brick texture commemorates the original setting: a brickfield strewn with dead bodies and soaked in blood. A square window was punched in the wall to show the skyline behind; this signifies hope. Early in the morning, the first rays of the sun pierce the window and land on the surface of the pool. Paths with planter boxes provide a simple approach to the memorial from the east; at the southwest end, a vast graveyard was laid out to bury the intellectuals who served this nation in the past, are serving it now, and will serve it in the future. A young banyan tree was planted to replace a dead old tree of the same species which in the wartime marked Dhaka's city border. A four-metre-high black-granite column stands alone and asymmetrically – a clear breach of traditional principles for positioning obelisks. The column represents Bangladesh's grief at losing its best intellectuals before they had seen the realisation of their long-cherished dream of an independent nation. In front, a flagpole always carries a huge national flag – a bold assertion that the intellectuals' 'Bangladesh' is now proud reality.

Saiful Amin Kazal

Asif Ahmed Mazumder

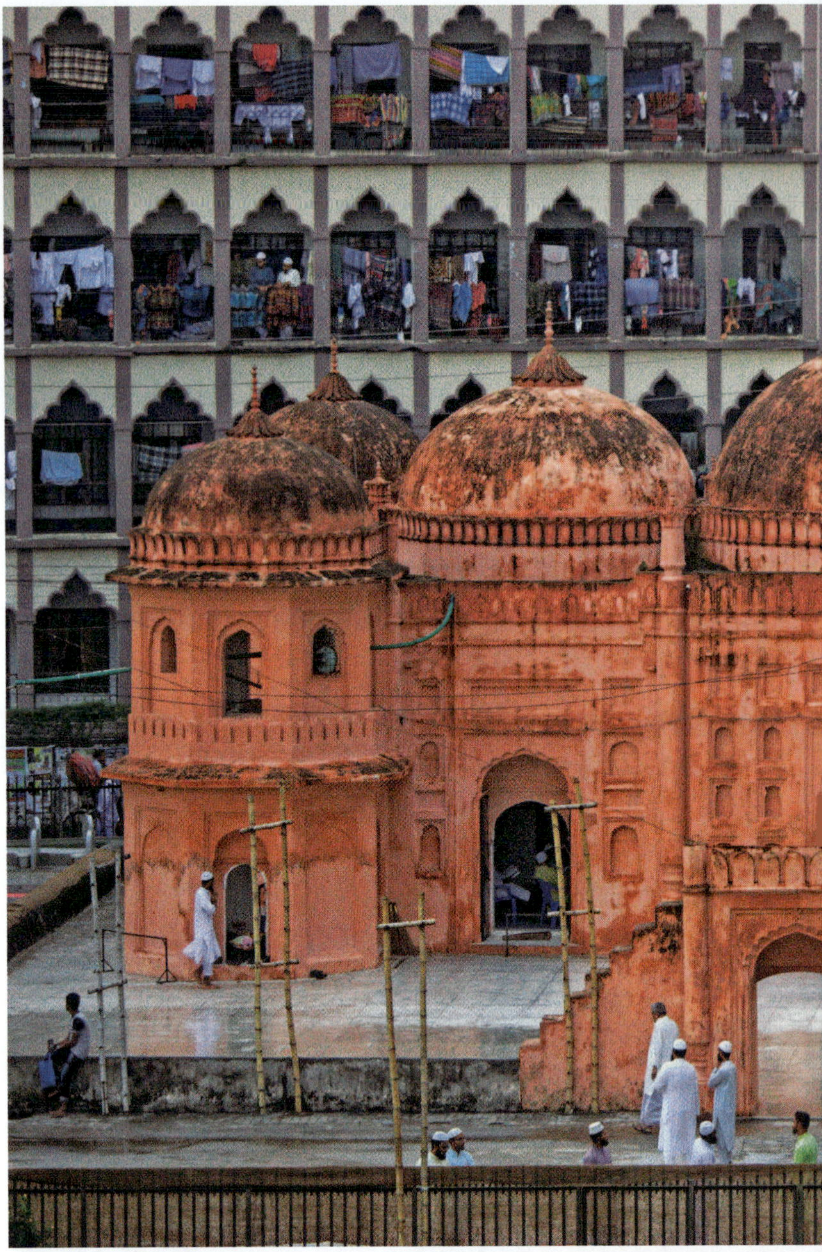

Philipp Meuser

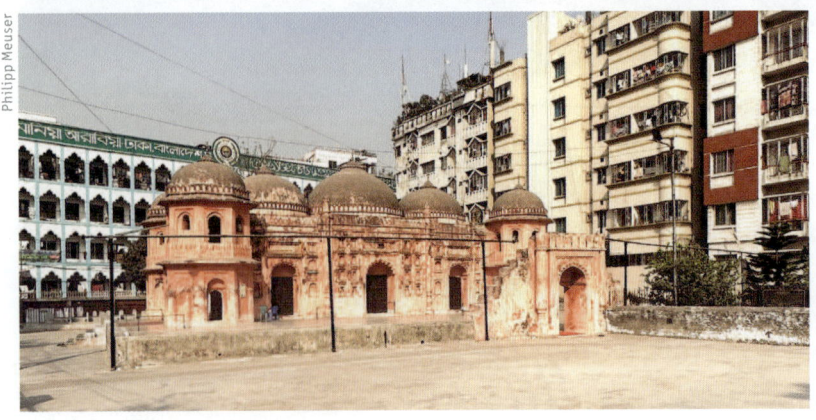

Saat Gombuj Mosque

Sat Masjid Road,
Mohammadpur
1680

070 B

This mosque was apparently built by orders of Governor Shaista Khan to provide a socio-religious centre for the village of Jafarabad and the surrounding agricultural area of Katasur in the *mouza* (revenue circle) of Sarai Begumpur. This was the main route by which shipping could reach the River Brahmaputra and the region of Mymensingh while avoiding the hostile River Shitalakshya. The exact date of construction is unknown. The mosque's architecture is in the provincial style of the period of Shaista Khan. Its main roof has three domes, while the corner *minars* (towers) have four more domes – making this a seven-domed mosque. All the bulbous domes are supported by octagonal drums decorated with pot finials on lotus-like bases. The middle dome is the largest. The mosque has a symmetrical plan. The gargantuan two-storey

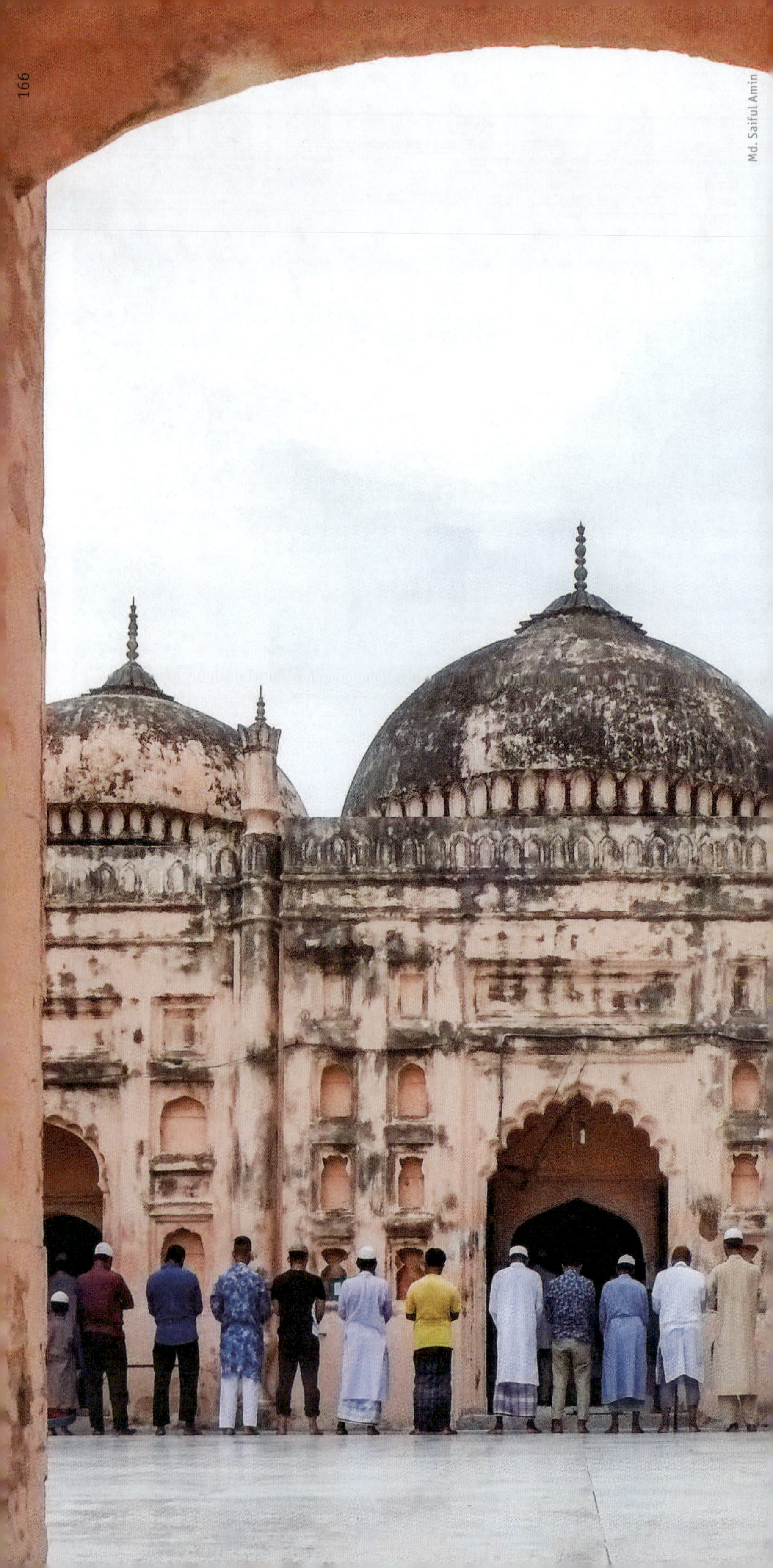

Md. Saiful Amin

Philipp Meuser

pavilions at each corner are octagonal and served as guardhouses or lighthouses. The three cusped-arched entrances, five exterior bays, prominent colonette, and slender engaged columns with bulbous bases make this the most innovative and unique piece of architecture in Mughal Dhaka. There are eight sunken panels on each side of the main door. The *mihrab* (prayer niche) echoes the entrance on the east wall and has slender pilasters with bulbous bases to indicate that this is the central bay. The corner turrets provide visual balance and structural stability. The building's plinth is buttressed by a 4.57-metre-high dam protecting the podium from flash floods from the River Turag and serving as a quay for shipping on the river. The dam is today obscured by a new madrasa. After 1760 the area as a whole was abandoned and became overgrown with vegetation. Nawab Ahsanullah renovated the mosque in 1900. In front of it was a garden, which has since been lost due to illegal development. The gateway is lower than its surroundings. Only four nameless tombs on the right of the courtyard still exist. There is also a nameless tomb on the opposite site of the road; this is octagonal, has a single dome, and stands on an elevated platform.

Philipp Meuser

Bangabandhu Memorial Museum

071 B

House 677 of Road 32, Dhanmondi
Iqbal Habib, Ehsan Khan, Vitti Sthapati Brindo Ltd.
2011

Once an ordinary family home, this three-storey building is considered the birthplace of Bangladesh. It is a monument to the gruesome events of the dark night of 15 August 1975, when Sheikh Mujib

Rahman, or Bangabandhu (Friend of Bengal), as he is also known, was assassinated, along with members of his family. Mujib moved here on 1 October 1961, and this house was witness to his political golden age: the anti-tyranny movement of 1962, the six-point movement of 1966, and, then the declaration of independence in 1971. This house was under military authority from 1975 to 1981, when Bangabandhu's daughter Sheikh Hasina returned to Bangladesh and had to pay the mortgage arrears to save the family home from being auctioned. After paying, she handed the house over to the Bangabandhu Trust. The Bangabandhu Memorial Museum opened to the public here on 14 August 1994. The museum has a simple layout. The drawing room displays Mujibur Rahman's international achievements. A long corridor connecting the drawing room to the office shows paintings of the martyrs of 1975. The adjacent meeting room, reading room, and personal library are historically precious; the table and telephone are emblems of Bangladeshi independence. It was here that Bangabandhu drafted the declaration of independence of 7 March 1971 before proclaiming it on 25 March, leading to his arrest. The room in the north-east corner of the house is the birthplace of his youngest son and is not open to visitors; this was where the family used to gather

and pray during the events of 1971. The bedrooms, dining area, and family living room on the second floor contain memorabilia of the family's ordinary lifestyle. The second floor also contains the famous balcony, where the leader used to appear in front of the public waiting on the street outside. The third floor contains a waiting room for foreigners with showcases of souvenirs and an office. The house's shattered windows, bullet holes on the walls, and bloodshed on the stairs are presented artistically. In August 2011 an extension of the museum opened with galleries named after Bangabandhu's parents, Sheikh Lutfar Rahman and Sheikh Sayera Khatun, and, on the fifth floor, a library and research centre containing 10,000 books and archival materials. The new building has been carefully inserted next to the original house in such a way as not to disturb it; its simple façade combines brick, concrete, and small *jali* (latticework) boxes.

Biswa Shahitto Kendro   `072` `B`
17 Mymensingh Road
Mahmudul Anwar Riyaad
2012

The teacher, writer, and activist Abdullah Abu Sayeed has spent 40 years nurturing this cultural centre as an expression of his belief in the need for human enlightenment and education. Sayeed started in 1978 with a desire to help Dhaka College students develop reading habits. Today his centre helps more than 100,000 persons. It was given a permanent home here on a 5295-square-metre site in a nine-storey building constructed with a grant from the Ministry of Education. Half of the ground floor was deliberately left unbuilt upon. The concrete ramp makes for an inviting entrance. The second floor contains an auditorium. The east and north blocks contain offices on every floor, while the south blocks contain libraries, a meeting room, an art gallery, three auditoriums, a theatre stage, archives, a guesthouse, and a café. The roof top has a garden and a small kitchen for serving snacks in the evening. The eighth floor is rented out to a well-known publishing company. The seventh floor has a cosy green lounge. The fact that this is a non-profit building meant that lots of space in it could be given over to greenery, ventilation, and opportunities for experiencing rain, making this a kind of urban oasis, a perfect blend of brick, concrete, glass, and vegetation.

Md. Mohaimin Ali Khan

Faruque Abdullah Shawon/Fozla Rabby Apurbo

Bashundhara City Shopping Mall   `073` `B`
3 Tejturi Bazar,
West Panthapath Road
Mohammad Foyez Ullah,
Mustapha Khalid Palash
2004

With a floor area of 18,000 square metres, this building used to be the largest mall in the country. Its right-hand part has 19 floors containing various offices of the Bashundhara group. The vast cylindrical atrium at the centre of the complex holds eight floors on its own. Its bluish glass dome with colourful stained glazing draws the gaze and is a source of abundant daylight. Arranged around this vast atrium are shops, megastores, cinema halls, a skating rink, and food courts. There are more than 2300 shops, some with their own prayer rooms and breastfeeding and changing rooms. Architecturally, the building's massing with interlocking of basic solids gives it a distinctive character. The façade consists of glazed Alocobond blocks, glass, and digital screens. Together with the imposing entrance steps, double-height pocket spaces, and rows of palm trees in front of the building, this makes the mall a true landmark of posh new Dhaka and a successful way of filling an urban void. With more than 1200 employees working here, this is the largest private employer in the country. The mall was built to endure an earthquake of 7.5 on the Richter scale. The authorities plan to extend the mall to make it one of the world's five largest shopping centres and serve increasing demand from one of Asia's fastest-growing cities.

Oriental Mirror

25/26 Road 8, Dhanmondi
Volumezero Ltd.
Mohammad Foyez Ullah
2014

This residential complex consists of two juxtaposed apartment blocks with a green playground at their centre. The two blocks are connected at each level by a service core of two lifts and two staircases. Each block contains apartment units of mostly similar size, and together they define a precise spatial response to the spirit of this site. The playground at the centre of the complex symbolises a traditional courtyard; the presence of a body of water is an allusion to traditional Bengali settlements. The division of the complex into two separate blocks of apartments allows air and light from the south to penetrate deep into the architectural and urban spaces; aesthetically, it creates long views both towards the building and from inside it. The outdoor area at the complex's centre facilitates the flow of indoor and outdoor spaces and connects the two mirrored building blocks with their urban surroundings. As an extension of the building's public spaces at ground level, the playground creates a comfortable environment for social interaction and is an important meeting point for the community.

Claudio Manzoni

F.M. Faruque Abdullah Shawon, H.M. Fozla Rabby Apurbo

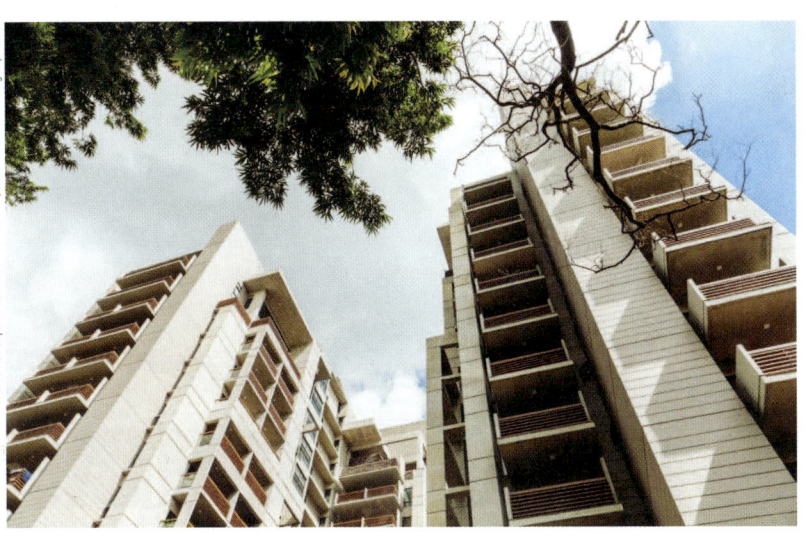

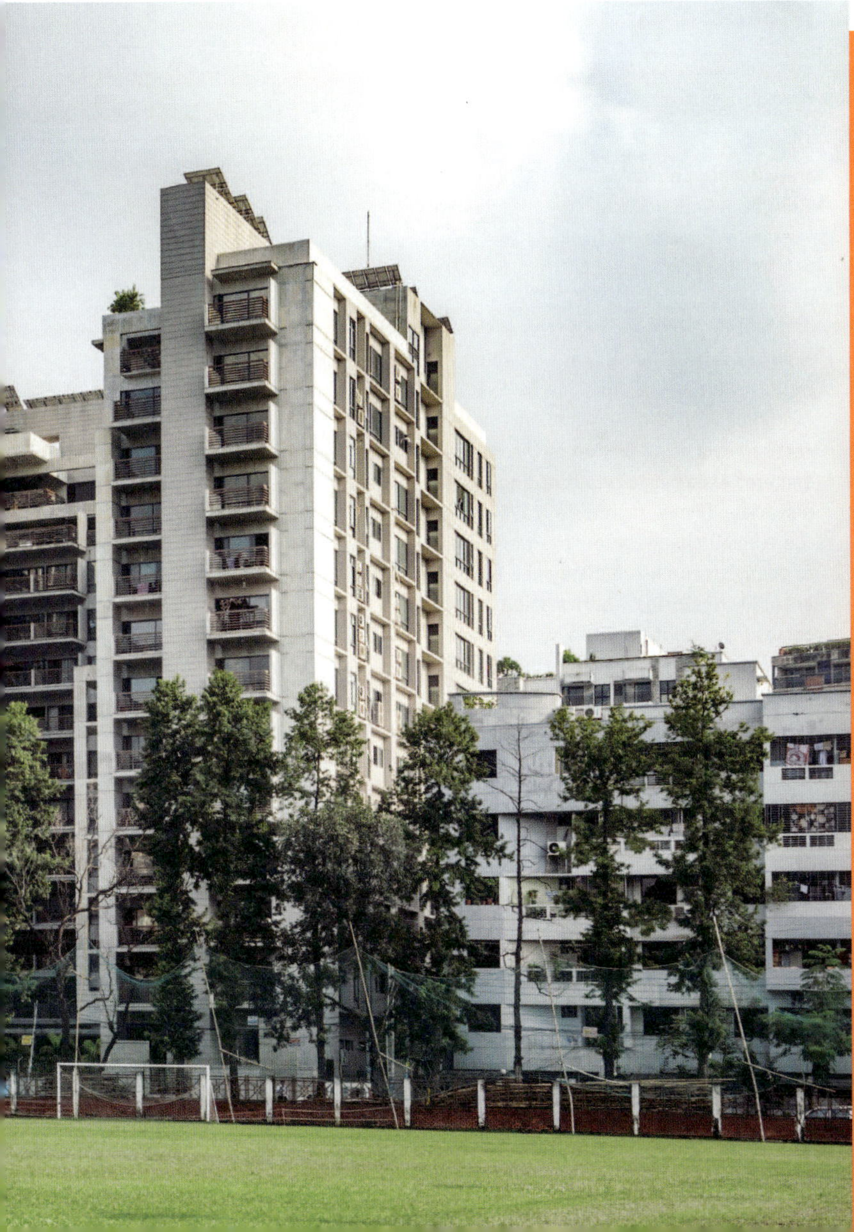

Philipp Meuser

Holy Rosary Church

075 B

Holy Cross College Road/
Farmgate–Tejturi Bazar Road/
Station Road
1677

Holy Rosary Church was established by Portuguese missionaries in 1580 at Tejkunipara on a site given to Portuguese settlers by a royal decree of the Mughal emperor Akbar in 1579. According to the historian James Taylor, in 1599 there was a small chapel here – the west block of today's church – built by the followers of St. Nestorius. Confirmation of this comes from a note written by the Italian traveller Ludovico di Varthema. Another source, however, tells us that the foundation of the Catholic church dates to 1714. What is certain is that after initially prospering, the church fell into decline after Kartalab Khan moved to Murshidabad in West Bengal and a large part of the church's congregation moved with him in pursuit of better trading opportunities. Fortunately, land was donated to the church by Catholic Franciscans and local residents, including half of the Tejkunipara area in 1854, allowing it to make ends meet. The church building was renovated three times: in 1714, 1940, and 2000. Its walls, more than

Philipp Meuser

one metre thick, were built using mortar made from brick dust. There is a gate on the north side. The main chapel is divided into two parts – the baptismal altar and the prayer hall. Differences in the thickness of the walls and in parts of the roof structure indicate that the east part of the building was a later addition to the main nave. The east hall is 25 metres long and 9.5 metres wide. The central aisles have two rows of circular Tuscan columns on each side. Two doors without porches on the north and south walls ensure sufficient light and airflow. To the north of the church is a Christian cemetery; to the south, the famous Holy Cross Girl's School and College.

Philipp Meuser

Md. Avijit Barman

3

Khwaja Amber Mosque
Mymensingh Road/
Kazi Nazrul Islam Avenue
Architect unknown
1678

076 B

Md. Avijit Barman

3

This mosque was erected in an attempt by Subahdah (Governor) Mir Jumla to make the journey along the Mughal Trunk Road to the province's northern frontier easier for his Mughal cavalry. In 1960 a three-domed veranda was added to the east side of the mosque; additional floors were built on to this during the 1980s, to the detriment of the building's authenticity and integrity. An inscription over the central doorway tells us that there was originally a well to the right of the gateway and a bridge built by Khwaja Amber, the head eunuch of Shaista Khan; these are no longer extant today. The mosque stands on a 3.66-metre-high platform whose upper edge is decorated with a row of blind merlons. The corners of the mosque are emphasised by large octagonal towers capped by kiosks and ribbed cupolas. The steps at the east entrance lead to an arched gateway housing a doorframe of stone. The front façade has three doorways, while the north and south sides have one doorway each. Stone is very rare in Bengal, so the stone for this building was probably imported from the Rajmahal Hills in India. To the north of the mosque a lone sarcophagus clad with brick is the tomb of Khwaja Amber. The mosque's plan is oblong, 13.41 metres long and 6.71 metres wide. All the doorways have projecting frontons flanked by turrets and arches

Philipp Meuser

made of black basalt. The west wall has three semi-octagonal *mihrabs* (prayer niches), mirroring the positions of the doorways. The protruding central *mihrab* has a rectangular frame made of black basalt with magnificent multi-cusped arches resting on semi-octagonal pilasters. The pilasters have slightly raised bands at regular intervals. The spandrels are embossed with relief rosettes; the in-between spaces have spiral scrolls. On the north side of the central *mihrab* is a three-stepped stone pulpit. Only the arches of the flanking *mihrabs* are made of stone. The mosque has three bays extending from east to west and divided by wide-span arches resting on brick pillars. The central bay is 4.27 metres wide and has a floor area of 18.23 square metres. On the roof three bulbous domes rise above octagonal drums decorated with friezes of blind merlons. The middle dome is larger than its fellows. A large medallion marks the apex of the largest dome. All the domes have crowns of lotus and pitch finials. This mosque was an important step forward in mosque architecture: it pioneered the use of bordering turrets, introduced a projecting fronton over the east doorways, and employed black basalt for the *mihrab*, pulpit, and arches – things never before seen in Bengal.

Krishivaban, BARC

Khamarbari Road, Farmgate
Rabiul Hossain,
Shaheedullah Associates
1981

077 B

Situated on an L-shaped site on the south-eastern edge of Sher e Bangla Nagar, this is the headquarters of the Bangladesh Agricultural Research Council. Three-storey, symmetrical, and clad with red brick, the BARC building is an important part of Bangladesh's Modernist heritage, alongside the works of Muzharul Islam: an example of aesthetic gravitas that demonstrates the evolution of a new architecture for a newly independent nation with an architectural legacy that goes back thousands of years. Since the old airport of Tejgoan was nearby, the building could not be more than four floors high. Its volume stretches east to west and is punctuated with staircases at either end. The architect's intention was to make the most of the southern breeze by using it for cross ventilation. There are three functional zones in the building. The first floor contains administrative areas; the second, executive offices; and the third, a conference room of 696.77 square metres flanked by a library and a meeting room (each with an area of 125.42 square metres). The building's total floor area is 2972.90 square metres. The corridors of the first and second floors are double-loaded; there is a single peripheral colonnade on the ground floor. The BARC building explicitly refers to Bengal's Mughal architecture. The brick shell protects the inner spaces from the sun and driving rain, creating a 'building within a building', an architectural type that emerged in medieval times as a response to climatic considerations. Brick is a great material for overcoming climate adversity and is part of Bengal's identity. Interior and exterior walls, columns, beams, floors, ceilings, and stairs: all were traditionally made of brick. This building's proportions and volume refer to the shape of this material: what we see here seems like a subtractions of masses from an enormous single brick. The vegetation at the road front and the play of light and shadow make for an experience that is easy on the eyes. Rabiul Hossain, the building's architect, was a patriot who was awarded the highest marks of recognition by the Bangladeshi government: the Bangla Academy Award in 2009, the IAB gold medal in 2016, and in 2018 the Ekhusey padak, the highest civilian award for Bangladeshis – the only occasion this award has been granted to a Bangladeshi architect.

Philipp Meuser

Krishibid Institution Bangladesh

Khamarbari Road, Farmgate
Vitti Sthapati Brindo Ltd.
2014

Designed for the Department of Agricultural Extension (DAE) and incorporating an international-standard auditorium which can accommodate 1000 people at a time, this building has a great mix of spaces, ranging from massive to cosily intimate. The 4014-square-metre built-up area is divided into two blocks: north and south. Its functions are layered and arranged around a revival of the traditional courtyard concept in three major zones: public, semi-public, and private. The different zones are connected optically by a plaza, a bridge, and a courtyard. The façade is an imposing combination of concrete, glass, wood, and steel. The south block is eight-storey with, attached to the front of it, an elevated convention hall for 500 people. The sixth and seventh floors contain a double-height convention hall for 550 people. This block also contains a 3D-projection hall for 200 people, three seminar rooms, office space for renting out, an administrative office, classrooms, club facilities, and a training centre. The basement has two floors of parking for 180 cars. The north block contains dormitories, a gymnasium, and a swimming pool. The site has a total area of 8028 square metres; the remaining 4014 square metres have been left as vacant space in front of the buildings. This empty space pays tribute to the landscape of village agriculture with its traditional grid pattern. The building is a climate-responsive structure. It makes the most of natural light and the south breeze, has shading devices on its west side, and is equipped for rain harvesting.

Md. Mohaimin Ali Khan

Md. Mohaimin Ali Khan

Philipp Meuser (all pictures of this object)

Bangabondhu Sheikh Mujibur Rahman Novo Theater

079 B

Bijoy Sharani Avenue
Ali Imam,
Government of Bangladesh,
Shathapti Shangshad
2004

Standing on 22,095.84 square metres of land and possessing a 21-metre dome, this planetarium is principally a theatre capable of accommodating 275 persons at a time. The dome's exterior reflects the light of the sky and simulates our blue planet. The seven columns on each side of it are an abstract take on a Greek order. Inside, the hemispherical structure enables visitors to float through space and experience the thrills of a vivid three-dimensional realm while travelling around the planets and satellites of the solar system. The planetarium's walls depict meteorological bodies, including stars and comets, with the help of 150 projectors set at a 120-degree angle. There is also a section showing the evolution of the Grand Canyon over the last 4000 years. Recently, a capsule ride simulator for 30 people was added to allow visitors to experience the horizontal and vertical movement of a space shuttle, as well as the entire story of human progress form ancient Egyptian civilisation to lunar conquest. Also new are a smart step floor, a 3D video screen, a gallery dedicated to world-famous scientists, and an information centre focusing on the nuclear industry. There are five shows every day. The planetarium also includes an auditorium for 150 persons, a conference room for 50 persons, and a parking area for 100 cars. Computer and internet fairs, scientific workshops, and seminars are regularly held here. This building's form rises over Dhaka's cityscape like a vision from a fantastic dream.

3

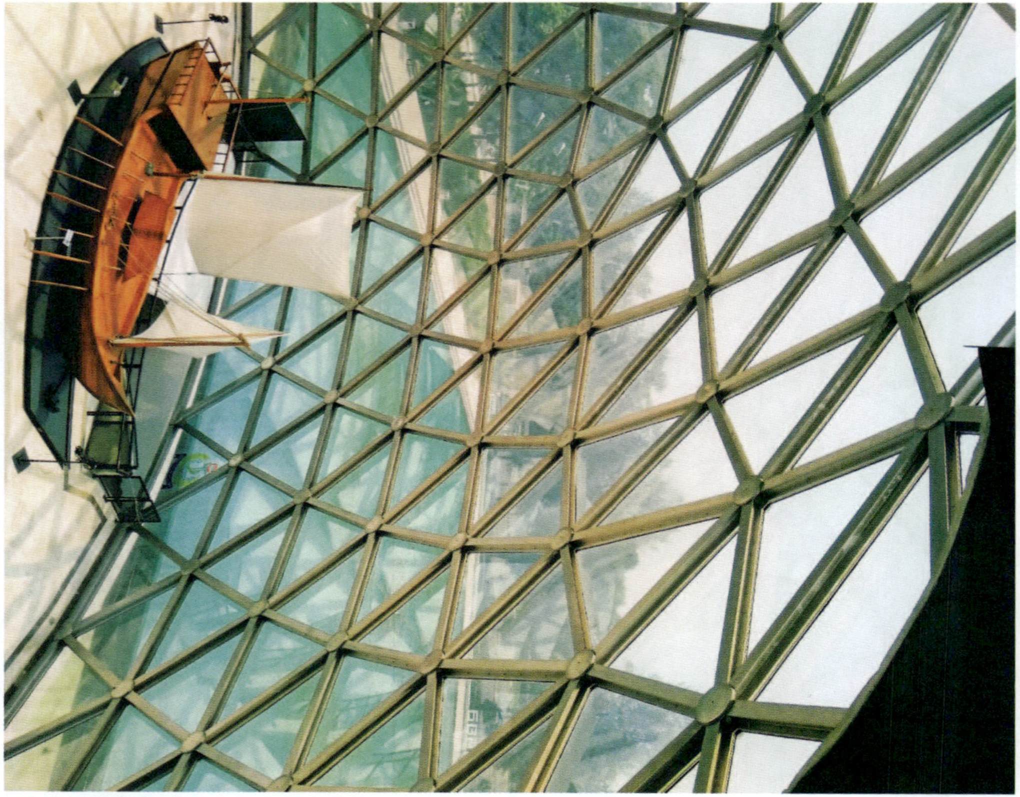

Samia Binte Azhar

Philipp Meuser

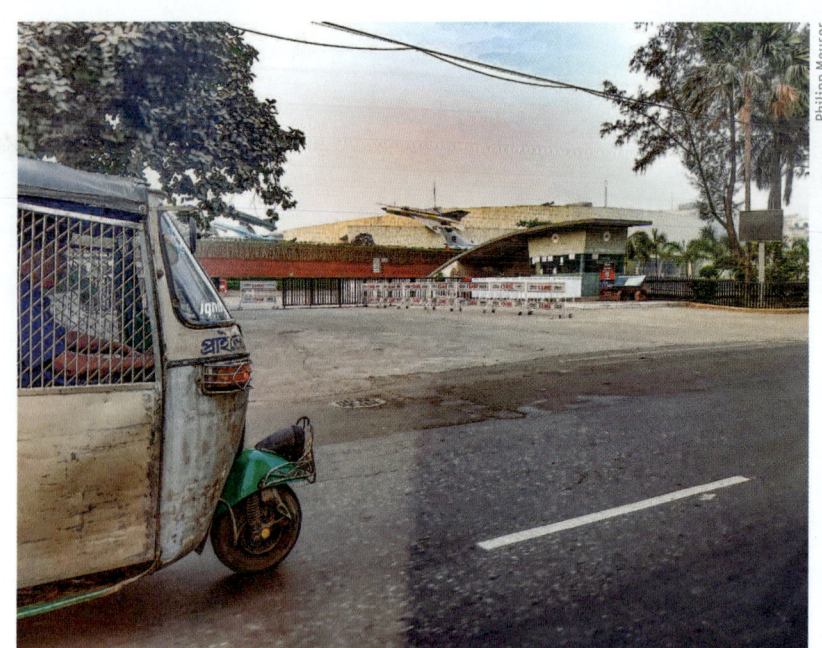

Bangabandhu Military Museum 080 B

Bijoy Sarani, Agargaon
Ali Imam and
Bayejid Mahboob Khondker,
Nakshabid Architects
2022

This compound is entirely dedicated to the glorious past of Bangladesh's military. The museum has stood here on a 37635-square-metre site since 1992. The plaza in front of the building is articulated by luxuriant greenery and a body of water. In place of a boundary wall, the site has 1.83-metre-deep trenches cut into its edges to provide security without interrupting visual links. Greenery planted symmetrically at regular intervals prevents the formation of heat traps. The landscape design is intended to satisfy citizens' needs for 'public recreational space' in their city, something which is notably lacking in Dhaka. The main challenge was to make a significant visual impact while abiding by the height limit (19.81 metres) imposed by the proximity of Tejgaon Airport, the city's old airport. Despite this constraint, the building's geodesic dome, made of low-emissivity glass and with a diameter of 36.58 metres, is a prominent landmark; it also prevents overheating and ensures a good balance of daylight. Variations in the heights of the storeys serve to give the elevation a fuzzy quality. There are three large galleries dedicated to the army, the air force, and the navy. Artefacts are arranged in six sections in a corkscrew pattern. Wartime relics from the Liberation War of 1971 are displayed on an outdoor spiral pathway, which uses the museum building as an ever-changing backdrop. Augmented reality, interactive displays, and selective illumination have all been woven carefully into the building. A special section on UN peacekeeping missions was added on the top floor, given that Bangladesh is the second largest contributor in the world when it comes to sending troops to conflict regions. The basement is used for maintenance, workshops, and stores. The ground floor is lined with marble, while the other floors are of polyurethane. The complex also includes a cafeteria, an art gallery, an amphitheatre, parking spaces for 450 cars, and a special gallery of *toshakhana* (gifts). The aim of the latter exhibition is to collect all the gifts received by the Bangladeshi government from foreign heads of state. 'Moondust' is the main attraction for visitors.

3

Bangabandhu Military Museum

National Assembly of Bangladesh

081 B

Manik Mia Avenue, Sher E Bangla Nagar Capital Complex
Louis Isadore Kahn
1961–1982

Located in the heart of Dhaka, this is one of the largest legislative complexes in the world, one of the twentieth century's most significant buildings, and a true *magnum opus* of this *magnus architectus*. Louis Kahn's mastery of light and shadow on grey concrete volumes has a timeless appeal. This monumental building wrests the attention of all who come near it. Whether you approach by the wide avenue in front or the road decorated with local flora at the back, you are bound to be surprised by the grandeur of the concrete façade with its colossal punched windows and the 'chiaroscuro' effect created by the pattern of primary shapes on the skin walls. The gigantic complex extends over an area of nearly 8.094 square kilometres. The main building at the centre of the complex is arranged around three squares: Main Plaza, South Plaza, and Presidential Plaza. While uniquely timeless, the architecture is nevertheless

Sayed Ahmed

3

deeply rooted in Bengal's deltaic context. The architect wanted to see his architecture as being capable of being archaeologised like the ruins of Mahasthangarh Buddhist monasteries. Along with the idea of 'served and servant' spaces, his key design tool was optimisation of spatial configurations. The supporting programmes (offices, a library, a mosque, hotels for parliamentary officials, and a restaurant) pivot around the 37-metre-high central volume, which is the seat of Bangladeshi democracy. The parabolic shell roof has clearance of a single storey to admit daylight. The brick plinth is similar in colour to a *viti* (mud platform); it contrasts both with the huge concrete mass above it and with the artificial body of water surrounding it. This artificial lake, an allusion to Bangladesh's riverine beauty, functions as a natural insulator and cooling system, creating an environmentally controlled setting for the interior. The entire complex is surfaced with a concrete texture with inlaid white marble, a Modernist statement of power and presence. Unfortunately, entry is restricted; acquiring permission to enter the building is a tiring and tiresome process.

Concrete and natural light as the main design materials
in the National Parliament of Bangladesh

3

Md. Mohaimin Ali Khan

Bangabandhu International Conference Centre

082 B

Begum Rokeya Avenue
Beijing Institute of Architectural Designs and Research
2002

Situated in the northern part of Louis Kahn's master plan for Shere Bangla Nagar, this is not only the largest international-standard conference facility in Dhaka but also one of the largest in the world. It stands on a 50,000-square-metre site and has a 20,000-square-metre footprint. The unbuilt-upon areas of the site have been left for gardens and fountains. The façade displays a convincing combination of yellow facing bricks and glazing. The join between the projecting eaves of the roof and the façade is covered by concave plates concealing the structural trusses that lie behind. The arches at the sides of the roof and the free-standing brick arches at the entrance allude to Dhaka's Islamic heritage. The car park has space for 700 vehicles. In all, the complex contains 17 venues catering to events of all sizes. The central conference space is the largest and is used for international summits for heads of states, state functions, export fairs, and various cultural events including national film and TV awards and convocations for private universities. This hall has capacity for 1700 viewers, 700 delegates, and 1000 spectators sitting in a second-floor gallery. The surrounding small halls are used for social events, school competitions, seminars, product launches, and reality shows. There are also two 200-seat meeting rooms, four negotiating rooms, a 700-seat banqueting hall, and a media briefing room for 300. In front of the building

3

Nahid Sultan

are 128 flag poles. The top of the building is covered by a 48-metre-wide spherical shell supported by 24 concrete columns; this provides a vast column-less gathering space and echoes the umbrella canopy of the nearby parliament building. The complex is centrally air-conditioned and equipped with facilities for simultaneous live telecasts in four languages, enabling coverage of any international event.

Md. Mohaimin Ali Khan

Shaheed Shuhrawardhy Medical College and Hospital

083 B

Mirpur road, Shere Bangla Nagar
Louis Isadore Kahn
1963

This building's neighbours include other medical institutes, but also the National Parliament. This Brutalist-looking hospital is the second project by Louis Kahn in Dhaka. Initially, in 1963, it was the Ayub Central Hospital with only 25 beds and an outpatient service. Renamed in 1972, it was upgraded to a 75-bed hospital. Kahn's iconic huge openings are again found here, this time in the form of circles and arches. The borders of the openings show brickwork laid in a centrifugal pattern that refers to the circular windows and arches. Interestingly, Kahn left the concrete lintels exposed, turning them into bold linear elements that intersect the brick arches and circular apertures. This treatment came from his search for spiritual 'beginnings'. Kahn often found inspiration in human anatomy – which is why he argued that a building's structural system should not be concealed but be expressively visible, just like the joints of our own hands. This building is oblong, a rare instance in Kahn's work since his earlier style had been defined by the volumes of basic shapes and their articulation. The reason for this is that a rectangular form is more suited to the functions of a hospital.

The punched apertures on the façades serve as sources of daylight and ensure natural ventilation for cooling. The porous quality of the double-height corridors with their series of arches allows patients and doctors to come closer. The same kind of idea is behind the small waiting room linked to a series of circulation spaces and the use of one-directional beams to give a sense of scale. This building is an aggregation of all the arch creation and brickwork that Kahn was so fond of. The medical college was inaugurated in 2005. Today this is a tertiary-level hospital with 850 beds. Ironically, though, the extension buildings are in a style so ridiculous that it obscures this complex's individuality.

3

Md. Mohaimin Ali Khan

3

083 B

Geneva Camp/Bihar Camp

Gajanabi Road/Babar Road
1971

Geneva Camp, aka Bihari Camp, holds more than 50,000 refugees, mainly from two groups: Urdu-speaking Muslims who migrated from Bihar in India after 1947 and Pakistanis stranded in Bangladesh after 1971. The camp occupies an area of just more than one acre. In 1971 the houses were one-storey, had rooms that measured 2.5 by 2.5 metres, and had shared latrines. Gradually, the original structures were extended upwards. The camp has only one school. Although a hotspot for drugs and crime, it also offers a fabulous range of street foods. In 2008 this 'stateless' community was given citizenship, but only members of it born after 1971.

084 B

Jonathan Raa

Bayazid Akter

Philipp Meuser

Geneva Camp/Bihar Camp (2023)

Bangladesh National Library and Archives

085 B

Justice S.M. Murshen Avenue
Muzharul Islam
1979

The Bangladesh National Library is in close proximity to Louis Kahn's National Assembly. In fact, it was also part of Kahn's master plan. The architect Muzharul Islam, who was Kahn's favourite student, wanted to establish harmony between Kahn's parliament building and his own equally bold library. So, he broke down the patterns of formal geometry and played with masses and materials. The library complex has a stereotypically grounded character, while most of Islam's other masterpieces are far more skeletally modern. It seems that here he has taken a square and then distorted parts of it to fit in with givens such as the site, context, and climate. Never giving up on his quest, Muzharul Islam slowly shaped the mass to the project's functional requirements. He divided the block into separate functional elements: the reading room and displays of books in the south, the administration in the east, and the ancillary facilities and storage in the west. The building has seven floors with concrete shear walls, except for the north wall which is a load-bearing brick structure. The walls act like a 25.60-metre-high envelope with cut-aways at the corners. This treatment of the façades allowed ventilation and light to penetrate deep into the interior. The library has a vast collection of 500,000 books and is operated by the Ministry of Cultural Affairs.

Md. Mohaimin Ali Khan

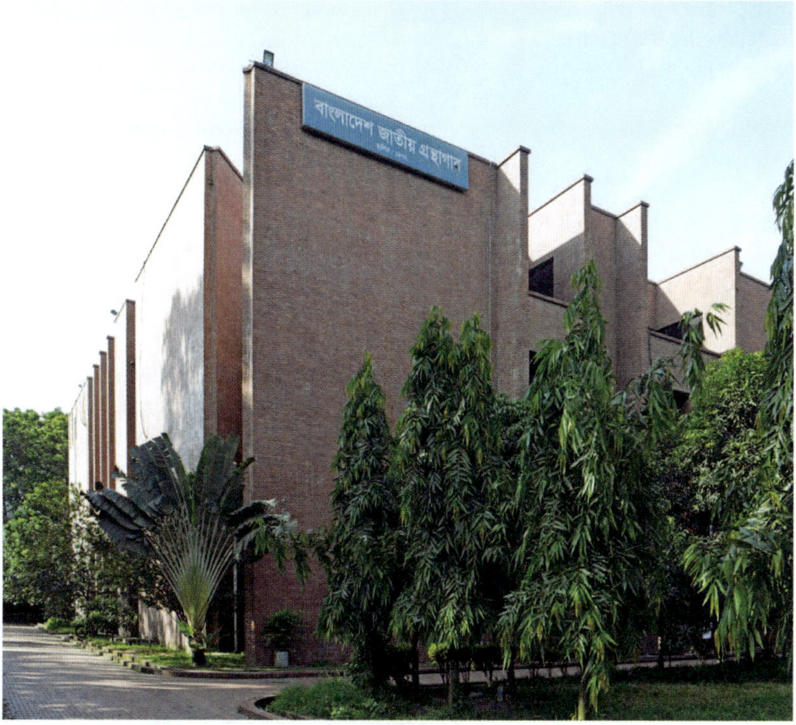

Md. Mohaimin Ali Khan

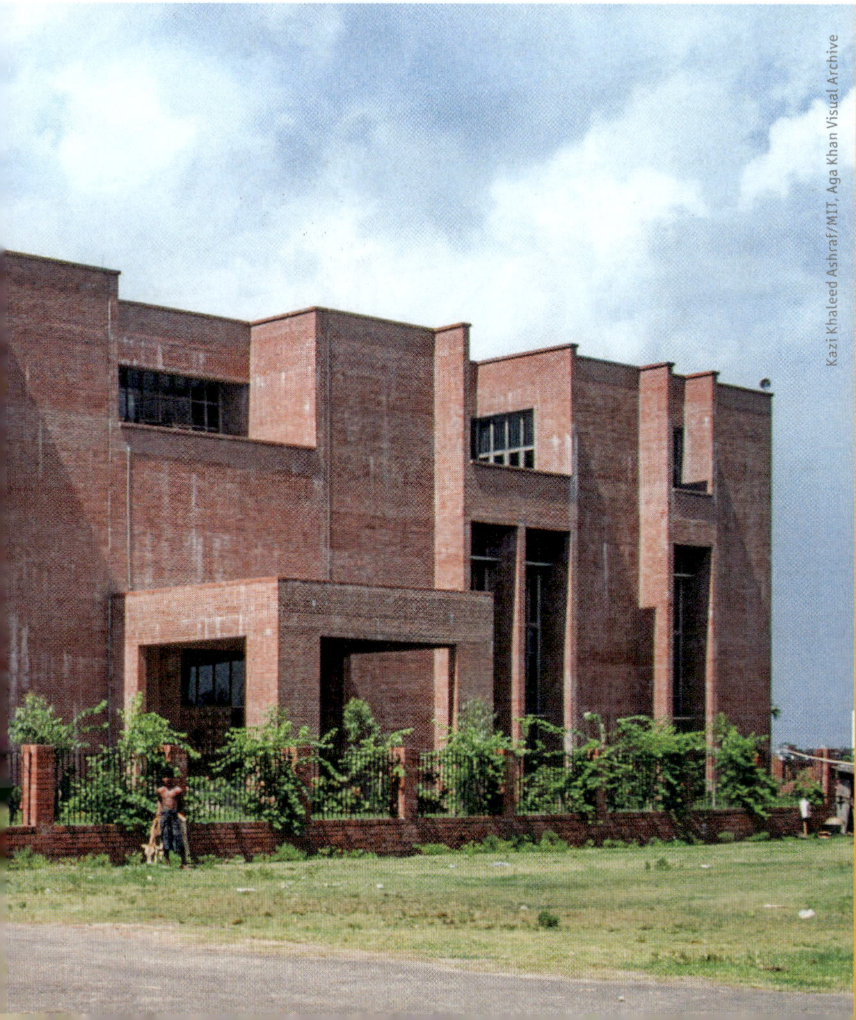

Kazi Khaleed Ashraf/MIT, Aga Khan Visual Archive

Institute of Architects Bangladesh (IAB) Centre

086 B

Plot 11, road 7, block E,
Agargoan,
Vitti Sthapati Brindo Ltd.
2016

This project is the epitome of simplicity. Its structural system allows a void at the centre of the building and a projecting roof that extends a welcome to visitors. The architect wanted to create an ambience of institutional unity. The introverted interior has a mezzanine floor, a double-height space, skylights, and natural ventilation through the wooden windows. There is an interesting interplay between the inner courtyard and the adjacent outdoor space. The brick façade, timber texture, and exposed steel panels interpret the lucidity of traditional architecture with a contemporary vitality. The double-height multipurpose hall for conferences is on the right-hand side. Other functions, such as the library, administrative offices, records room, seminar room, and training room, are on the left. As a gathering place for architects, this building offers the maximum of interactive spaces along with a luxuriant green courtyard in front. The oblique entrance ramp is the perfect way to approach this building.

Md. Mohaimin Ali Khan (all pictures of this project)

3

Islamic Development Bank Complex
Begum Rokeya Avenue
E/8-A, Agargaon
M Mahiuddin Khan, Shathapti Shangshad
1999

087 B

This 20-storey building is Dhaka's computer city and the largest technology-based market in the country. It also accommodates a weather station and UN's Bangladesh office. Its total floor area is 9293.30 square metres; the adjacent four-storey building houses 322 computer showrooms, an IT hub, and an atrium where computer fairs are held each year. This complex is regarded as

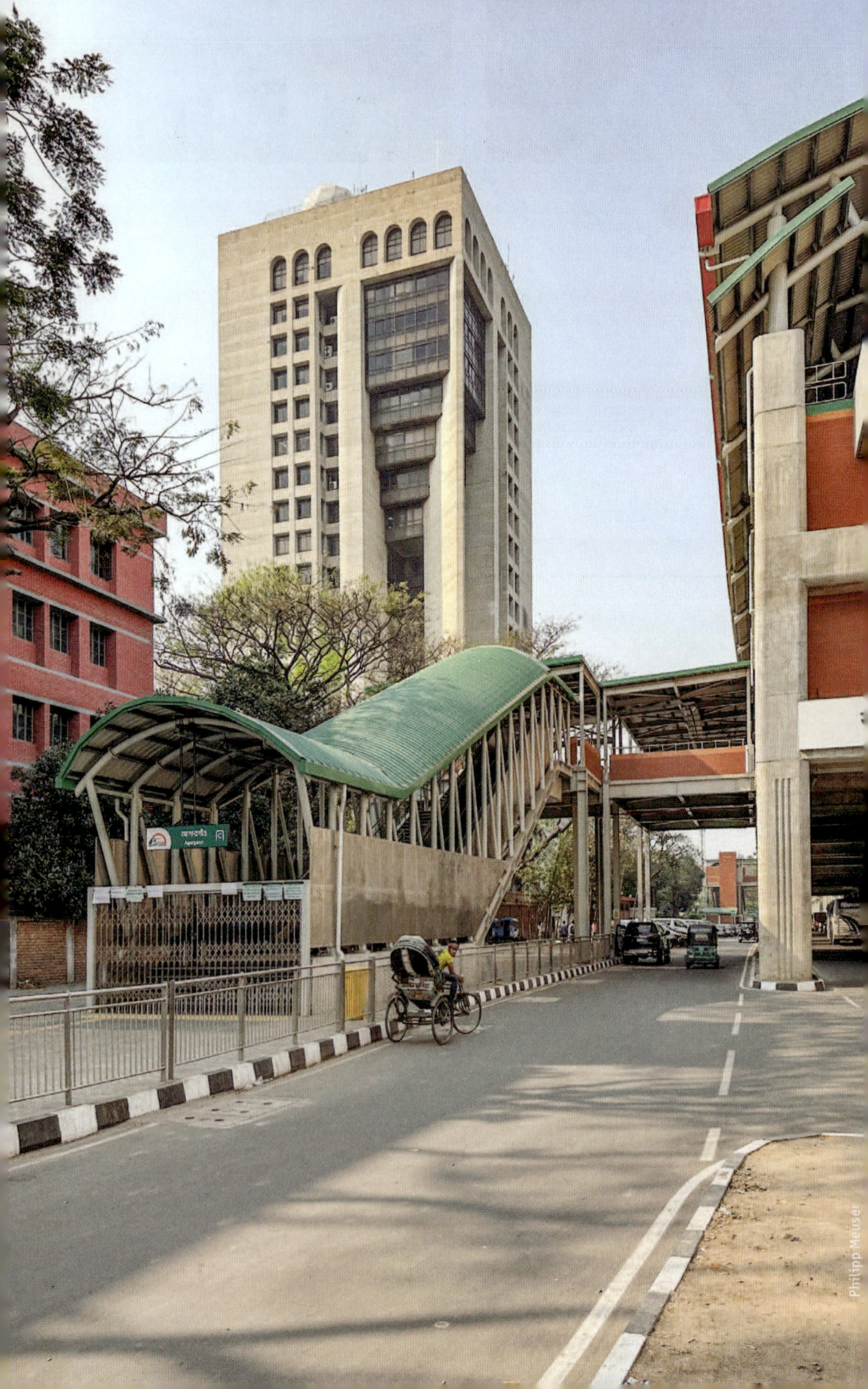

Philipp Meuser

3

an early successful example of high-rise development in Bangladesh and a landmark in the Agargaon business district. It has a fair-face concrete façade dominated by recessed square windows with hemispherical arches on the top floor; the arches allude to Islamic architecture – appropriately, given that this building is owned by Islamic Development Bank. The treatment of the corners is also interesting: a towering strip of wall indicates the building's entrance; to maintain a sense of scale, the expanses of glass on the upper floors become progressively larger towards the top of the building.

Grameen Bank Headquarters `088` `A`

5 Mirpur Road,
Mirpur Section-2
Mubasshar Hussein
1990

Twenty storeys and 76.71 metres high, this building was designed to be the home of Grameen Bank, which won the Nobel Prize for Peace in 2006. The objective of Muhammad Yunus, the pioneer of micro-financing, was to endow Bangladesh's poor with self-confidence. This is a model which is followed today in more than 100 countries all over the world. The Grameen Bank bank building has an octagonal plan. It rises boldly from a podium, its façades shaped by alternative horizontal bands of solid wall and glass panels. At the right-hand corner of the main façade, the bands turn to wrap onto the lift core; on the top four storeys, however, they keep going. The lift core, positioned on the west side, is a distinctive vertical presence. The lower floors of the building contain seminar rooms, archives, galleries, a showroom for fabric crafts, and a media room. The upper floors accommodate Grameen Bank's 12 directories. In front of the building is a small garden. Standing on a 3437.41-square-metre site and having a footprint of 1068.38 square metres, this simple building is a landmark in the Mirpur area.

Aashaa

Philipp Meuser

Shere Bangla National Cricket Stadium

Mirpur 2
Masud Rahman Khan,
Bashat Architects
2006

This is the 'home of cricket' in Bangladesh, the home ground of the national team, and the ultimate destination for one of the most cricket-crazy nations in the world. Shere Bangla National Cricket Stadium is named after the great leader AK Fazlul Haq, aka 'the Tiger of Bengal' – a sobriquet which, incidentally, echoes the nickname given to Bangladesh's cricketers, 'the Tigers'. Constructed in 1978, the stadium was originally for football and athletics and so had a rectangular field. When it became the permanent home of Bangladeshi cricket in 2004, the stadium was renovated: the turf was dug up, nearly one metre of red clay was excavated, a layer of rock chips and sand was put down, and grass was grown on top. The grass is angled at a gentle slope: there is a difference of 76.33 centimetres in level between the wicket in the middle and the boundaries at the edges of the field. The stadium's field now measures 186 by 136 metres. Its capacity has increased to 25,416 spectators. The complex also includes a cricket academy and a practice centre with both indoor and outdoor facilities. The renovation also included the creation of two elevated plazas with commercial shops underneath. The conversion project faced challenges because it retained the stadium's existing structure while reconfiguring circulation routes and the zoning for the VIP lounge, corporate lounge, press and media centre, players' pavilion etc.

3

Other notable changes included improved floodlighting for day/night matches and a new grandstand and corporate stand with a canopy of zinc alloy supported by tall steel columns. The new drainage system ensures that rainwater runs off quickly. A turnstile ticket-control system was introduced. The main materials used in the stadium are glass and brick. The first international match, between Bangladesh and Scotland, took place here on 18 December 2005. Shere Bangla National Stadium has hosted a number of important international events, such as the ICC Cricket World Cup in 2011, the 20 World Cup in 2014, and the Asia Cup Championship in 2012, 2014, and 2016. Since 2012 it has also regularly hosted matches in the Bangladesh Premier League (BPL). A common venue for finals, this stadium is an important seat of Bangladeshi national pride and emotion.

Nurunnaby Chowdhury

Shakkyamuni Buddhist Temple 090 A

Mirpur 14, Minto Avenue/
Mirpur Road
Salauddin Potash,
Shaheedullah Associates
1993

This is one of Dhaka's four Buddhist temples. It was built for the Buddhist community from three Chittagong Hill Tract districts who live in Dhaka. In recognition of the unceasing service of the Buddhist chief priest, Vikkhu Vedanta Bimaltishya, the then president of Bangladesh, donated land to the organisation known as 'the Hill Tract Buddhist Council' in 1976. The site has an area of 4180.64 square metres, of which 1858.06 square metres are occupied by the temple itself. A Buddha statue of white marble was presented by the Dharmarajika Buddhist Monastery of Kamalapur at the temple's inauguration. In 1992 the temple became home to a Buddhist primary and secondary school, children's homes, and a college, turning this into an important educational and social welfare centre for orphans. There is a large playground in front of the school. A 10.67-metre-tall figure of Buddha by the renowned sculptor Mrinal Haque has stood at the entrance since 2015. The L-shaped, three-storey building accommodates 208 children ranging from five to 11 years of age. Educational activities here involve 114 teachers and 2237 students. The school has classrooms, a library, a multipurpose room, a dining hall, and a kitchen. There are offices on the ground floor of the building. The upper floor contains dormitories. The building's structure consists of load bearing-walls of exposed brick and concrete slabs. Wooden windows were chosen as the type of fenestration. This building was nominated for the Aga Khan Prize in 1998.

SOS Youth Village and Vocational Training Institute

1 Mirpur Road, Shamoli
Raziul Ahsan
1985

The devastating Independence War of 1971 left many Bangladeshi children homeless and without parents. Hermann Gmeiner, the Austrian philanthropist and founder president of SOS-Kinderdorf International, the largest non-profit organisation for childcare in the world, visited Bangladesh in 1972 to establish a branch here. SOS-Kinderdorf was granted a 10279-square-metre piece of land in Shaymoli, and the youth village and training institute was established here in 1974. The present buildings date to 1985. There are 15 family houses arranged in three wings of five houses each; each house can accommodate eight to ten children. The playful design of the spaces, social amenities, and educational facilities imitates the scattered order and low, ground-hugging structures of a traditional Bangladeshi village. The architect wanted to give the children here a happy childhood, so the L-shaped site is full of vegetation and greenery. The vaulted roofs of the houses encourage natural ventilation, while the pronounced concrete overhangs protect the windows from tropical rain. The buildings here are all the same width but differ in length in accordance with their function. The water tank clad with brick is a key point of interest.

3

Navid Zaman Dhrubo

Navid Zaman Dhrubo

Navid Zaman Dhrubo (all pictures of this object)

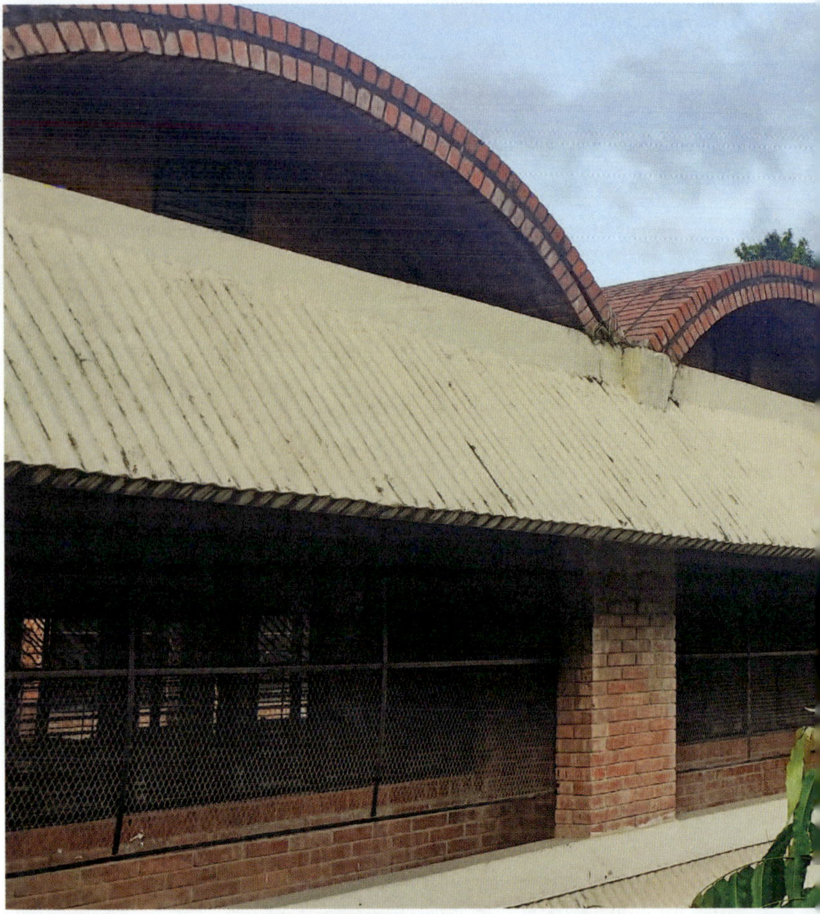

SOS Hermann Gmeiner School 092 A

Mirpur, 13 no Sector/
Minto Avenue
CAPE Architects,
Raziul Ahsan,
Nahas Ahmed Khalil,
1988

The SOS-Kinderdorf International college was established to provide a start in education to village orphans and underprivileged children from kindergarten age to 12th grade (4–18 years old). Today the college accepts bright students from every social class; nearly 1200 study here. Situated on a 8100-square-metre piece of land at Mirpur, the school complex is a two-storey brick building with 20 classrooms on either side of a corridor. The roof is of brickwork vaulting. The complex is arranged around a central playground with a basketball court and large open spaces for outdoor activities. Rows of vaulted structures line the north and south parts of the site; the east side includes scattered vaulted structures and some structures with flat roofs. Vaulted structures were chosen for a number of different reasons: they are easy to construct using bricks; they resemble traditional projecting elements such as eaves; and, most importantly, rainwater runs off them quickly. The east wing contains three laboratories, a multipurpose hall, a gymnasium, a library, and a large dining room. The U-shaped entrance approach reveals a visually

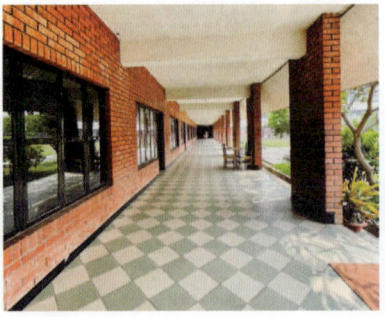

stimulating view of the façade: whitish horizontal bands combine with the oblong shapes of the vaults on different levels to give this complex an effective identity. The staggered angular sides of the buildings create a cosy setting that is ideal for children's play. Structurally, the buildings are a combination of a reinforced-concrete frame and brick infill. The frame is coloured white; the brickwork is red. A colonnade of brick pillars in the corridors supports a sloping overhead roof; the corridors have good visual links with the inner courtyard. The complex as a whole is notable for the fluidity and variety of its spaces.

Kakoli Manor Residence

093 A

Plot-20/A/3, Road-17, Block-G,
Bashundhara Residential Area
F2A+Partners
2022

Located on a corner plot in the Bashundhara residential area, Kakoli Manor was designed as a demonstration of contemporary building techniques. With roads on two sides, the site was an interesting opportunity to flip the typical set up of suburban housing. The result is a project with a feeling of clarity and composure – a home that enhances the life of the growing family residing within its walls. The building has an introverted form. The solid, static mass of concrete makes a bold impression from the outside. It is only when you enter the building and walk through the different spaces inside that you notice the vigorous interplay of mass and light. This is a complex network of spaces of different characters and functions linked by continuous visual links and physically connected by double-height spaces and passages. The ground floor has parking for vehicles, a formal living area, a dining area, a pantry, and a patio area with a swimming pool. The second floor contains a family dining zone with a coffee bar, two separate kitchens, a TV room, and a large walk-in closet for the lady of the house. This floor is where the residents spend most of their time. The third floor is a private zone with two bedrooms for children and one for the parents, each of which opens onto a terrace. The fourth floor is dominated by open spaces. Here there is a gym, an indoor lounge, and elegantly furnished outdoor sitting areas. The landscaping of the terraces and external areas is predominantly tropical with low-maintenance species, creating a lush tropical ambiance. This four-storey residential building is built entirely of fair-faced concrete, resulting in a timeless feel. Engraved on one part of the interior wall is a graphical motif that brings out the details and beauty of the concrete. Altogether, this is an all-season urban escape space with a bright and airy ambiance.

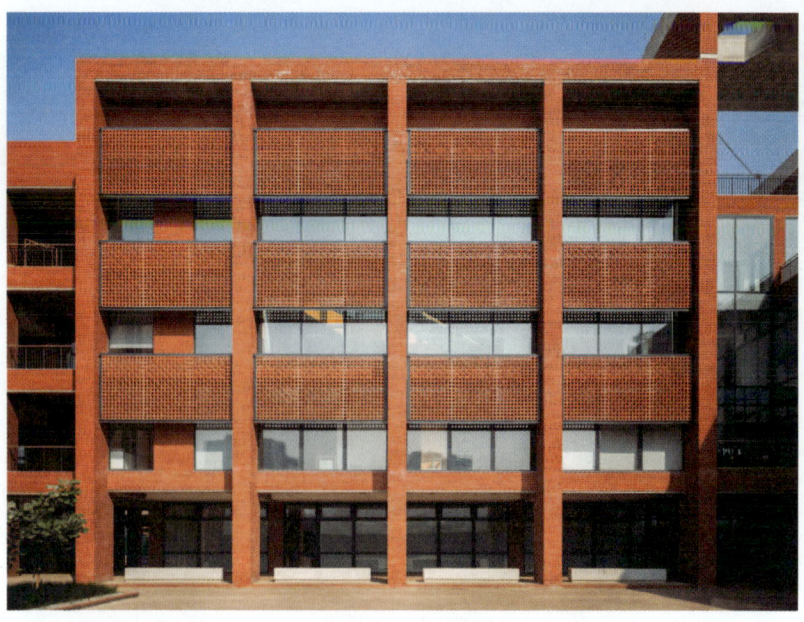

Asif Salman

Aga Khan Academy

Purbachal Express Highway/
Sayem Sobhan Anvir Road
Feilden Clegg Bradley,
Rafiq Azam
2022

094 A

Situated on an approximately 80,000-square-metre site, the Aga Khan Academy has 1200 boarding students and is part of an integrated network that includes 14 other countries. This is a purpose-built campus with state-of-the-art classrooms, dormitories, and extensive sports facilities arranged around a *maidan* (community gathering place). The *maidan* is a reference to the foundation's core concept but also an allusion to the layouts of historical Buddhist monasteries in North Bengal. Local materials and technologies have been used to tackle climatic factors such as humidity and monsoon rain. The complex of buildings has natural ventilation and cooling, giving it low energy consumption. Spaces specially designed for informal education have been incorporated; these include: indoor outdoor spaces, extensive decks, and informal open-air areas. The complex's lavish brick façade recalls the long tradition of Bangladesh's architectural past. The design by Feilden Clegg Bradley won the prize for best future project in the educational category at World Architecture Festival in Berlin in 2017.

Asif Salman

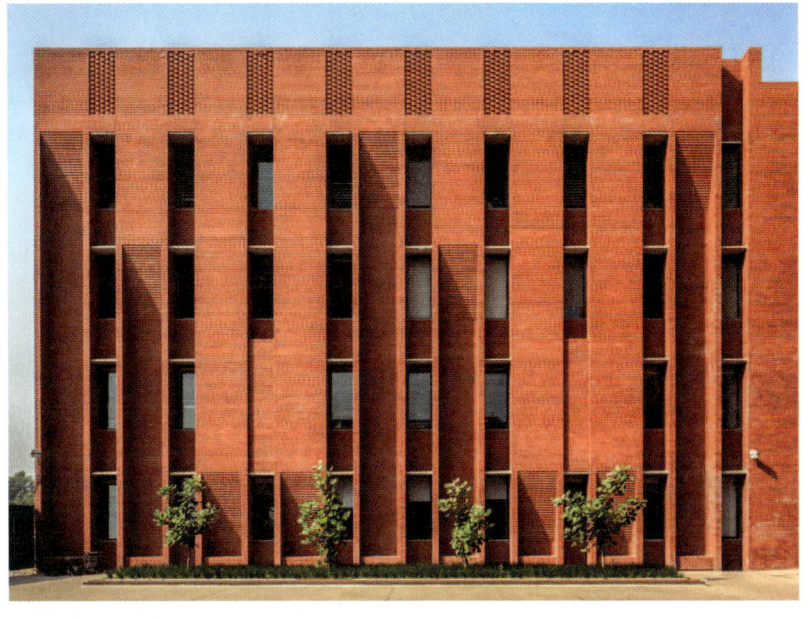

International Convention Centre Bushundhara (ICCB)

095 A

Next to 300 ft. Purbachal
Express Highway
Volumezero Ltd.
Mohammad Foyez Ullah
2014

Spread over 17 acres, the ICCB is a unique initiative by the country's largest real estate conglomerate, Bashundhara Group. The site's irregular shape posed a challenge for the design of the master plan. The site is approached via the Asian Highway, a 30-metre-wide, six-lane expressway that links Dhaka with the emerging satellite township of Purbachal to its east. The four convention halls have been pushed to the edges of the irregularly shaped site. There is an efficient traffic-management system channelling traffic around the one way loop on which the convention halls are placed. Interspersed with the buildings are canopied parking spaces. The modular convention halls executed in metal, concrete, and glass exude a gracious simplicity and can be used to hold a large number of different events simultaneously, including social occasions, expos, concerts, seminars, and examinations. The landscape provides a neutral and soothing backdrop, and the ICCB's location between Dhaka and the emerging satellite city to the east puts it in the perfect position to capture a growing market.

F. M. Faruque Abdullah Shawon, H. M. Fozla Rabby Apurbo (all pictures)

4

Grameenphone Headquarters
Bashundhara R/A
Vistaara & Icon Architects,
Mustapha Khalid Palash,
Mohammad Foyez Ullah
2010

This is a masterpiece by Mustapha Khalid Palash, a prolific exponent of the twenty-first-century contemporary style in Bangladesh's corporate architecture. Palash's motto is architecture that stands out for 'appropriate use of land, combined with invigoration of spaces for public gatherings.' The 7466-square-metre site is rectangular. The basement contains a three-level car park with an area of 16,800 square metres. The two wings on the east and west sides are gently asymmetrical but contain similar functions. Linking them in the middle is a vast plaza-like courtyard with bridges, lifts, gardened terraces, and monumental flights of steps. A pedestrian ramp makes the entrance staircase more human and inviting. The complex has a total floor area of 45,200 square metres. Almost 22% of the building is given over to circulation, and there are 4000 square metres of landscaping. To encourage a 'democratic character', Mustapha Khalid Palash divided the building's spaces into two rough categories: public and private. The tri-spatial relationship (courtyard-pond-garden) found in traditional architecture inspired him to put a large circular pool in the middle of the plaza and a garden in the south plaza. In terms of materials, this building is a harmonious marriage of traditional brick and contemporary glass and metal. Like his choices of materials and construction technology, Palash's maximisation of daylight and natural ventilation is a design strategy that makes for environmentally responsive architecture. The top of this nine-storey building has a metal shield that floats above the concrete slab in a 75-metre sweep, forming a kind of urban canopy. This has the additional advantage of improving thermal performance and air flow inside the building.

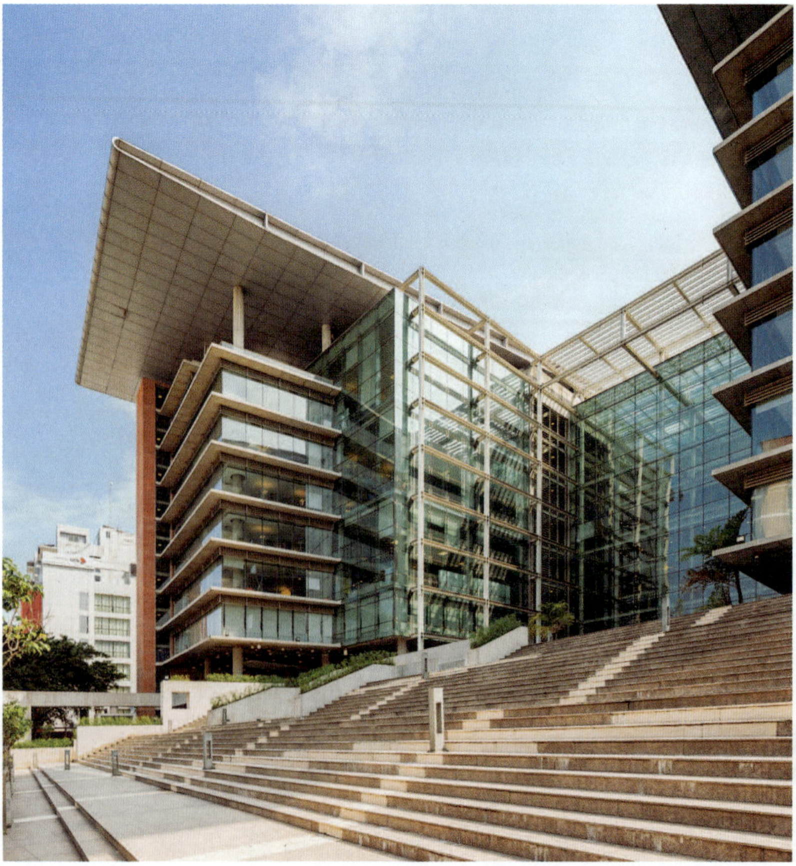

Mohammad Mashiur Rahman (all pictures of this project)

Blues Communication Ltd.

Plot 3880, Solmaid
Bashundhara New Road, Vatara
Rashed Chowdhury,
Sayedil Ashrafin,
Desharworks Architects
2019

This bespoke office for a premier event-management company puts an equal emphasis on productivity and creativity. When asked by the architects, the employees said they wanted something to motivate them as they worked: a good work/play mix, combined with freedom from repetitive, rigid patterns. Hence this building, which offers homely but glossy warmth, a flexible working environment, cosy workspaces, and a lavish and interactive landscape. The free flow of the plan allows a degree of zoning while promoting flexibility, reducing space dedicated to circulation, and promoting overall unity. Hospitable hubs, including coffee bars, informal lounges, and meeting tables, have been placed in various calm corners. There are numerous alcoves where employees can enjoy privacy or quick chats with one another or talk on the phone. The two-storey building has a rectangular plan and a footprint of 687.48 square metres. A pre-fabricated steel structural skeleton was installed to make the project effective in terms of time and money. Double-layered polycarbonate roofing helps regulate the internal temperature. The building's transparent shell and the height of its spaces draw daylight into the core. The building's LED lighting makes it a twinkling presence throughout its neighbourhood when in use at night. The wooden staircase functions as a bookshelf and links with the open central lounge. The red elevated mezzanine floor is a contrasting but focal element of the building's façade – an eye-catching platform which serves as a venue for events, art exhibitions, and lectures. Underneath it is a fun terrace where both employees and employers can play cricket. To block the heat coming from the west and north, the artist Reesham Tirtho painted colourful graffiti, adding an element of fantasy. This building's interior and furniture exude zestful vitality.

DIU Administrative Building 098 A

Badshahi Mosque Road
Nabi Newaz Khan Shomin/
Archeground Ltd.
2015

This volume of simple shape is the result of a determination to minimally occupy the plot while implementing a fixed programme: a library to inspire both teachers and students in their research. The architects applied hand-made brick chips to the façade using a pebble-wash technique, resulting in an expressive monolithic appearance which is easy to maintain and at the same time has a strikingly powerful colour. The structural system is steel columns and bracing, a choice determined by concerns about seismic activity. The steel columns are clad with brick and concrete to protect against fire. The non-load-bearing walls divide the spaces into small units. Steel louvres protect the western façade from both heat and the very strong winds that blow in this location. The recessed windows cast a variety of shadows at different times of day and allow interior light to emerge at night. The building is a climatically adapted and is an iconic presence on the university campus.

4

Bashundhara Sports Complex

N block, Mouza Dumni,
Bashundhara R/A
Volumezero Ltd.
Mohammad Foyez Ullah
2018

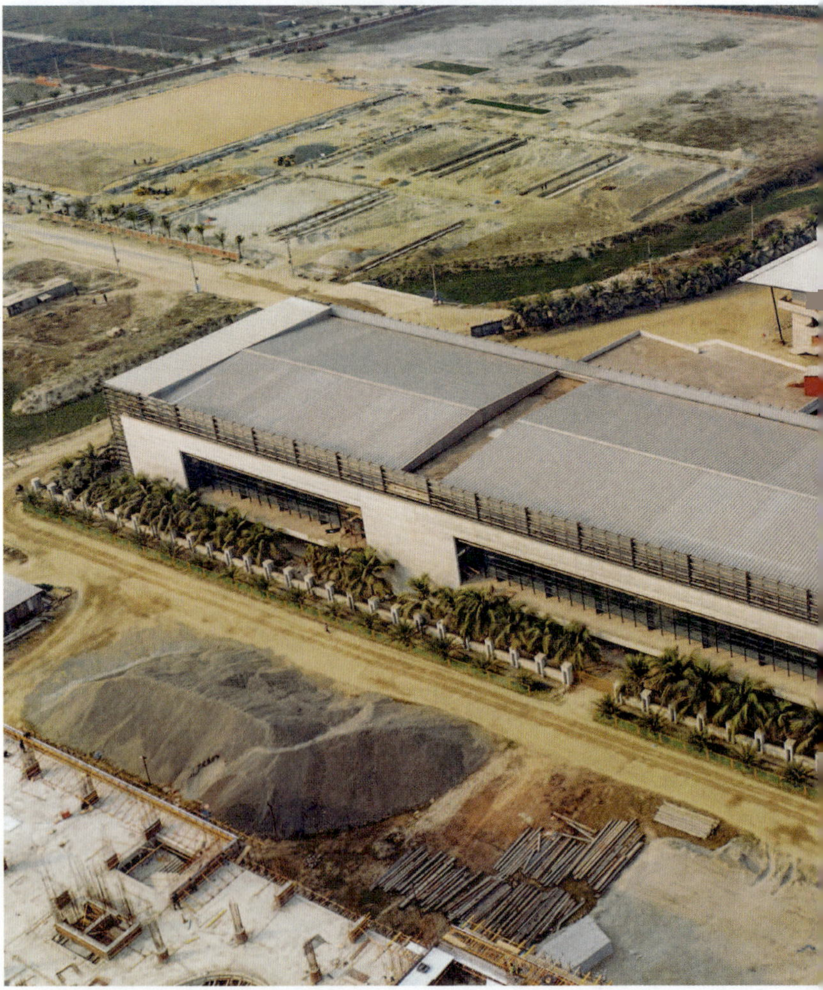

Sports are an integral part of a person's growth and physical well-being. Institutions dedicated to generating physical development are a rarity in Dhaka's ever-expanding city. For the larger part, planned development has ignored the need for institutions, complexes, and playgrounds. On Dhaka's eastern fringe this is even more noticeable. Bashundhara Sports Arena has addressed this void. Sprawling over more than 56 acres, this sports ensemble comprises three distinct zones: an indoor sports complex and playing areas in the north, an academy and club facility and multiple grounds in the south, and a gated cricket facility in the southeast. The north zone consists of an indoor complex with two swimming pools, an indoor multi-sports facility, squash courts, gyms, and a yoga studio, as well as multiple outdoor facilities, including a cricket ground, football and futsal grounds, and tennis courts and hockey courts (all of which meet the international requirements for court sizes laid down by FIFA, ICC, FINA, FIBA etc.). The football ground is a state-of-the-art natural grass playing area built to FIFA standards. It is accompanied by international-standard dressing rooms for both home and away teams and match officials, a 6000-seat gallery, VIP boxes, a press-conference room, an international-standard press box, and broadcast-quality lighting. The cricket facility comprises a state-of-the-art natural-grass playing area built to ICC standards, accompanied by international-standard dressing rooms for both home and away teams and match officials, a 2500-person gallery, and broadcast-quality lighting. Additionally, there is a nets practice facility with five indoor practice lanes and five outdoor lanes. A fenced-off futsal facility with three futsals with artificial turf completes the outdoor sports zones. The south zone comprises an academy building with residential facilities, a shooting complex, and a club with a dedicated area for archery. Adjacent to the club is a sports zone for basketball, volleyball, and kabaddi. The outfield facilities include a football practice ground, a hockey practice ground, a tennis facility, and a futsal compound with six fields of artificial turf. In the east of the site is a golf driving range with teeing facilities. These

state-of-the-art sports grounds are laid out as an ensemble in a park intended for visitors from the general public. The focus of the park is a water feature whose laser light shows and water fountains are a major attraction. The east extension is a gated cricket facility dedicated to the development and cultivation of cricket as the sport that drives Bangladeshis' passions. It comprises a natural-turf cricket stadium with seating for up to 15,000 spectators, an outfield, and practice nets with seven indoor lanes and seven outdoor lanes. Bashundhara Sports Arena is not only one of the most extensive sports facilities in the country but possibly one of the largest in South Asia. The overall planning and architectural grammar aim for functionality and appropriate zoning while ensuring that every individual function of the complex is part of the overall whole.

4

EIIL Moriyum Residence

House 03, Road 03, Block K,
Baridhara
Volumezero Ltd.
Mohammad Foyez Ullah
2018

100 D

concrete are well integrated with the building's overall mass. High-end materials, a rooftop pool, landscaping, and gardens complete the image of luxury and sophistication. The window shutters were custom-designed for this project.

New embassies have made this one of the most exclusive and desirable neighbourhoods in Dhaka. The main idea behind this design for an ultra-luxury residence was to create a vertical microcosm in which the lawn at ground level is part of the vertical shaft of the courtyard space. The inwardly oriented balconies reflect the fact that there is just one residential unit per floor. The balcony screens of perforated

4

Franco-German Embassy

101 D

11 Madani Avenue/
Park Road, Baridhara
Stephane Paumier Architects
2017

As part of the friendship treaty concluded between Germany and France in 1963, the two countries agreed on the possibility of sharing diplomatic premises – a first in human diplomatic history. In 2009 a competition to design the Franco-German embassy in Dhaka involved ten teams from France, Germany, and Bangladesh. It was won by Stephane Paumier Architects. The result is a building with a floor area of 6635 square metres on an 8000-square-metre site. The plan is asymmetrical. There is no clear division into front/back, left/right or top/bottom. The low podium contains offices and a section for issuing joint Schengen visas; the six-storey tower accommodates the diplomats. Dictated by considerations of safety, this layout gives the embassy a resemblance to a medieval fort. The building contains two parallel spirals – a double DNA helix with the two brick-coloured masses wrapping around one another. This unified duality represents the bond between the European Union's two economic powerhouses and is to be found even in the solid walls of the communal interior spaces, such as the lobby, the atrium, and circulations: the red clay brick symbolises Germany and north Europe, while the grey cement brick represents the more stony

4

qualities of south Europe, the birthplace of concrete, especially France. The walls were built using the Dutch bond bricklaying technique. Rising from a base shared by the two countries (containing the visa section, reception, and spaces for cultural events), the tower is, by contrast, a bulwark of duality: there are separate chancelleries for the French and German ambassadors. In keeping with other embassies in Dhaka's diplomatic quarter, the Franco-German Embassy has a large garden, which, like the Mughal Char-Bagh, consists of a number of parts with different functions. There is a formal arrival court for official cars, a *cour d'honneur*, a 'terrace de café' for cultural events, and a formal garden for receptions, garden parties, and national celebrations. Structurally, the building is RCC (reinforced cement concrete) with a brick cavity wall filled with insulation. The beautiful exterior is dominated by double glazing and glazed terracotta louvres. Black ceramic bricks are inlaid with 30-millimetre strips of white marble. The central octagonal tower is a faceted cocoon of steel and glass inspired by Dhaka's traditional Islamic *minars* (towers). An empty triangular structure contains a panoramic lift and serves as a light well. In this project the architects found a balance between high technology and ecology.

Turkish Embassy

6 Madani Avenue, Baridhara
Semra Uygur, Özcan Uygur
2020

102 D

The Turkish Embassy in Bangladesh is situated on a small plot of land adjacent to other embassies (belonging to the USA, France, Germany, South Korea, Saudi Arabia, et al.). Due to the limited size of the plot, the extensive programme, and contemporary requirements, users are separated and their needs are accommodated through a focused design strategy. The tropical climate here played a leading role in the design language, along with characteristic materials and cultural factors. The design features open and covered outdoor spaces, walkways, and carefully designed traffic areas, which together create a multifaceted sensory experience that reinterprets the neighbourhood. There is a central courtyard with private living areas and areas for exterior use arranged in a transit pattern. The prism shapes of the masses are enriched with architectural elements that create fascinating patterns of light and shadow in the bright sunlight. Finally, the architects identified and reinterpreted emblematic architectural symbols from the history of Byzantium and the Osman Empire to give the building a unique contemporary identity.

ids consult (all pictures of this project)

Royal Embassy of Saudi Arabia 103 D

40/2 Madani Avenue, Baridhara
ids consult
2020

Consisting of the embassy chancery building, the ambassador's residence, and 12 modular staff villas, the royal embassy complex of the Kingdom of Saudi Arabia in Dhaka is a modern and luxurious foreign mission. Combining handworked natural stone and woodwork and state-of-the-art IT and security technologies, the complex stands out as a success achieved in spite of obstacles such as tough geographical conditions, limited technological resources, and an exacting timeframe.

US Embassy

12 Madani Avenue, Baridhara
*Kallmann McKinnell and Wood,
Bashirul Haq*
1989

104 **D**

This embassy building, nicknamed 'the Red Fort' for its surrounding moat and walls clad with terracotta brick tiles, was inspired by Bengal's Mughal architecture. Kallmann McKinnell and Wood, a Boston-based architecture firm, invited Bashirul Haq to work on the project as their local collaborator. Standing on a 14,660-square-metre site, this building has a square plan. The ground floor, in the form of a workspace for 400 members of staff contains, offices, amenities, and the security service. The upper floors are for delegates and diplomats. The design features red lintels, black railings, and projecting inclined eaves of thick masonry. The rectangular windows of the upper floors contain *jali* (latticework) windows, while the lower-floor windows are ornamented recessed arches.

U.S. Department of State

Navid Zaman Dhrubo

U.S. Department of State

4

The *jalis* are combinations of triangles. At the building's four corners and in its centre are bastion-like towers standing on square bases. The central tower is larger than the others and has two bands of three windows – an arrangement found in the 'five-jewel' temples of medieval Bengal. The entrance porch is an additional tower; its relative lowness provides a well-proportioned approach to the building. The green lawns are adorned with rows of palm trees.

![Bay's Edgewater building]

Bay's Edgewater

12 North Avenue, Gulshan-2
Mahmudul Anwar Riyaad,
Mamnoon Murshed Chowdhury
DWm4
2013

105 **D**

A perfect expression of the corporate lifestyle, this building's adherence to the highest international standards has made it popular with multinational companies. The 1821-square-metre site is in the most expensive and prestigious business district in Dhaka. The project conspicuously breaches the rules governing building height for the Gulshan area, where commercial buildings are mostly six-storey – but does so in a most fertile way. With special permission from RAJUK (the Dhaka agency responsible for urban development), the building combines residential and commercial functions in a total floor area of 11,150 square metres, permitting more space than usual under floor-area-ratio rules. The lower floors contain communal spaces; the middle floors, offices; the upper floors, residential units. The challenge was to segregate the residential and commercial zones. This was done by careful segregation of routes on the ground floor – just like in an airport terminal. Everywhere from the entrance zone to the garden areas, visitors and users find a welcoming environment with green spaces, landscaping, pools of water, and soft pavements, all of which complement the natural beauty of the nearby lake. The basement has spacious parking for 160 cars with a one-way traffic system designed to ensure easy navigation. A 'scissors ramp' splits the basement levels and makes it possible to fit all necessary services into a compact space. The building also has rainwater harvesting and comprehensive backup power generation. The offices on the upper floors enjoy stunning views of the green landscape and curving shore of Baridhara Lake. The west side of the building is screened by a solid concrete façade to counteract the sun. Double and low-E glazing was installed to prevent heat building up inside the building and reduce noise pollution. Meticulous detailing, precision in the design of the concrete blocks, and high-tech glazing make for a bold contemporary façade. This building won the Berger Award for Excellence in Architecture in 2015.

Maison Park

House 01, Road 86/88, Gulshan 2
Volumezero Ltd.
Mohammad Foyez Ullah
2022

Located on an exclusive corner site, this luxury complex contains spacious apartments with floor areas of more than 500 square metres. The units have clear separation of public and private zones and an invigorating environment shaped by functional flow. At ground floor level the landscaped outdoor spaces intermesh with the building's interior, creating bold visual frames that welcome residents and guests alike to a refreshing ambiance.

Claudio Manzoni (all pictures)

The Way Dhaka Hotel

107 D

10/B/2 Road 54B, Gulshan 2
Rohit+Matin
2016

Situated in the heart of Gulshan and conceived by the New Delhi-based architects Rohit Tewari and MA Matin, the Way Dhaka Boutique Hotel is easily accessible, being just eight kilometres from Hazrat Shah Jalal International Airport. The interior designer Jiraprann Tokeeree has here fused modern design finesse with traditional techniques, creating a memorable mix. The hotel has nine floors with a total of 38 guestrooms and two upscale suites, including specially designed rooms for individuals with limited mobility.

Justice Shahabuddin Ahmed Park

108 N

Gulshan North Avenue,
Road 06/Road 03, Gulshan 2
Vitti Sthapati Brindo Ltd.
2019

This is the first park in Bangladesh to achieve a Sustainable Development Goal (SDG). The architects saw their role as involving policy making as much as landscape design. 1765 existing trees belonging to 40 different species were retained, and the bio-diversity present on the site was preserved intact. Five types of pavement were used: brick chips, CC pavement, soft paving, weather-treated wooden planks, and, for the cycle paths, a paving mixture containing an advanced chemical compound to make the surface more permeable. The drainage system incorporates rainwater harvesting. The lake in the middle of the park is surrounded by winding walkways and three decks that reinterpret the traditional concept of the *ghat* (stepped embankment); a fountain sprays vitality and freshness. The lake is the backdrop for a green amphitheatre. Supplementary functions include a snacks bar, a community library, a prayer space, kiosks, a small gym, a children's playground, an outdoor exercise zone, and a women's corner. The traditional solid boundary wall has been replaced with transparent fencing, enhancing visibility and permeability.

Noor A Alam

Philipp Meuser

Philipp Meuser

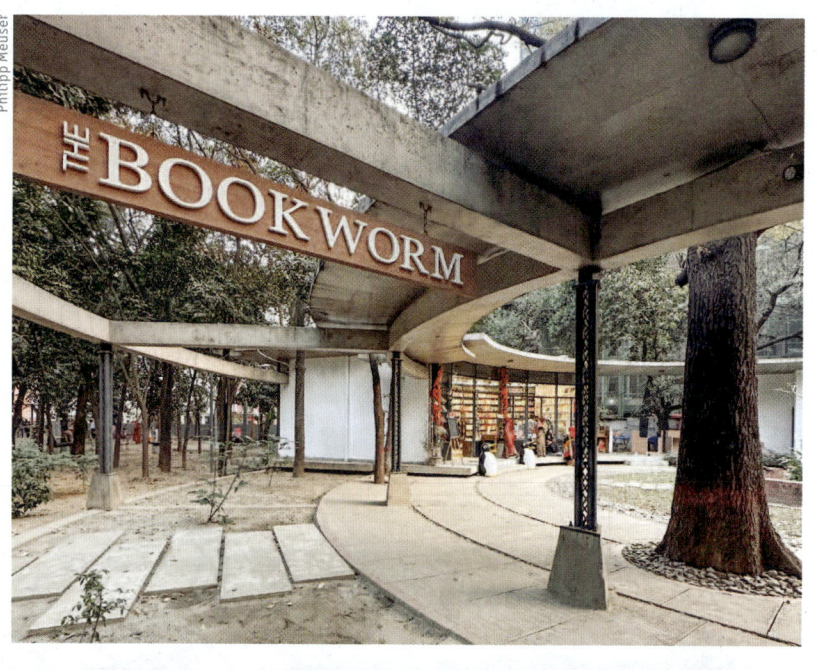

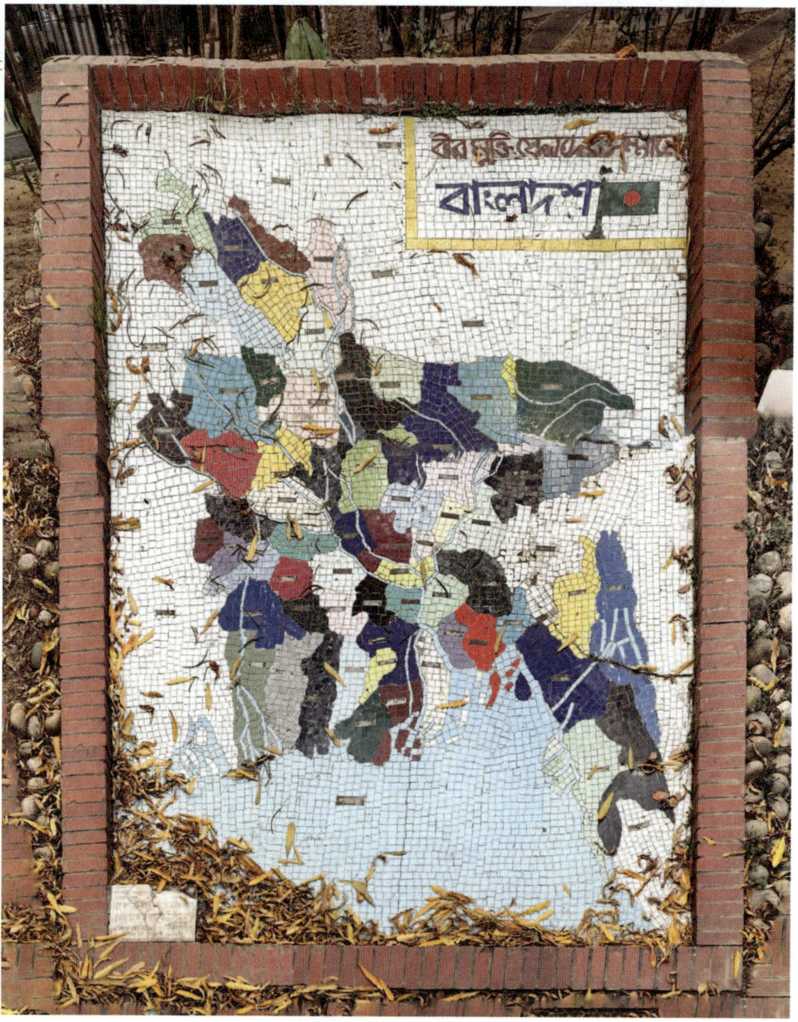

Justice Shahabuddin Ahmed Park (2023)

4

Gulshan Society Mosque

Road 17/A, Road 12,
Gulshan 2
Kashef Mahboob Chowdhury
2017

109 D

This mosque occupies a relatively small site (741 square metres) yet needed to accommodate a large congregation (nearly 2500) for Friday prayers, a requirement which led the architect, Kashef Mahboob Chowdhury, to adopt a vertical solution. The traditional layout with an outdoor courtyard and interior prayer hall is here replaced with a pragmatic perpendicular volume. The flight of steps up from the pavement leads directly to the vestibule and prayer hall. On two sides are stairs and elevators extending to the seventh floor. Natural light and ventilation have always been a prominent concern in Mahboob's works, and this building is no exception. The dominant feature of the façades is innovative full-height *jalis* (latticework) an abstract representation of Arabic letters. Inscribed continuously in seven lines covering all seven levels on all four sides of the building is the sentence, 'Allah is the only one to be worshipped'. The white concrete gives this building a strong monolithic character, distinguishing it amidst the surrounding urban fabric, which had until this point been made up of either commercial or residential buildings. In terms of spatial organisation, the building follows a symmetrical order. The huge arches in the middle of each façade draw the eye from a great distance. The mosque is so popular today that it attracts more than 4500 people for weekly Friday prayers, even if some have to pray in the road in front of the building.

F.M. Faruque Abdullah Shawon, H.M. Fozla Rosby »purbo

Hashi

House 135, Road 4, Block A,
Banani
Volumezero Ltd.
Mohammad Foyez Ullah
2018

Hashi is a ten-storey residential building whose simple design resembles a playful interlocking of cubic volumes shifting on a vertical axis. The site is linear; the east side is open to a road junction, permitting a clean vista through the neighbourhood; the west side overlooks a state-run nature reserve nursery with views of preserved forest. The building's layout takes advantage of this situation. Its core is on the north side, while bedrooms are located on either the east or the west sides, where the best views are. The kitchen, dining space, and living room form the heart of each apartment. The cubic volumes that make up the building's composition are enlivened with screens of glass or wood that serve as railings.

Sayed Khokon's Autograph

House 67/68, Road 21, Block B,
Kemal Ataturk Ave, Banani
Volumezero Ltd.
Mohammad Foyez Ullah
2018

111 D

The design of this building is a response to the dynamics of its site's geometry. The forms juxtaposed here differ in terms of both their orientation and the treatment of their exterior. A clean glass facade has been placed over the building's structural skeleton. Concrete shapes and frames provide the shade that is so important in this climate, minimising solar heat gain while optimising permeability to daylight.

EHL Loqman Husain Centre

59/B Kemal Ataturk Ave,
Banani
Volumezero Ltd.
Mohammad Foyez Ullah
2020

112 D

Eastern Housing Limited is one of the most reputable organisations in Bangladesh. The company's headquarters building combines all the high-quality facilities required of a corporate office with an atmosphere of aesthetic sophistication. Its total floor area of 22,000 square metres is spread over 14 floors and three basements. The upper floors give a clear view of the city on all sides.

F.M. Faruque Abdullah Shawon, H.M. Fozla Rabby Apurbo (all pictures)

Lighthouse

House 53, Road 21, Block B, Banani

Volumezero Ltd.
Mohammad Foyez Ullah
2020

Standing on a corner plot on Kemal Ataturk Avenue, Lighthouse was conceived as a landmark in the belt of commercial high-rises dotting the city's skyline. Its corner position, facing the avenue to its south and a secondary road to its west, gives this building considerable advantages, and the building responds gratefully with a design that is responsive to both its site and the climate. Approached along the main thoroughfare, its form seems a play of layered planes. The planes express a hierarchy of tactility: first, there is a concrete slab that folds at the top; it is followed by planes of glass and louvred screens with regular folds. Pockets of gardens have been incorporated throughout the building; these open up to become urban windows, pockets of green space on the office floors providing employees with the chance to take a tranquil break from the race against time. A tree at basement level penetrates ground level. Similar trees will in time break through in a similar way at different levels in this tall building – almost as if nature is looking for a way through this man-made structure in a bid to coexist. The plates fold and terminate at the top of the building, leaving a glimpse of exposed structure; here a 16-meet infinity pool has been positioned to give views of the sunset in the west.

F.M. Faruque Abdullah Shawon, H.M. Fozia Rabby Apurbo (all pictures)

4

4

Sheraton Hotel Dhaka

44 Kemal Ataturk Ave, Banani
Volumezero Ltd.
Mohammad Foyez Ullah
2017

Situated in Banani and originally conceived as a mixed-use development with a commercial tower atop a shopping arcade, this building was completely redesigned for use as a five-star hotel. The architectural expression is based on omni-directionality. A vertical mass is plugged into a base, resulting in an L-shaped volume that imparts a sense of stability and functionality.

F.M. Faruque Abdullah Shawon, H.M. Fozla Rabby Apurbo (all pictures of this project)

Urban Forest

Road 12, Banani
Selim Altaf Biplob,
Tamanna Sayeed,
Khalid Bin Kabir,
Inquest Design Studio
2018

115 D

Populated with both flora and fauna from the local environment, Urban Forest is a precious breathing space in Banani, the city's busiest commercial area. This commercial building has ten floors and a built area of 2730 square metres. The challenge was how to design the principal, west, façade where the low angle of the sun generates heat. Instead of screening the west side completely, as is conventional practice, the design by Inquest Design Studio blends opaque, translucent, and transparent materials on the west and south façades. All the large openings are louvred with slats of wood. The louvres run vertically to decrease heat absorption and reduce consumption of energy needed for cooling. Floating bridges from the sixth floor upwards act as a shield against heat gain and cast comfortable shadows. The introverted design involves a semi-internal courtyard with pools of water and vegetation. The influence of the garden is so strong that it can be felt by users in every corner of the building; the horticultural vegetation continues at different levels on the various floors, ensuring a natural flow of air, helping to drive heat through the open-air courtyard instead of trapping it inside. It also attracts birds and bees – a very rare scenario in the middle of this chaotic concrete jungle. The solid parts of the façade are finished with unfired flexi-clay cladding (a modified clay material mixed with sand). Recyclable, non-toxic, and fireproof materials of this kind are an effective solution for an environment-friendly building like this.

4

Philipp Meuser

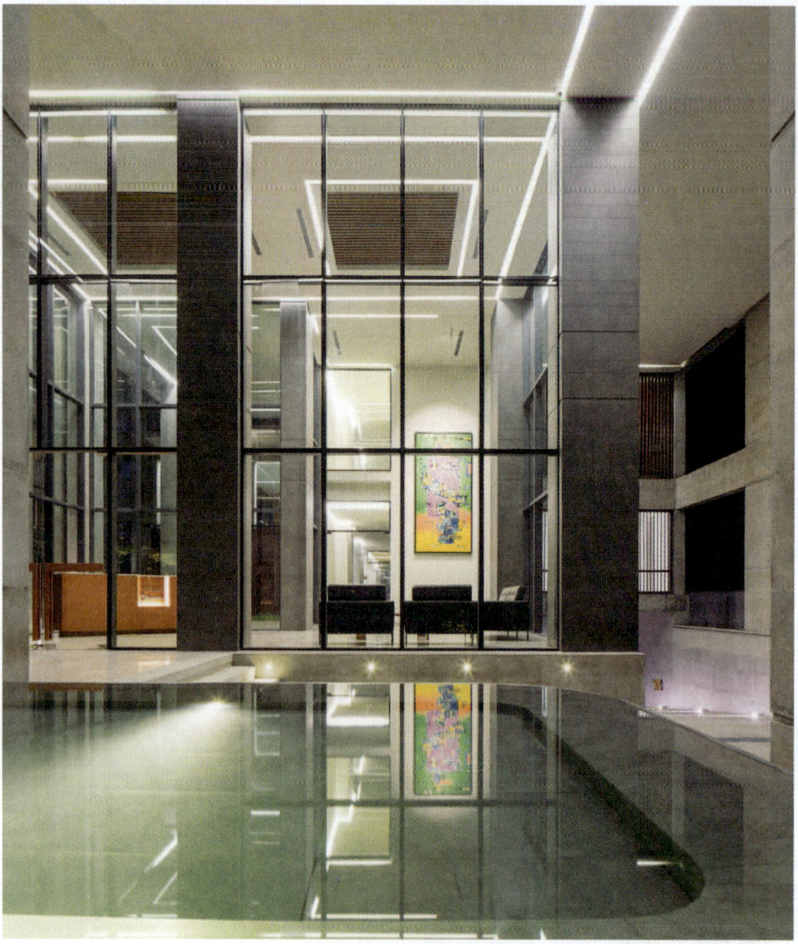

The Altair

116 D

House 20, Block CWN(A),
Road 47, Gulshan R/A
Volumezero Ltd.
Mohammad Foyez Ullah
2019

This 13-storey luxury residential building combines climatically responsive architecture and bold design. The L-shaped plan derives from the shape of the site, maximising the area of building exterior in the two blocks positioned on two sides of the lawn at the foot of the building. The maximised exterior surface facilitates the interplay of natural light and ventilation created by walls (planes) which vary in permeability from solid to open. The fragmentation of the walls facing the lawn on the east side is an unparalleled design feature. Together with the box balconies on the north side, this gives the building a strong identity.

![building photo]

South Breeze Square

52 Gulshan Avenue
Nahas Ahmed Khalil,
Farzad Ehsan,
Rehman Taki Ferdous
2019

117 D

This commercial building is a concerted attempt to solve energy efficiency and climate problems. There were two main concerns: to prevent heat gain from the west and ensure natural light in the workspaces while minimising glare. Expensive glazing and shading devices were avoided. Innovatively, the architect opened up a view to the north-west by designing a staggered west façade with random twisted bands which 'more or less' serve as a solid surface. This interpretation of brise-soleils exploits the plasticity of concrete while creating sufficient openings and preventing the sun from penetrating the building. The west part of the site was landscaped and a fountain was erected in order to harmonise the entrance into the built mass. The setback is shaded by an extended block containing full glazing that guarantees daylight in the interior. Cantilevering verandas with planter boxes provide additional shade and breathing spaces for office employees. To counter glare, the lower middle section of each window has been installed in such a way that it can be screened. Its inner extension acts as a light tray to bounce light off the ceilings. The semi-basement is a partially sunken space whose landscape serves as a private open-air garden. The duplex offices occupying the lower floors up to the third floor have a direct connection with the ground floor in order to reduce the traffic load on elevators serving the remaining 12 floors of offices. The architect removed the toilet stacks from their traditional position in the service core and placed them in the corners of the office space to reduce circulation. The small lobby is used as a garden-cum-dining space for lunch in the southeast part of the building.

Kafil Manor

House 20, Block CWN(A),
Road 47, Gulshan R/A
Volumezero Ltd.
Mohammad Foyez Ullah
2018

118 D

Standing on a corner plot at the heart of Gulshan, Simpletree Kafil Manor is a marriage of architectural complexity and technological ingenuity. A play of projecting planes forms an exterior layer which creates a bold architectural appearance while also providing ample shading for the interior spaces. The architectural design is rooted in the semantics of contemporary design ideology, while simultaneously challenging the standard approach to apartment design. With parking spaces for more than 60 vehicles, the basements have sufficient space for both drivers and staff working in the apartment complex. Three state-of the art elevators serve the residential storeys. These elevators can be customised to open inside the private lobbies of each residential unit. This 15-storey building contains two spacious apartments on each floor, arranged around a luscious greenscape with a dynamic play of outdoor spaces. The living spaces and bedrooms invite gentle breezes.

The circle of Gulshan 2 at night (2022)

4

House 10

House 10, Block CEN(D),
Road 101, Gulshan Model Town
Volumezero Ltd.
Mohammad Foyez Ullah
2020

Located in a prime location in Gulshan, this 10-storey residential building is a response to both the client's needs and conditions imposed by the site and the climate. Sandwiched between three low-rise houses, this much taller structure has a base of four generic apartments supporting an exclusive simplex and two likewise unique duplexes. The simplex and duplexes incorporate luscious green spaces in the form of terraces and courtyards overlooking the landscaped garden at ground level.

F.M. Faruque Abdullah Shawon, H.M. Fozla Rabby Aprurbo (all pictures of this project)

Claudio Gustavo Manzoni

4

Sahjalal Islami Bank
Plot 04, Block CWN(C),
Gulshan Avenue
Volumezero Ltd.
Mohammad Foyez Ullah
2016

121 D

The brief for the corporate headquarters of Shahjalal Islami Bank Ltd. called for a sophisticated use of architectural grammar to match the sophisticated image of this successful corporate entity, one of the oldest financial establishments in Bangladesh. The design incorporates sustainable features. Expressive of sobriety and discipline, its clean lines and bold forms stand out on the city's skyline. The bank building stands on one of the most influential avenues in Dhaka. The main façade, consisting of layers of glass, faces east towards the avenue. Incorporated in the first layer of glass are horizontal bands of ceramic fritting for enhanced thermal resistance. The purpose of the second layer, which consists of glass fins with low-emissivity thermal properties, is to provide shade. The fins run the full height of the façade. Aluminium louvres serve as horizontal shading devices on the south side, reinforcing this structure's credentials as a climate-responsive design. The building's core is on the west side – the optimal position for maximising usable space on each floor, while also acting as a buffer protecting against heat coming from the west.

F.M. Faruque Abdullah Shawon, H.M. Fozla Rabby Apurbo

Noufel Sharif Sojol (all pictures)

4

Shanta Skymark

18 Gulshan Avenue
Ehsan Khan
2020

122 D

Standing on a 1779.28-square-metre site, this high-rise accommodates office and commercial functions. The façade is double-glazed with low-E glass, which allows natural light to penetrate the interior and also minimises heat gain. This is the first building in Bangladesh to be fully wrapped with curtain walls. This sort of façade is durable, energy-efficient, heat-resistant, and water- and dust-proof. Elegant metal fins cast shadows and subdue the shine of the glass. The matte texture of the materials enhances the building's aesthetic appearance. The building automation system (BAS), UL-certified fire doors, HVAC system with water-cooled chiller, LED lighting, four levels of basement parking, and automated mechanical ventilation system are all cutting-edge for Bangladesh. Structural columns have been kept to a minimum so as to maximise open space. This benefit of a free plan makes the building flexible and adaptable to different functions to suit changing individual needs. The layout includes nooks and breathing spaces for social recreation. The 11.58-metre-high reception area is clad in natural stone. The public spaces have furniture of leather, wooden details, and walls of exposed concrete. The site contains diverse landscaping; the open connections between the pedestrian pavement, the gateless entrance, and the ground floor make for a sophisticated urban social space – not only for users of the building itself, but also for the ever-changing cityscape.

F.M. Faruque Abdullah Shawon, H.M. Fozla Rabby Apurbo (all pictures)

Simpletree Anarkali
89 Gulshan Avenue,
Gulshan
Volumezero Ltd.
Mohammad Foyez Ullah
2015

123 D

Simpletree Thikana
House 2/A, 2/B Block S.E(D),
Road 138, Gulshan
Volumezero Ltd.
Mohammad Foyez Ullah
2017

124 D

Anarkali was the first commercial building in Bangladesh to be granted gold LEED certification in recognition of its ability to conserve water and electricity. The intelligent use of double low-E, ceramic fritted glazing panels on its west façade ensures the requisite solar heat gain coefficient value. At the same time, however, this building makes a strong aesthetic impression. The delicate concrete frame and even more delicate glazing conjure up a sense of clarity and lightness. According to the architect, the design 'reflects the evolution of Dhaka's socio-economic values: within the chaotic randomness lies a regulating grammar, a repetition of order that breathes life into its expression.'

Thikana is a residential complex consisting of two blocks. Thikan 2A has two apartments per floor; Thikana 2B, just one. The two blocks share the same compound and service core. They are aligned with the south-west boundary of the site, leaving space for a landscaped forecourt on the north side with access from the street. The units have an asymmetrical layout in response to both the climate and the site. The architectural expression is defined by planes of concrete that shift as they move upwards. The inner layer of brick has intricate details that reflect the natural light. The multiple layers encourage an interplay of light and shade.

Philipp Meuser

Korail slum, rehabilitation

Bow Bazar, Korail, Banani
J A Architects Ltd, BRAC
2016

125 **D**

The aesthetics of informality should be taken into account when judging Dhaka's context. Korail and Saattala are both slum districts in Dhaka. More than 40 per cent of the city's inhabitants are slum dwellers and, as such, face the daily threat of fire. Platform of Hope was a project initiated by the architect Hasibul Kabir in Korail, Dhaka's largest slum in 2008. Construction ended in 2011. Korail provides a home to 120,000 deprived and impoverished people on 90 acres of land. Kabir and his team gave the slum a new dimension by creating a public gathering space, a playground for children, and a gardening area using cheap materials such as bamboo, bolts, and nails. On the shore of Gulshan Lake, Ashar Mancha (Platform of Hope) was a platform measuring 5.5 x 11 metres. A bamboo bridge connected it with a small but luxuriant communal green. The platform has a small library. Abir successfully educated the inhabitants and cultivated in them an awareness of pollution, sanitation,

Students at architecture department, BRAC

Aditya Kabir

proper ventilation, and natural illumination, transforming their mindset and allowing them to believe that their slum could be a better place. Backed by BRAC, the largest NGO in the world, the project had a substantial impact on the overall cityscape, thanks to its simple motto, 'pleasure in living with less'. The project was showcased at Cooper Hewitt National Design Museum in New York and received much international attention. Unfortunately, the 'platform of hope' was demolished in 2012. J A Architects Ltd. and BRAC carried out community-based participatory restoration in the slums of Korail and Saattola in Dhaka's Gulshan area in 2016, as part of BRAC's Urban Development Programme. This involved site planning to ensure proper ventilation and sunlight. The following planning principles were followed: cluster development with open-air spaces, community mapping, and research into existing patterns of use. The team then drew up a site layout showing the pattern of ownership. Continuous and wide-ranging community consultations were carried out; it was unanimously agreed that the roads in the neighbourhood should be widened.

Students at architecture department, BRAC

Smithsonian Cooper-Hewitt/Khondaker Hasibul Kabir

4

Philipp Meuser

Aerial view of Korail (2023)

BRAC Centre

75 Mohakhali,
Gulshan Badda Link Road
Mazherul Qader,
Shamsul Haque,
Asad Uz Zaman
1996

126 D

This high-rise building was designed for BRAC, the largest NGO in the world. The brainchild of a legendary personality, the late Sir Fazle Hasan Abed, BRAC has been working to improve the lives of deprived people for over 50 years. The building is roughly divided into two parts. The lower part up to the fifth floor contains blocks of different sizes and shapes which have been carefully grouped to achieve intimacy of scale. This grouping has resulted in a sequence of spaces in layers leading off the entrance. Since the site is irregular in shape, the podium is important for restoring harmony; it serves as a base for a robust 21-storey square tower. This simple barbican is elegant and sufficiently eye-catching to be considered a landmark. The building's total height is 80.59 metres, and its total built area is 10,570 square metres. The central lift core, situated in the west part of the building, constitutes 25% of its total area. The building's simple façade combines horizontal concrete bands with strips of glazing. There is a waffle canopy over the entrance on the north side.

Philipp Meuser

Teach For Bangladesh office building

House 210/A-2 Bir Uttam
Mir Shawkat Road
Studio Dhaka Architects
2017

127 D

Situated in Dhaka's most densely commercialised district on a site with an area of only 1008 square metres, this building contrasts with the surrounding urban fabric in both function and characteristics. Teach for Bangladesh's office is a down-to-earth, unassuming structure woven from the available natural resources: trees, plants, water, breezes, rain, and most importantly, sun (the shade cast by the sun expresses the changing time of day). This is architecture that employs cost-saving, eco-friendly choices of materials and construction techniques: local gas-burnt brick, custom-made mild-steel window frames, corrugated CI and plastic sheets, cement-finish floor, etc. The circulation flows straight across the site to keep movement to a minimum. The corridors merge with the landscape, and all the corridors are semi open-space with a herringbone treatment of the brick floor. There is a series of seven pods, ordered in an axial pattern. Between the pods are pocket-like open spaces where communal functions create stories, just as happens with courtyards in vernacular architecture. These small courtyards are food courts, discussion and workshop areas, play arenas, and places for exercise. For events, the grassy steps of one of these courtyards can become an amphitheatre with capacity for 100 persons. This courtyard can be covered with overhead tensile structures during the monsoon season. Polycarbonate sheeting is used to let daylight penetrate the translucent shelters. Under the canopies there is seating. The trusses made of MS rods are light in weight. The garden has lavish vegetation: mango, fig, and neem trees and lilies in the pond. All the trees that stood on the site were preserved by the architects and incorporated in the design.

Asif Salman (all pictures of this project)

Reza Noor Muin

Rangs Babylonia Vaban

128 D

Plot 246, Tejgaon Link Road,
Bir Uttam Mir Shakhawat Road
Mohakhali
M.K. Palash, Vistaara Architects
2018

G M Shifatur Rahman

Another extraordinary creation by the
architect M.K. Palash, who has here
taken lifeless materials and turned them
into a vivid sculpture that redefines the
commercial architecture of the Gulshan
area. The dynamic façade seems a snap-
shot of a juggler at work: concrete-and-
glass boxes thrown into the air have fro-
zen at different distances from the street
in front and the ground below. Some of
the boxes at the top are concrete outlines
containing cuboid quantities of sky. This
building has 15 floors: three basement
floors of parking and 12 floors containing the offices of Rangs Group.

4

Nina Kabbo

227/A, Gulshan
Tejgoan Link Road
Enamul Karim Nirjhor,
Systems Architects.
2011

Nina Kabbo is an office building which uniquely marries poetry and business. The building's façades are patterned with vertical lines of text engraved in different font sizes on its concrete surfaces. The texts are quotations from 12 leading Bengali poets (including Rabindranath Tagore, Kazi Nazrul Islam, Michael Madhusudan Dutt, Sukanta Bhattacharya, Jasimuddin, Jibanananda Das, Sufia Kamal, Shamsur Rahman, Ahsan Habib, and Nirmalendu Goon). The poetry flows indoors, where each of the 12 main floors has no number but is named after a poet and features a portrait of the latter and one of his poems. The subjects of the poems include humanism, patriotism, independence, and morality. This building occupies a site of 2007 square metres and has a total built area of 22,900 square metres. There are 13 floors and a mezzanine level with an area of 760 square metres. Five split levels of car parking accommodate 106 vehicles. The building's central core is a full-height atrium connecting generous circulation spaces with the light of the sky above; this ensures maximum penetration of daylight into the building's interior to save energy during the day. The welcoming entrance has waterwalls, a pool, and abundant vegetation. A small wall on the pavement outside is somewhere where both passers-by and those working in the building like to sit. At night Nina Kabbo is a fascinating pattern of light when seen from outside. This building won the Berger Award for Excellence in Architecture in 2014.

Reza Noor Muin

Reza Noor Muin

4

Akij House

House 198, Gulshan Link Road,
Tejgaon I/A
Volumezero Ltd.
Mohammad Foyez Ullah
2016

The aim was to create a unique architectural entity that would make a substantial contribution to the city's skyline. Cutting-edge solutions and efficient building technologies here go hand in hand with a chic interior which is predominantly neutral in its textures and colours. Akij House contains workspaces with an open plan layout that allows them to flow into and interweave with one another.

F.M. Faruque Abdullah Shawon, H.M. Fozla Rabby Apurto (all pictures)

Tower 117

House 117/A, Tejgaon I/A
Volumezero Ltd.
Mohammad Foyez Ullah
2017

The corporate headquarters of Knit Asia was conceived as an iconic emblem for the commercial and industrial district of Tejgaon. This 18-storey commercial tower is defined by its façade, a smooth sheet of delicately reticulated glazing which at the bottom crumples – or rather folds neatly like a masterful piece of origami work – to frame a tall, canopied entrance. This design reflects state of art construction material and technology that consolidates the presence of elite clientele.

Sarak Bhaban,
RHD Headquarters
Love Road/Hatirjheel Link Road,
Tejgaon
Masum Iqbal
2020

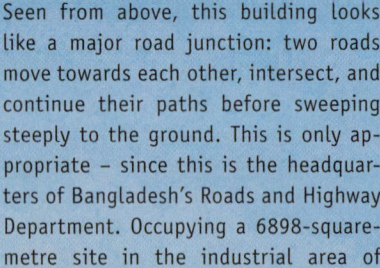

132 **D**

Seen from above, this building looks like a major road junction: two roads move towards each other, intersect, and continue their paths before sweeping steeply to the ground. This is only appropriate – since this is the headquarters of Bangladesh's Roads and Highway Department. Occupying a 6898-square-metre site in the industrial area of Tejgaon, the 12-storey RHD building has a floor area of more than 180,000 square metres. It contains multi-storey offices, a mosque, a library, an archive, a day-care centre, an audiovisual hall, cafés, community networking spaces, a fire-fighting floor, a staff lounge, several large rooms for seminars, and an 800-seat auditorium. The building's car park accommodates 200 cars. The podium-like base includes a public plaza. A rectangular punch-out makes it possible to see through part of the lower floors. The landscaping, which leaves a large empty space in front of the building, is admirable. The building's structural system is RCC and steel frame. Special glass imported from China forms horizontal blue strips with narrow concrete edges. The building's roof combines a garden with a field of photovoltaic cells. The garden is used for rainwater harvesting; the solar cells generate power for the building.

Skyscraper City

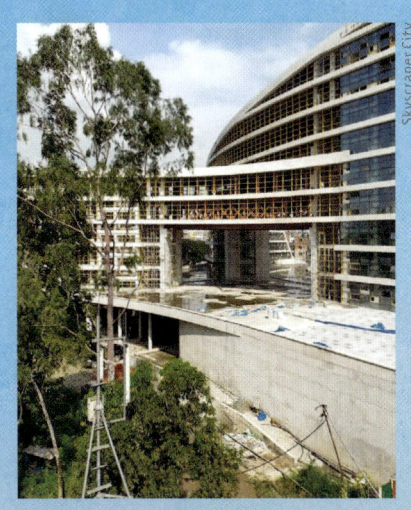

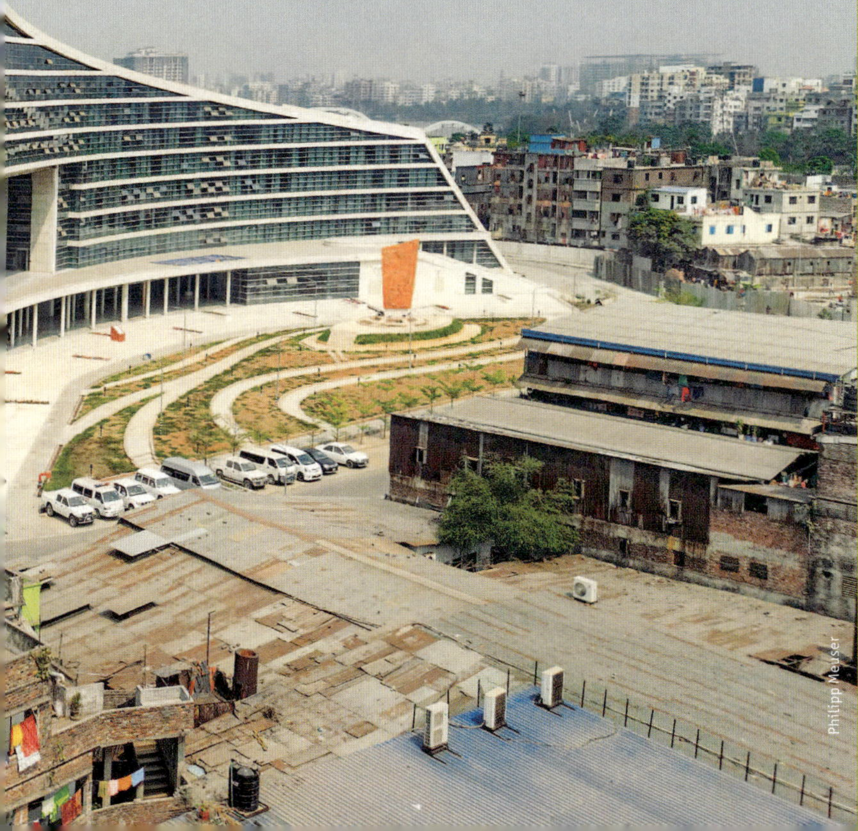

Philipp Meuser

Hatirjheel: integrated renewal for water retention

Hatirjheel
Vitti Sthapati Brindo Ltd.
2015

133 D

In the nineteenth century the landlord of Bhawal used to keep his tamed elephants at Pilkhana (the name means 'elephant shed'). The beasts used to come here from Pilkhana to bathe – which is where the name Hatirjheel ('lake of the elephants') comes from. The client for this water-retention project was Bangladesh's Local Government Engineering Department (LGED). Following the adoption of the Waterland Protection Act in 2000, in 2007 the LGED launched initiatives to reclaim Dhaka's wetlands as bodies of water that are open to the sky. Today this is one of the most popular places for citizens of Dhaka to spend their free time – an urban oasis which is the principal symbol of water retention in the heart of the capital. In the dry season Hatirjheel Lake holds roughly 3.06 billion litres of water; in the monsoon season this swells to nearly 4.81 billion litres. Improvements have also been made to public transportation in adjacent areas. This new connectivity makes it possible to travel from west to east Dhaka in the shortest possible time, a blessing for dwellers who previously had to use the city's heavily congested streets. This project has picked up three international design awards and has ensured Dhaka's water-retention capability, bringing hope for the city's other dwindling bodies of water. Its example has ignited ecological preservation measures in other cities throughout the country.

Ishtiaque Ahmed (all pictures of this project)

4

Sarak Bhaban with Hatirjheel in the background (2023)

4

Sazzadur Rasheed

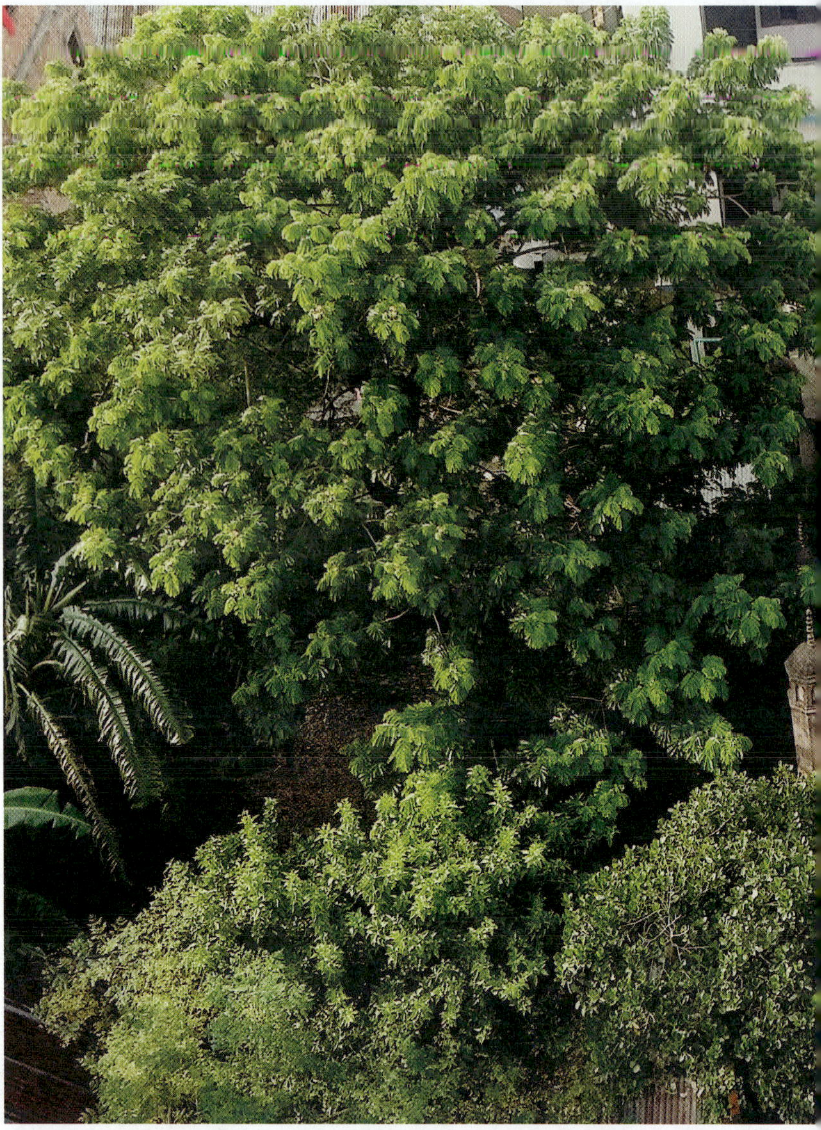

Nahid Sultan

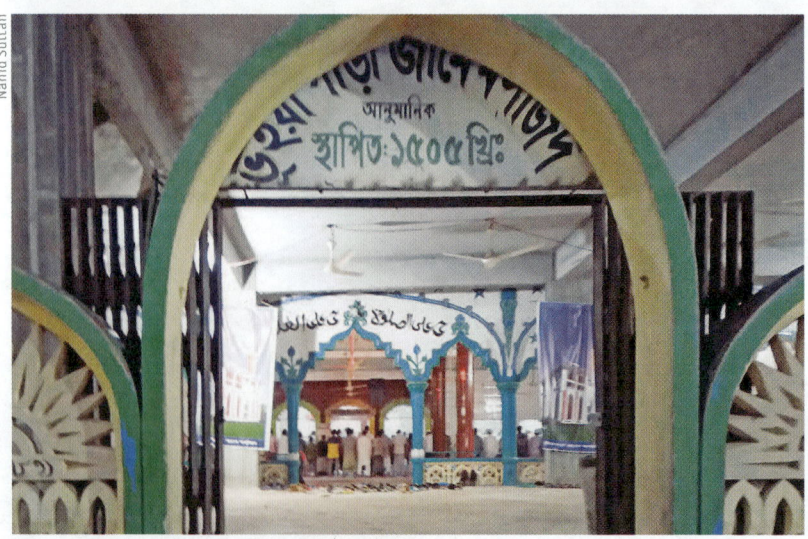

5

Bhuiyanpara Mosque
Beraid, Badda
1505

134 A

This piece of the urban fabric was known as Dhaka's 'mosque village' since there were ten ancient mosques here before the Mughal era. Bhuiyanpara Mosque was listed as heritage in 2002. It is a single-dome mosque with a total area of 371.61 square metres and a square plan. Its height, excluding the height of the dome, is 5.35 metres. Today only the western side is preserved as heritage. This historical monument is being squeezed by the city on all sides.

Sazzadur Rasheed

Zinda Park

Purbachol, Rupganj,
Narayanganj
Sayedul Hasan Rana
2012

Occupying 607,028 square metres of land, this community eco-resort with a staff of 4000 is 37 kilometres from central Dhaka. It has five enormous water reservoirs crossed by traditional bamboo bridges and with huddles of paddle boats lining their shores. Approximately 10,000 trees belonging to 250 different species of flora are to be found here. The park complex includes a library, a mosque, a restaurant, a school, a memorial to the Liberation War, a community clinic, and a number of mud-and-straw bungalows and rental cottages in which tourists can stay overnight. This was, in fact, an ordinary village in the 1980s, when four young friends from the neighbourhood came up with the idea of creating an ideal village that would marry a rural setting with urban facilities while also generating revenue and providing employment through community cooperatives. The most striking element in this park is the cylindrical five-storey library. Built from eco-friendly, sustainable materials which merge with the surrounding landscape, its design encourages light and air to fill its interior. This building has a floor area of 1335.46 square metres and a façade defined by the grey texture of fired-clay hollow bricks. To preserve local agriculture, the bricks were not made from topsoil; and, due to environmental concerns, they were not fired in a kiln. Using this distinctive ecofriendly material not only reduced construction costs by 26% but also speeded up construction since the bricks are so easy to make. A further advantage is that the bricks' hollow insides enable temperature control. The building's floors and railings are of wood. In the middle a circular cut-out provides a visual connection and sufficient daylight for reading. The pergola on top of the building makes it visible from all corners of the park. The ten classrooms in the school building enjoy sufficient daylight not to need additional lighting. The mosque, which has capacity for 400 devotees, is inspired by the sultanate era; the use of zinc *surkhi* (mortar) gives it a unique monumental character; it is also notable for the rare terracotta collected from different parts of Bangladesh and installed in its interior.

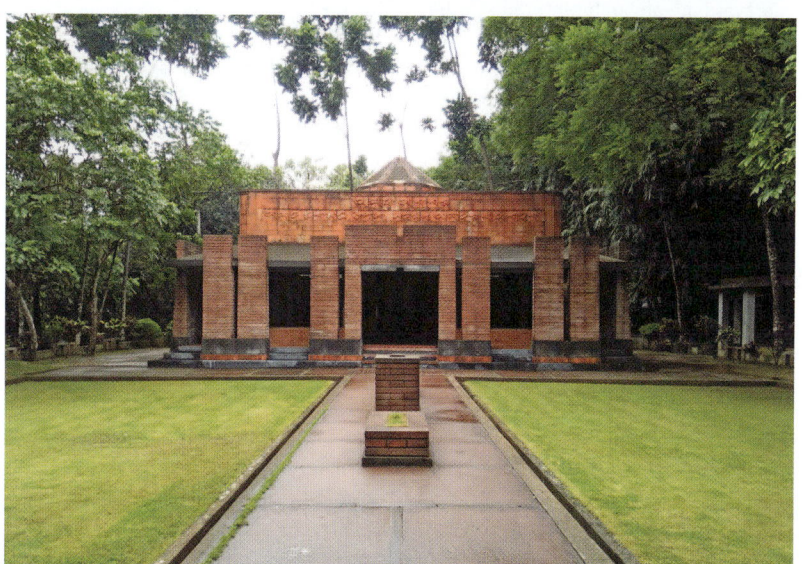

Volumezero Ltd.

F.M. Farruque Abdullah Shawon, F. M. Fozla Rabby Apurbo

Rupayan City Uttara

136 A

Road No 14, Sonargaon Janapath
Volumezero Ltd.
Mohammad Foyez Ullah
2021

This housing estate is situated at a point where the city's boundary is being extended towards surrounding satellite cities. Rupayan City Uttara is an attempt to create sustainable housing in harmony with nature. This premium gated community is in virgin hinterland, a location which made it necessary to create enclaves of vegetation for recreation and visual respite. The modular residential units are arranged around a green courtyard in an architectural strategy which echoes traditional practice in the tropics. The project's two phases are linked by two major axes: an experiential axis in the form of a vista connecting the green enclave, built forms, the road, and the amenities; and a vehicular axis which distributes and manages the transport network serving the housing. The project occupies a 14.1-acre site. There are six types of residential unit here in all; ranging from 150 to 220 square metres, they are aimed at people with different needs. Rupayan City Uttara is an autonomous project in which all facilities required by inhabitants are to be found within a short distance of their homes. Amenities such as mosques, schools, and local shops are all located on the periphery of the neighbourhood, allowing them to be used not only by residents of the estate but also by those living round about.

Sharif Uddin Ahammed (all pictures of this project)

Little Wonder School 137 A
Sector 4, Uttara
Vistaara & Icon Architects (VIA)
Sharif Uddin Ahammed,
Sthapotik
2015

This project involved local building materials and community participation, was inexpensive to build, and was completed in a short time – only two months. Existing vegetation and structures were left in place. A nine-storey building on the north side of the site was also left intact and used as a backdrop and source of diffused light. The school's pitched roof enables light reflected from the adjacent building to penetrate the classrooms. Standing on a 545.53-square-metre site, this early-learning school is for children from two to eight years old. The site is zoned to take account of climate, surrounding structures, existing trees, and an open-air expanse. The architect created a pavilion-like space in which, instead of permanent partition walls, there are removable folding doors. These establish a flexible relation with the outdoor space and ensure an uninterrupted natural flow of wind through the building. They also allow a larger floor area and more spacious classrooms. Entrance to the building is from the southwest, while the classrooms, teachers' room, library, therapy room, and services are arranged in the north, west, and east corners in an L formation. The semi-outdoor corridors covered with a sloping roof can be easily transformed into an extended classroom for larger numbers of students. The choice of materials focuses on low energy emissions and thermal balancing: walls and floors are of exposed brick; doors have wooden panels; windows are of glass and metal; ceilings are supported by detailed bamboo framing and lined with coloured NCF GI sheeting. Since the school is for children with special needs, its spaces have been designed to enhance communication, social skills, and sensorial development.

5

F.M. Faruque Abdullah Shawon, H.M. Fozla Fabby Apurbo (all pictures)

Arham Tower

Sector 7, Road No. 5, Uttara
Volumezero Ltd.
Mohammad Foyez Ullah
2016

138 A

Arham Tower in Uttara achieves a simple portrayal of corporate identity through a bold interlocking of planes. The L-shaped tower sits on a rectangular podium overlooking the Dhaka-Mymensing Road. It faces south-east to take advantage of the natural light. Its façade is double-glazed using glass with a low-E coating to minimise heat gain. The fritted panels create an interesting work of art against the backdrop of the Dhaka cityscape. The carefully designed landscape in the forecourt is complemented by terraces and a rooftop garden providing visual and physical refreshment for users of the tower's office spaces.

MIKA Cornerstone

139 A

16/17 Road 12, Sector 6, Uttara
Volumezero Ltd.
Mohammad Foyez Ullah
2016

5

The MIKA Cornerstone building rises from a corner plot in Sector 6, Uttara with the Dhaka-Mymensingh Highway to its west and a secondary road to its north. This is an important location on the way in and out of the city, so the client naturally wanted a bold architectural statement. The design concept is based on the divergence of the two rectangular surfaces that constitute the building's west façade. The concrete frame remains aligned with the directions of the compass, while the plane of glazing defining the volume of interior space diverges from the frame, receding inside the building at an angle and reemerging on the south façade. The divergence of the two surfaces creates a recess that shades the west façade from heat and glare, while a screen of aluminium louvres supported by a steel frame structure provides additional shade. The building's core has been placed so as to ensure optimal conditions in the workspaces.

Scholastica School Uttara

Plot 2, Road 8 And 9, Uttara
7 II Ahmed,
JAA Architects
2000

140 A

Given the smallness of the site (4046.86 square metres), the architect had no choice but to design a multi-storey building to accommodate students from grade five to advanced level at a reputable English middle school in Dhaka. The building's inviting double-height entrance, elevated ground floor, circulation corridors focused on outside courtyards, staircases of different sizes, and interconnection between different levels make for a varied and intricate composition. To break up the solidity of the side corridors overlooking the central courtyard, the architect deployed green plants and exposed brickwork. Large, perforated overhead parasols filter the rays of the sun and cast poetic shadows. The façades are a coherent composition of reflective glass, exposed brick, and plastered surface. In plan, this is an asymmetrical building. The blocks of classrooms have deliberately been arranged in an arbitrary way to encourage playfulness among the students.

Reza Noor Muin (all pictures of this project)

5

The Artisan Hotel and Aarong Commercial Centre

7, Jashimuddin Avenue
Plot 7, Sector 3, Uttara
Patrick d' Rozario,
Synthesis Architects
2010

141 A

The brief was to create an international image for Aarong group's flagship shop. Aarong started in 1978 as a way of empowering rural artisans and is now a major fashion and lifestyle brand. The nine-storey building has a total built area of 5800 square metres on a 765-square-metre site. There is a three-level basement car park. Above ground, the building is divided into two parts: the bottom six floors contain Aarong outlets; the top three floors have accommodation for expatriates. The brand shops are interlinked to form a series of continuous spaces. Each individual shop reflects its origins in rural crafts: there are wooden railings and showcases. On the top three floors are 21 rooms. These are only accessible from the road at the back of the building and have a separate lobby and restaurant on the ground floor. The roof has a canopy of green vegetation, and there is an open-air terrace for outdoor activities of various kinds. In terms of architecture, this is a bold design. Two sides of the building are entirely closed to their surroundings. A dynamic mass at fifth floor level seems to be supported by a single slender circular column. Rough-textured concrete contrasts with smooth reflective glass. The square perforations on the principal façade recall *gobakshas* – small windows in vernacular architecture. This project won the 22nd JK Cement Architect of the Year Award in 2019.

Sandro de Carlo Barsa

Bait Ur Rouf Mosque

Fayedabad
Marina Tabassum/MTA
2012

142 A

City Syntax

Bait Ur Rouf Mosque was MTA's first commission. It is situated in the northeastern outskirts of Dhaka and was conceived as a place of tranquillity and a neighbourhood meeting place for an otherwise densely populated area of Dhaka. The land once belonged to Marina Tabassum's grandmother, who gave it to the community after the deaths of her two daughters. Her grandmother commissioned Marina to design a mosque on the site. The project was funded by family members, friends, the local community, and other donors, all of whom were involved in the design process. It was important that MTA should keep the architecture simple and clear; this led to the abandonment of traditional mosque iconography such as the dome, *mihrab* (prayer niche), and *minbar* (pulpit). Instead, the emphasis is on calibrated structures of space and light that create a spiritual experience. In addition, brick was used because its texture has had a lasting impact on mosque architecture in the Ganges Delta. The result is a perfect square with a cylindrical volume in the centre – the prayer hall. The different geometrical shapes create open courtyards on all four sides; these keep the building well ventilated during the summer months. The other functions are arranged around this spatial structure. To compensate for the irregularly shaped terrain, the mosque stands on a plinth, which has numerous functions: it protects against flooding and is somewhere where people can sit and talk while waiting to pray, but most importantly, it separates this religious place from the hustle and bustle of the street. The project received the Aga Khan Award in 2016 for pushing the boundaries of a religious place of worship and encouraging communal spirit.

Dhaka's Periphery and Other Places

5

5

Dholeshwar Hanafiya Mosque 143 A

Bashundhara River View Road,
Keraniqanj, 1868
Abdullah Abu Sayed,
Kashef Mahboob Chowdhury
2019

This is a perfect example of cohesion between historical and contemporary edifices. The family-owned old mosque has stood here for 150 years and four generations. It includes a family graveyard. This was carefully and sensitively restored in 2017–2018. The new mosque building has rows of steel columns whose branching tops give them a resemblance to tree trunks; they support a flat roof. The interior imitates the colour of the adjacent historical mosque. The open spaces and surrounding walkway have red-brick paving. There is a pool of water along two sides, to keep the air fresh and improve its circulation. The roof consists of slabs separated by narrow slits that allow daylight to enter the building in precise alignment with the marks indicating the rows for prayers. The dome is unusual for any mosque: an ovoid bulge rising from the otherwise flat roof. The choice of red for the façades was a reference to the Mughal architecture of the adjacent structure. Since Bengal lacks the red stone of Delhi, its builders traditionally mixed brick dust with calcium carbonate to create the appearance of a red-stone exterior; the same process was used here. The extensive use of tall panes of glass in the new mosque's envelope preserves the visual connection with the old mosque.

Jinjira Palace, ruins

Baroghortola,
Keraniganj
1697

144 C

Also known as 'Qasr I Jazira' (Island Palace) or simply 'Howli', Jingira Palace was built by the Mughal governor Ibrahim Khan as a recreational resort in the late seventeenth century. It is situated opposite Bara Katra and the south bank of the River Buriganga. Rumour has it that a wooden pool used once to connect these two buildings. Until 1703 the palace was used as a residence for Nawab Murshid Quli Khan when collecting revenues. During the rule of Nawab Alivardi Khan it was a residence for Naib Nazim of Dhaka. After the fall of Nawab Shirajuddaula, the female members of his royal family were kept in strict captivity here. The complex included a palace-like edifice, a rectangular, two-storey hammam (bathhouse), and a two-storey gateway with two flanking octagonal towers in the south of the site. The rooms are rectangular; there is a traditional vaulted roof resembling a *chauchala* (four-roofed Hindu temple modelled on the Bengali thatched hut). The walls are plastered with lime mortar. The surviving broad foundations for defensive walls along the moat that surrounds the site may indicate that this was a fortified palace. Today only seven rooms, a narrow stairway leading to the roof from outside, and the gateway housing rooms for the gatekeepers remain. But these too are in a poor state and may collapse at any time. The rest of the complex has been encroached upon and obliterated by illegal development.

5

Kazi Karar Naier

Kazi Karar Naier

Loom Shed for Amber Denim

Banglabazar, Rajendrapur,
Gazipur
Jubair Hasan,
Archeground Ltd.
2015

The RMG (ready made garment) sector is the backbone of Bangladesh's economy. This simple loom shed combines space for large loom machines with a high ceiling that ensures comfort in the workplace. Also accommodated here are a buyers' room, dining spaces for staff, and a prayer room. The entire building stands on an artificial waterway and is supported by upcycled gas pipes that function as steel columns. Innovative and simple bamboo screen walls and floating decks not only ensure natural light and proper ventilation in the interior workspaces but also offer cosy breathing spaces, to the relief of the employees, who spend long hours at monotonous work. Maximised use of daylight helps save energy and reduce costs; and the building's all-round permeability reduces expenditure on air conditioning. This project took top prize in the commercial category at the prestigious 2A Asia Architecture Awards in 2015 and was also shortlisted for the Aga Khan Award in 2019.

Sandro di Carlo Darsa (all pictures)

Khelaram Data Temple

146 E

Kolakopa, Bandura,
Nawabganj
1900

5

This temple was built 1.5 kilometres from Dhaka by Khelaram, a robber who in later life turned pious and became a *data* (benefactor) of poor people – which explains the temple's name. This two-storey brick *nabaratna* (nine-jewel) Hindu temple is very unusual in its marrying of Mughal and European architecture. Erected at the location of an important trade hub beside the River Ichamoti, its volume constitutes a 'cuboidal sanctum', which is rare in Bengal. The square plan and the proportions of the rooms, arranged in a grid pattern known as *vastupurushamandala*, relate to mythical cosmology. The ground floor has 15 chamber-like rooms; the second floor has nine chambers. The two floors are connected by two staircases, which are symmetrical to the central axis. The *garvagriha* (central hall or cella) is sllghtly raised above the plinth and is topped with a *shikhara* (conical tower). This central focal point is aligned with the daily path of the sun from east to west. On the top floor the tower is surrounded by dormitories for worshippers – again a rare phenomenon in the architecture of such temples. These eight separate rooms on the top floor are shaped like traditional Bengali huts in the *dauchala* and *chauchala* styles (the styles of huts with double-pitched and four-pitched roofs respectively). The open-air passages between the *shikhara* and the dormitories have a courtyard-like feel. Here devotees can perform rituals and offerings – again an innovation in Bengal's temple architecture. The temple also has a bathing compound for the use of those staying in the dormitories. A tunnel still runs to the riverbank; this was probably the route by which looted wealth was taken to the upper part of the *shikhara* for storage. The temple walls are 0.762 metres thick and consist of bricks bonded using a mortar that is a mixture of calcium carbonate and brick chips (*surkhi*) – a Mughal technique. The vaulted ceiling on the ground floor also derives from Mughal architecture. The flat roof recalls the architecture of the Gupta Empire from the fourth to fifth centuries. The beam-joist system of construction is a European technique. The combination of floral (Hindu) and geometrical (Islamic) ornamentation indicates a transitional point in Bengali temple architecture during the colonial era. The temple was listed as protected heritage in 1989 and was restored in 2015 under the supervision of the Department of Archaeology.

Syed Nazrul Islam Convention Centre

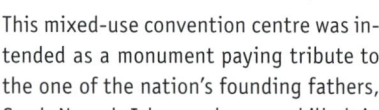

Borobazar, Mirpur Beribadh Rd.
Ruqun Uddin Bhuiya,
Radia Sultana,
Metropolitan Architects
2013

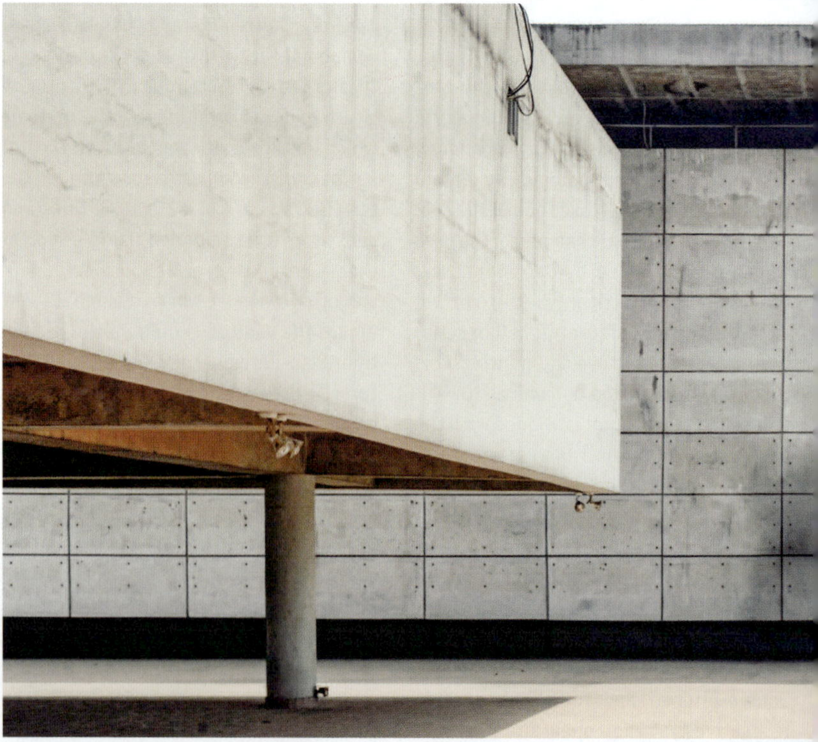

This mixed-use convention centre was intended as a monument paying tribute to the one of the nation's founding fathers, Syed Nazrul Islam, who was killed in Dhaka's Central Jail in 1975. The building stands on pillars on a plaza-like platform which leads under the building and out towards the river. The plaza is an open space where people come to take breath, meet one another, and enjoy the riverside view. The building itself accommodates reasonably priced public facilities such as a multipurpose hall, a library, a community health provider, and offices in a neighbourhood in which these amenities had previously been lacking. The hierarchies of its spaces are designed to resemble the day of the assassination of Syed Nazrul Islam in jail, an event which was a dramatic political turning point in Bangladeshi national history. Small rectilinear perforations on the building's surface allow daylight to penetrate in an uneven and distracted manner, forcing visitors to feel the cruelty of that dark night – but also light up the complex during the evenings, whenever an event is held in the hall. The building's raw-concrete envelope is an exterior that stands as a bulwark against the changes of time and simultaneously a capsule that preserves the ideals of patriotism inside. This project shows Syed Nazrul Islam's personality in its historical context.

5

Asif Salman

University of Liberal Arts

688 Beribadh Rd., Chadd Uddan
Kashef Mahboob Chowdhury
2020

148 **A**

5

When he created this outstanding building for the University of Liberal Arts Bangladesh, Kashef Chowdhury had already designed a number of climate-sensitive buildings in Bangladesh's deltaic landscape, including the award-winning Friendship Centre in Gaibandha (Aga Khan Award 2016) and the Friendship Hospital in Sathkhira (RIBA Prize 2021). The ULAB building stands out for its high porosity and abundant unprogrammed spaces. In a hot and humid climate where permeable construction is essential, spatial openness facilitates natural cross ventilation. The new building's layout is linear, simple, and practical, in keeping with the limited budget and the narrow site between a canal and a row of large trees. Stacking the extensive building programme vertically made it possible to preserve the tall, shade-giving trees on the site. Despite the building's compact volume, the sophisticated distribution of solids and voids creates rich spatial qualities. In addition to the spatial porosity of its layout, the building features innovative materials and construction technologies. The entire structure, including the ceilings, is made of locally produced ceramic bricks. Thick cavity walls reduce thermal conductivity, while the dimensions of the windows in the teaching wings are carefully adjusted to reduce solar heat gain. Circular skylights in the deep circulation zones provide additional illumination and allow hot air to escape upwards. The roof is covered with a thermal mass of earth and greenery, which has a positive effect on the internal climate. The plants hanging like green lampshades from the circular skylights and the screens of overflowing greenery shielding the stairways and semi-open gathering areas from heavy rain are an integral part of the building. Set against the vibrant red brick, the greenery creates a cheerful, stimulating atmosphere. The ULAB building embodies a balance between compactness and porosity. Its openness and permeability demonstrate that pragmatism and poetry can coexist in the creation of sustainable educational buildings. The design bears witness to a contemporary integration with Bengal's building history and brick-making traditions, which have been used to create structures that provide identity, durability, and permanence in a landscape where everything appears to float. This building offers a glimpse into the future.

Arcadia education project school

South Kanarchor, Alipur, Keraniganj
Saif Ul Haque
2016 (demolished)

The client for this school was Maleka Welfare Trust, which is owned by Razia Alam, who returned to Bangladesh after a life spent teaching in the UK to use her pension to help underprivileged children. She purchased a site in the countryside outside Dhaka near the River Dholeswari which is submerged to a depth of three metres for one third of the year. Her nephew, the architect Saiful Haq, came to her help with an innovative idea. By designing the building as a series of amphibious modules, he made the school capable of floating during the monsoon season and resting on the ground during the winter. The terrain was levelled using retaining walls made of sandbags filled with sand, soil, brick chips, and, on top, recycled tyres acting as cushions. Bamboo posts were inserted to a depth of two metres on average to act as anchoring points interconnecting the eight rectangular structures. Three of the structures were multipurpose classrooms with bow-arched bamboo roofs and post-free interior spaces. One was an office with lavatories and utilities; another was an open-air platform. All were linked by a

corridor with a pivoting thatched panel overhead and a ramp to connect it to the ground. The structures were kept afloat using 30-gallon steel drums installed inside bamboo frames. Three types of bamboos were chosen for their lightness and durability; these were treated with a liquid made from a boiled local fruit (gaab), a traditional method to protect against climate and rotting. Dominant textural elements in the school's interior were traditional fencing (*bera*) and mats (*pati*). Joints consisted of rope knots to avoid the use of corrodible steel. Simple hand tools were used in construction. This project served as a daycare centre, a shelter for orphans, and a vocational training centre with a nursery. The school's total built area was 486 square metres. This was a perfect example of sustainability, responsibility for humanity, creation of social value, and preservation of the river's ecosystem. The school won the Aga Khan Award in 2019 cycle but was destroyed by a flood in 2020.

Dewanbari Mosque

Dhaka-Savar Highway
Amin Bazar, Mirpur
1880

150 A

This *chini tikri* (broken china) mosque was built by Haji Janab Ali, a wholesale leather trader. The approach to it is a platform which serves as a space for ablutions. This is a three-domed mosque. Instead of having the standard square plan, it is rectangular with a 2.11-metre-wide antechamber. The high podium on which it stands leads to an open veranda giving access to the main prayer hall. The mosque itself is 7.42 metres long and 7.20 metres wide. There are three bays; the middle bay is square and topped with a semicircular dome, while the side halls are rectangular with half vaults springing from the north and south walls. The north and south walls have a single window in their centre. The three *mihrabs* (prayer niches) in the west wall are multi-cusped arches in rectangular frames and echo the three entrance arches in the east wall. The central *mihrab* is larger and semicircular; the others are shallow and rectangular in shape. On the outside of the building six slender octagonal turrets have blind kiosks extending beyond the roofline. The four larger turrets are at the corners of the mosque; the two smaller turrets flank the main entrance. The base of the central dome is decorated with blind merlons and projecting mouldings. The ante-chamber is divided into two equal bays by three lateral arches supported by brick pilasters on the west and east walls. Façades decorated with pieces of beautiful broken blue and green china make the mosque highly visible from a distance.

5

Syed Zakir Hossain (all pictures)

Adib Ehsan

Shahriar's Scrapbook

Raja Harish Chandra Dhibi

 151 A

Rajashan, Savar
7th century

This area started to grow as a business and administrative hub on the bank of the River Bangmshi from the seventh and eighth centuries forwards. An inscription on a burnt block found here, dated to approximately 829 AD, names a Buddhist king called 'Haris Chandra Pal'. Haris Chandra Pal migrated from Rarh in west Bengal. His new kingdom was called 'Kirat' and stretched over the Brahmaputra Plains to the Himalayas in the north. Its capital was Savar. From 1918 to 1921 this site was excavated by the famous archaeologist Nalinikanta Bhattashali, who was a curator at the Dhaka Museum. In recognition of the site's importance, the government of British India gave it protected heritage status. In 1988 scholars revealed that there had been a Buddhist monastery here, based on the discovery of numerous bronze sculptures from the Buddhist era, including of Lokeshwar-Vishnu, Bojrojani, Amitav, Bodhiswatta, Padmapani, Obolokiteswar bodhiswatta, Avaya mudra Buddha, and Praygyaparmita. The red, black, and grey pottery that has been unearthed here is decorated with distinctive patterns in black, including geometric designs in horizontal bands on the bodies and necks of the vessels. All these artefacts are today kept in the National Museum in Dhaka. The archaeological site is a rectangular mound with a scattering of three *moths* (towers). A square with three culturo-historical layers was later excavated nearby. Its purpose seems likely to have been similar to that of other Buddhist sites in north Bengal.

IFAD Autos Industrial Park

Dhaka-Aricha highway,
Dakshin Naogaon, Dhamrai
Nishat Afrose,
Saklayen Bulbul
2015

152 A

This industrial park has a total area of 3994.83 square metres, of which the built area is 668.90 square metres. The architects transformed a structure with a traditional simple folded roof (*dauchala*) into a series of interlinked dynamic volumes. Parts of the building are tilted in order to improve illumination and ventilation. Another feature of this design is that simple construction techniques have been used to build a structure which houses all the required industrial activities under one enormous roof canopy, with capacity to assemble up to 10,000 cabins for small and large trucks each year. The two ends of the building are designed to simplify the production line: one gate processes incoming vehicle parts; the other releases the final product. The functions of the different parts of the shed are in keeping with this circulation. The windows on the inclined sides of the building are special: fixed and openable parts alternate from top to bottom. This design allows fresh air into the building but keeps out the heat of direct daylight. The inclined roofs are highly effective on rainy days.

5

Jahangirnagar University

Asian Highway or
Dhaka Aricha Highway Road
Muzharul Islam
1970

153 A

Modelled on the famous Aligarh Muslim University, Jahangirnagar University was inaugurated on 12 January 1971 but failed to open properly due to the Liberation War. The master plan drawn up by the architect Muzharul Islam envisages an entirely residential public university – the only one of its kind in Bangladesh. The bold composition and geometrical layout with angular lines and slanted squares harmonises with the surrounding topography. This is a vast rural campus stretching over an area of 2.8 square kilometres. The natural landscape contain bodies of water with sprawling vegetation, as well as gentle ascents to plains. The architect took advantage of this to create orders of space with light, greenery, and air flow in between. Every element in this well-woven master plan enhances rather than disrupts the topographic continuity. The red-brick detailing on the building masses sets up a dialogue and makes room for the lush green foliage. Muzharul Islam placed the administrative

and teaching buildings at the centre of the campus. There are 16 student halls at the north end; the teachers' dormitory and staff residences are in the south. The internal courtyards are reminiscent of Bangladesh's vernacular architecture. The buildings have been slanted diagonally for two reasons: to create spatial enclosures within the volumes and to ensure the same degree of exposure to the sun, as well as proper natural ventilation. Unfortunately, a large part of the original master plan is still to be implemented. Jahangirnagar University is an example of an architect's alternative proposal for an urban planning and housing project. The communal amenities and streetscape reveal a collective spirit and civic order. The *shahid minar* (martyrs' tower) designed by the famous architect and poet Rabiul Hossain (1943–2019) is the tallest such tower in Bangladesh, at 21.64 metres high with a base that is 515.84 metres wide. It represents two historic events: the Liberation War of 1971 and the language movement of 1952. *Sangsaptak* is a famous sculpture in the front of the library and cafeteria. Every winter, birds migrating from Siberia take shelter in the lakes here, making this the perfect spot for birdwatchers. The butterfly-shaped Mir Mosharrof Hossain Hall and Jahanara Imam Hall are especially impressive when seen from a bird's-eye viewpoint. The complex also includes a medical centre, an auditorium, a gymnasium, a swimming pool, and an amphitheatre. These buildings are scattered over the university campus.

5

Syed Golam Rabbani

Sunshine Resort

154 E

Meghna Chat, Tetoila, next to N1
Framework Architects,
Faysal Kabir Himun,
Anup Kumar Basak
2016

A remodelling of vernacular and contemporary architecture, this building accommodates multiple activities under a central roof behind a brick perimeter wall – an approach which represents an extraordinary solution for a hot humid climate such as in Bangladesh. The challenge was to erect the building in only four months and yet create a homely environment. The building's plan resembles a slanted square fitted inside another square. This interlocking of geometrical forms gives four identical courtyards at the sides of the central square. Streams of sunlight create patterns on the seemingly handcrafted brick walls.

The interior spaces, including toilets and service areas, are lit by ordinary sunlight. All the accommodation units are grouped around a courtyard with which they have a deliberately blurred indoor-outdoor relation. The complex includes 54 rooms, two lounges, sun decks, a gym, a dining hall, a kitchen, a laundry, and a medical centre. The quiet backgrounds and brick *jali* (latticework) screens in the corridors serve to keep out aural and air pollution and to enhance the circulation of air. Torrents of rainwater spouting from the conduit in the central courtyard are a major sensory attraction in the monsoon season. Rainwater harvesting is carried out by means of a central reservoir, which can also be used as a source of water for fighting fires, if needed. Traditional fruit and flower trees have been planted on the site to convey to foreigners the richness of Bangladesh's nature as the seasons change.

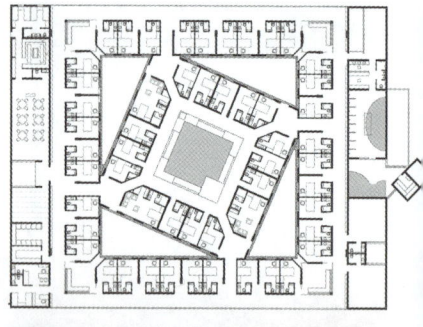

Sayed Ahmed (all pictures of this project)

Housing for Bangladesh Livestock Research Institute

155 A

Savar
Shamsul Wares and
Aparesh Das,
Shisrikkhu Sthapatis
1989

Known as BLRI, the Bangladesh livestock Research Institute was established as an autonomous research centre with six divisions. It comprises 65 scientists and 83 members of staff. The beautiful housing design was led by Shamsul Wares, the respected guru of all Bangladeshi architects. Located just two kilometres from the periphery of Dhaka, the site encompasses 2,023,500 square metres of flat land and is surrounded by a typical terrain with red soil mounds. The complex has only two-storey buildings, all of which have forms that are staggered to take advantage of the southern breeze, natural ventilation, and the diffuse light coming from the north. The buildings' slanted roofs harmonise perfectly with the scale of the surrounding landscape and echo the local traditional homesteads. This is considered a cost-effective project. Instead of plasterwork, use was made of red machine-made bricks, which make a vivid impression alongside the green vegetation. The architects' aim was to ensure comfort while creating well-proportioned spaces of simple design.

5

Mosque at the National Monument

Savar
Abdur Rashid
1984

156 A

This symbolic and religious structure is part of the National Martyrs' Monument complex. Its humble symmetry is an attempt to harmonise with the latter monument. The main prayer hall is square in plan with sides of 6.86 metres. Unusually for mosque architecture, the concave prayer niche is in a square shaft which is also part of the surrounding veranda. The width of the verandas on the four sides is 2.29 metres. There are four pillars on each side; the middle pillars are full pillars, while the two at the edges are embedded in L-shaped walls. The roofs of the verandas are lower than the adjacent prayer hall. Four hollow brick columns drain rainwater from the flat roof of the prayer hall. The façade is of red bricks, nearly 25 centimetres thick. There are cosy corners for meetings and preaching. The brick vaulting over the pillars depicts traditional Islamic arches with a semicircular brick borderline. Exposed lintels connect the spans of the arches. The recessing of the verandas and inner walls provides protection from drifting rain.

Four clerestory windows in the middle of the prayer hall ensure abundant natural light in the upper part of the building. Three niches on the north and south sides are interspersed with windows. There are three doors on the east side. The detached minaret is notable for its band of arches and small dome.

National Martyrs' Memorial

North West, 35 km,
Dhaka Aricha Highway Road
Syed Mainul Hossain
1982

In 1976 the government of Bangladesh decided to build a public monument to reflect the sacrifices of the martyrs in the Liberation War. A nationwide design competition was held in 1978. Of the 57 entries, the design by the architect Syed Mainul Hossain was unanimously chosen by the jury. Construction took place in three phases and was completed in 1982. The architect was awarded the highest state honour for civilians, the Ekushey Padak. The monument is surrounded by a holistic landscape. The 99,957.35-square-metre site includes an artificial lake and luxuriant greenery; the buildings have a floor area of 339,936 square metres. The monument is of concrete; the pavements are of red brick, turning the site into a geometric tapestry. In front of the monument is a rectilinear pool carrying its reflection; access to the monument is via a connecting bridge over the lake. Differences in pavement levels with reference to an axial point are intended to call to mind the sacrifice in bloodshed made in order to achieve a single goal, freedom. The complex also includes – carefully concealed from sight – mass graves, a helipad, parking spaces, a cafeteria, and housing for staff. The monument is a series of seven pairs of prisms – isosceles triangles of different heights and base lengths, placed parallel to and at a distance of 2.79 metres from one another in such a way as to look like a unified structure, a pyramid, when seen from the front. The innermost pair of triangles is the tallest at 46 metres high but has the narrowest span – 6.09 metres. The architect was inspired by changes in the monument's shape when seen from different viewing angles; when seen from the sides and the front, the monument describes a parabolic curve. The seven pairs of triangles represent significant stages along the path to independence. The number seven also represents Bangladesh's seven national heroes, *birshesthros*, the most outstanding freedom fighters in the 1971 war. The seven national stages/events are as follows: the language movement of 1952, the landslide victory of the United Front at the provincial elections in 1954, the constitution movement of 1956, protests against the education commission in 1962, the six-points movement in 1966, the mass uprising of 1969, and, finally, independence in 1971. On 26 March (Independence Day) and on 16 December (Victory Day) every year the nation celebrates here with collective vigour.

5

5

METI School

Rudrapur, Dinajpur District
Anna Heringer,
Eike Roswag-Klinge
2006

158 E

This school was created by the German architects Anna Heringer (design) and Eike Roswag-Klinge (technical planning). The building was highly praised by the jury of the Aga Khan Award for Architecture for its ability 'to create beautiful, meaningful, and humane collective spaces for learning.' Poverty and lack of infrastructure have driven many in the Rudrapur region in the north of the most densely populated country on earth from the countryside to the cities. To address this issue, Dipshikha, an NGO, launched a development programme to give the rural population prospects for the future while helping them appreciate the value of village life. To instil self-confidence and independence in the region's children and strengthen their sense of identity, a new concept of the school was introduced. Architectural critics were impressed with the approach taken in developing this project, which allowed new design solutions to emerge from an in-depth understanding of the local context and traditional ways of building. They noted that while the design solution may not be replicable in other parts of the Islamic world due to the different local conditions, the project still serves as a fresh and hope-bringing model for sustainable building globally. Locals in the area have also praised the project, recognising the unique use of available materials and techniques and the joys of building together to create a successful project. Traditional materials and techniques were preferred to expensive and energy-inefficient imports; as a result, the project represents the local identity and is a refreshing sight for the area's developing communities. For Anna Heringer the project's true success is not the building itself, but the people who worked on it and the joyful community atmosphere it creates. The children at the METI school are flourishing in a space they love, one that was created with them in mind.

5

E. M. S. Inan

B. K. S. Inan

Interior of the METI School

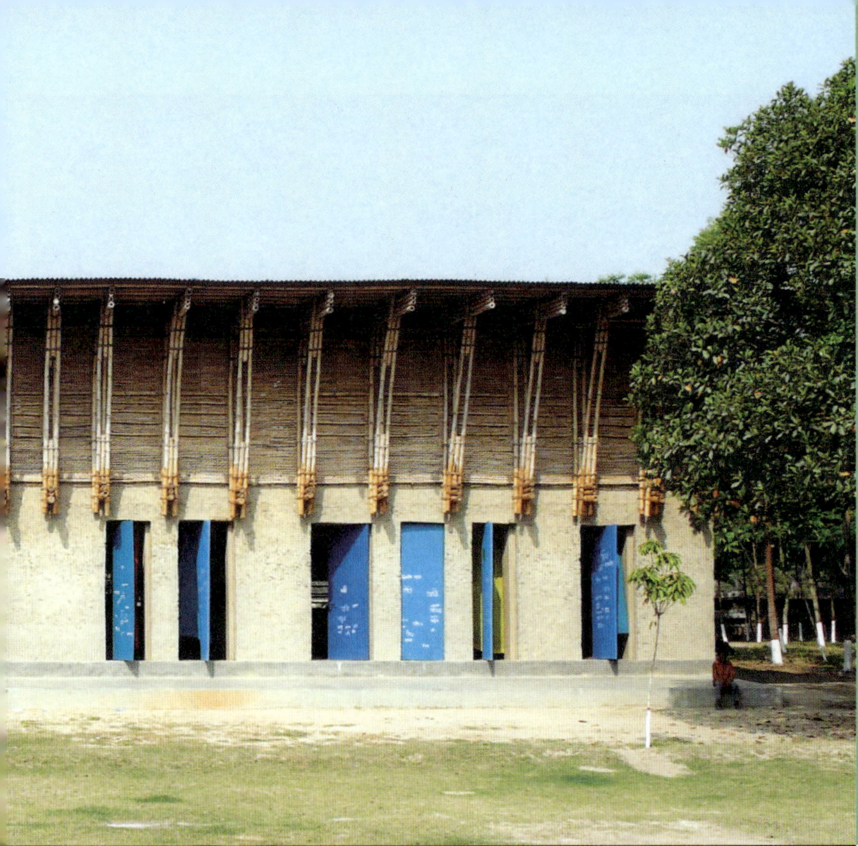

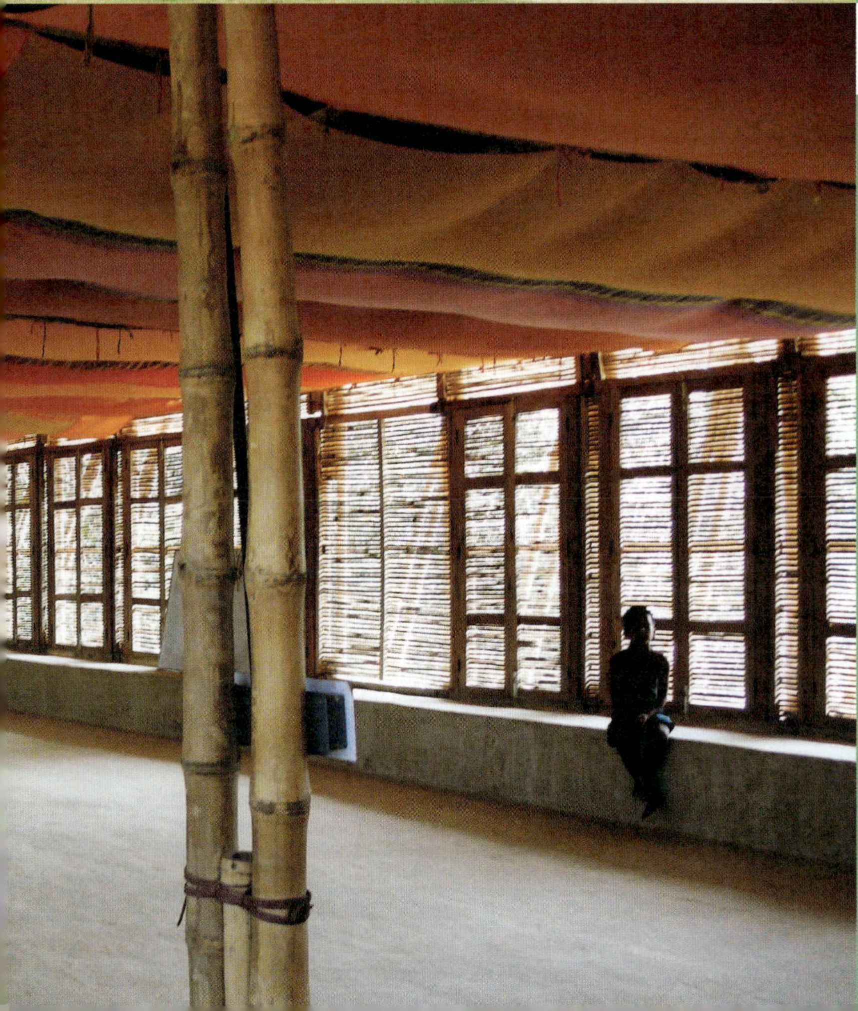

Kurt Hoerbst (all pictures of the project)

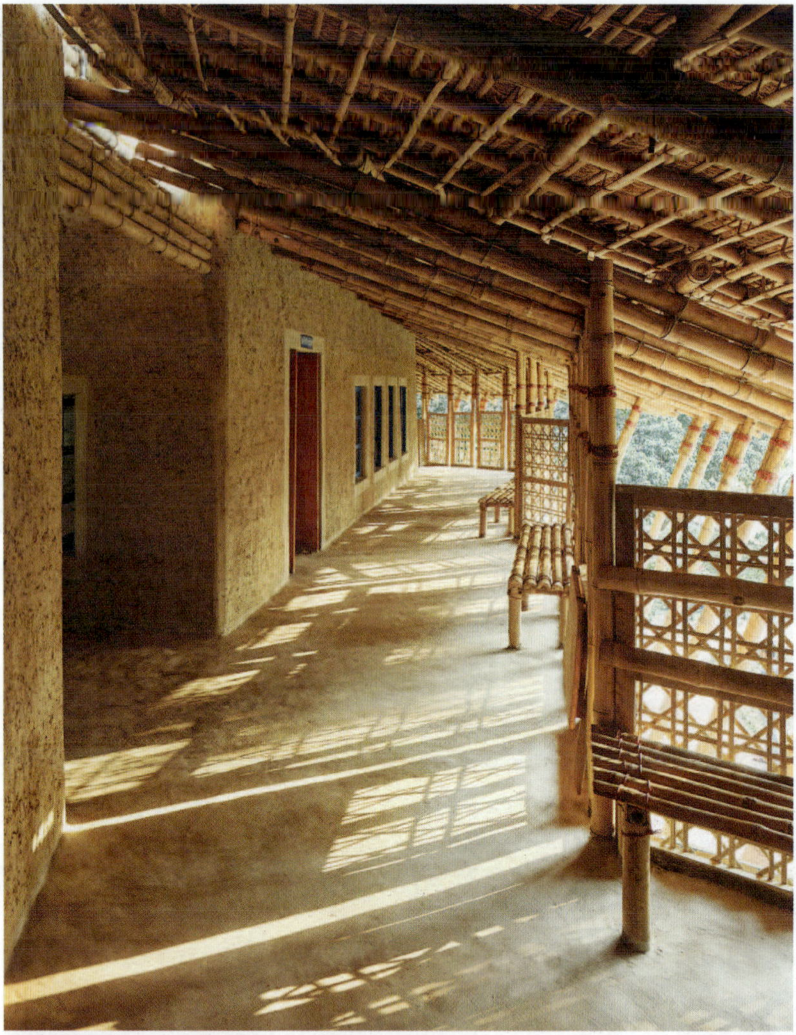

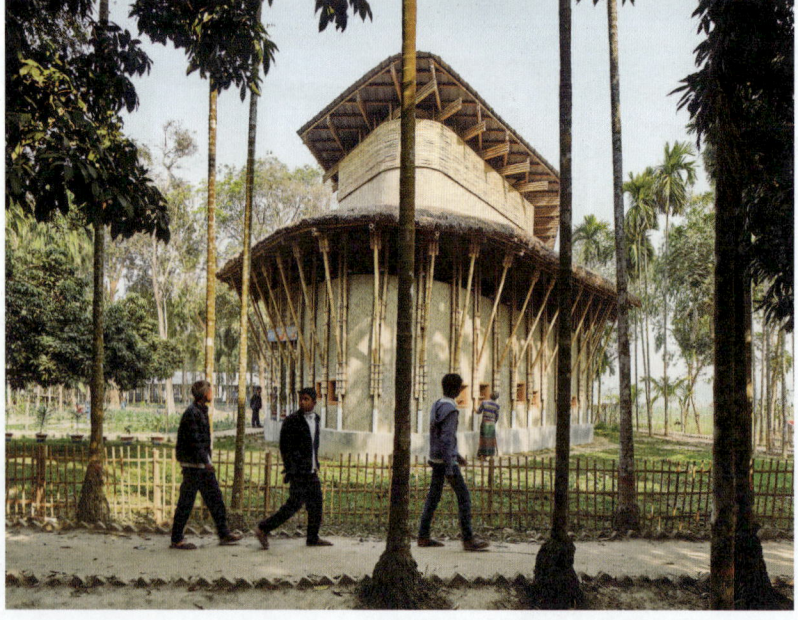

Anandaloy: Centre for Disabled People & Dipdii Textiles Studio

159 E

Rudrapur, Dinajpur District
Studio Anna Heringer
2020

Situated in a rural setting in Bangladesh, the Anandaloy Building is a centre for people with disabilities that also includes a small studio producing fair textiles (Dipdii Textiles). The primary building construction materials were mud and bamboo obtained from local farmers, and a substantial amount of the budget was allocated to employing local craftspeople (both men and women). Accordingly, this building has taken on a significance beyond that of a mere structure and become a catalyst for local development. The staging of the construction is the culmination of a learning process from earlier projects by Studio Anna Heringer in Rudrapur, including the METI School. In contrast to those earlier projects under German supervision, this site was supervised by the Bangladeshi contractor Montu Ram Shaw with a team of mud and bamboo workers from the village, including some with disabilities. In Bangladesh disabilities are concealed rather than accommodated because they are typically

viewed as a punishment for past misdeeds. Sadly, therapy and treatment options tend to be scarce or non-existent, particularly in rural areas like Rudrapur, leading to the exclusion of disabled persons from their communities. Initially conceived as a therapy centre, Anandaloy was subsequently expanded to include Dipdii Textiles, a studio for female tailors from the village. Co-initiated by Anna Heringer, this enterprise offers women an opportunity to work close to their homes, alleviating the need for migration to urban areas. The project offers individuals with disabilities not only therapeutic support but also an opportunity to learn and work in the facilities and become an active part of the Rudrapur community. The large ramp rising upwards from the ground floor, the only one of its kind in the area, is a visible sign of this commitment toward inclusiveness and has sparked discussions among visitors about the importance of access for everyone, regardless of their state of health. The architect has a contemporary take on materials, regardless of the relative cost or popularity of traditional materials. A special technique mens that sturdy forms can be made without the use of moulds, and curved forms are as straightforward to create as straight walls. Unlike other buildings in the region, with their rectangular floor plans, the Anandaloy Building is gracefully curved, its playful ramp twisting around the interior structure. From a symbolic viewpoint, the building's appearance embraces diversity while radiating the joyful message that difference is something to be celebrated.

5

Studio Anna Heringer

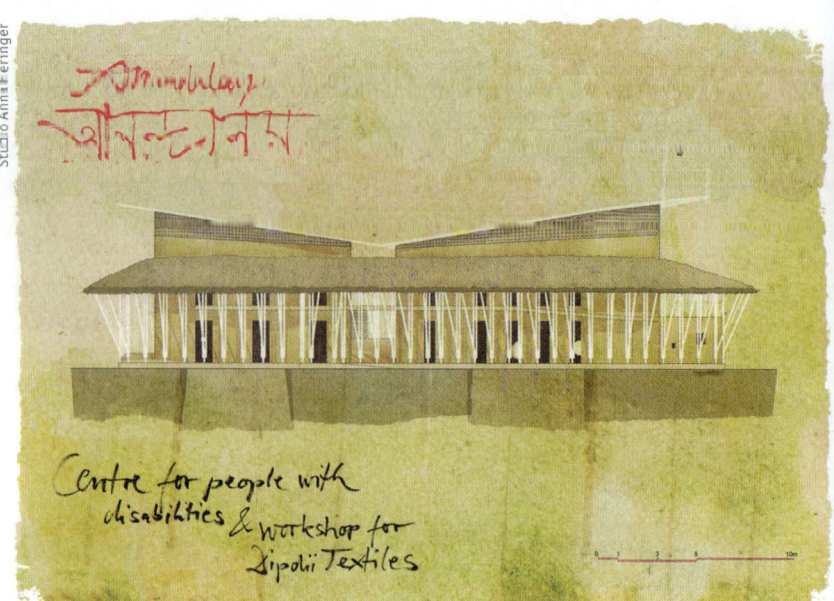

Centre for people with
disabilities & workshop for
Dipdii Textiles

Elevation

Stefano Mori

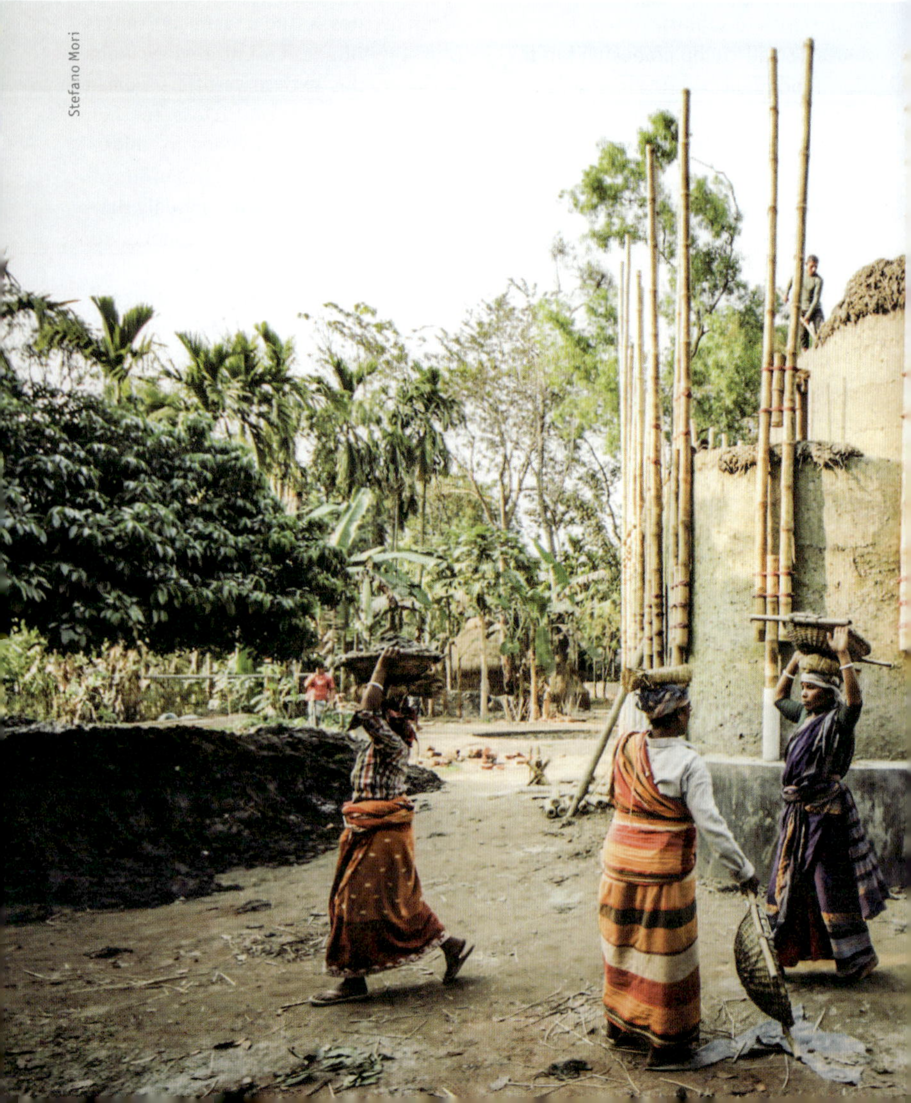

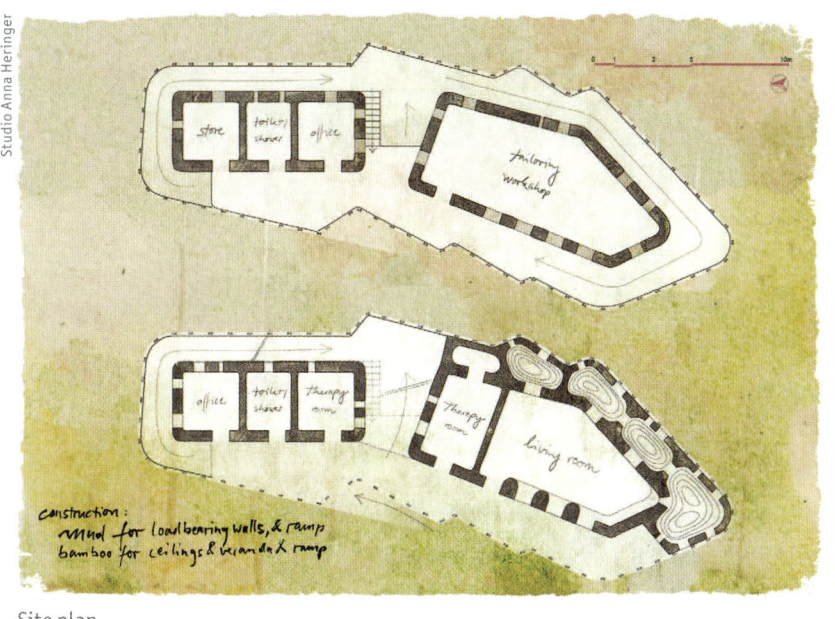

Studio Anna Heringer

Site plan

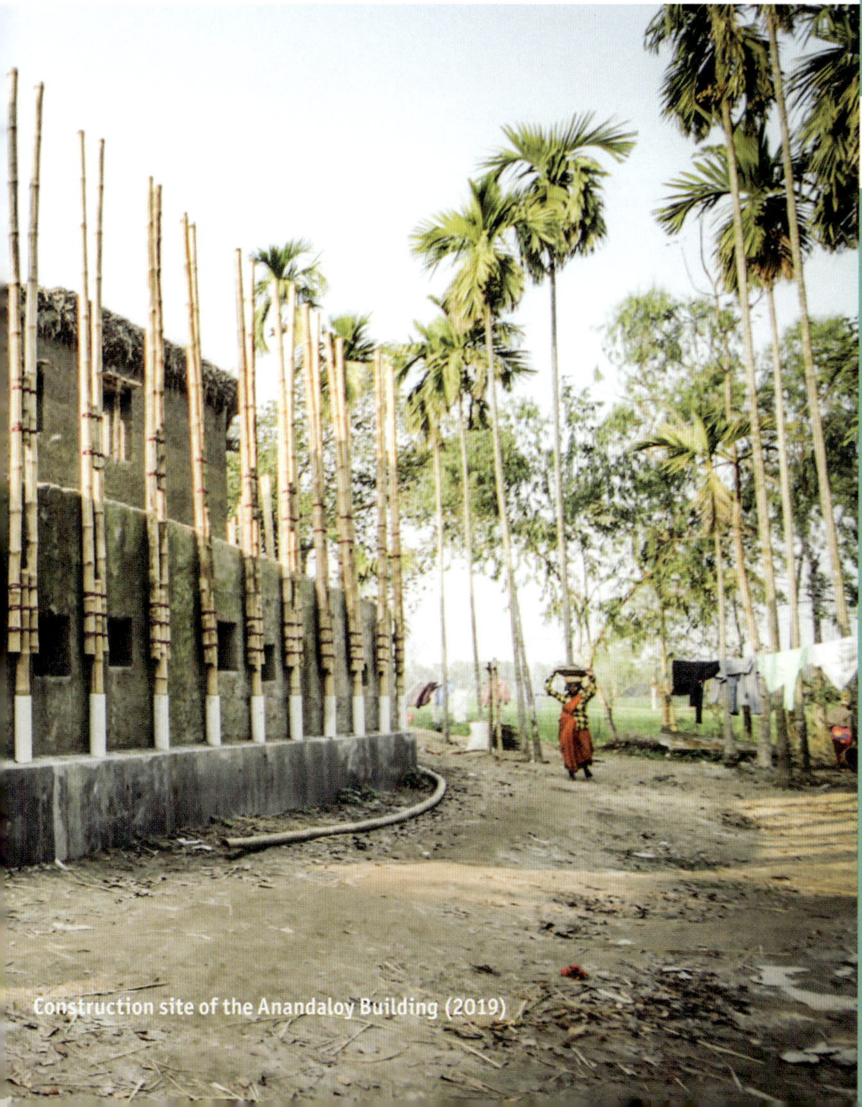

Construction site of the Anandaloy Building (2019)

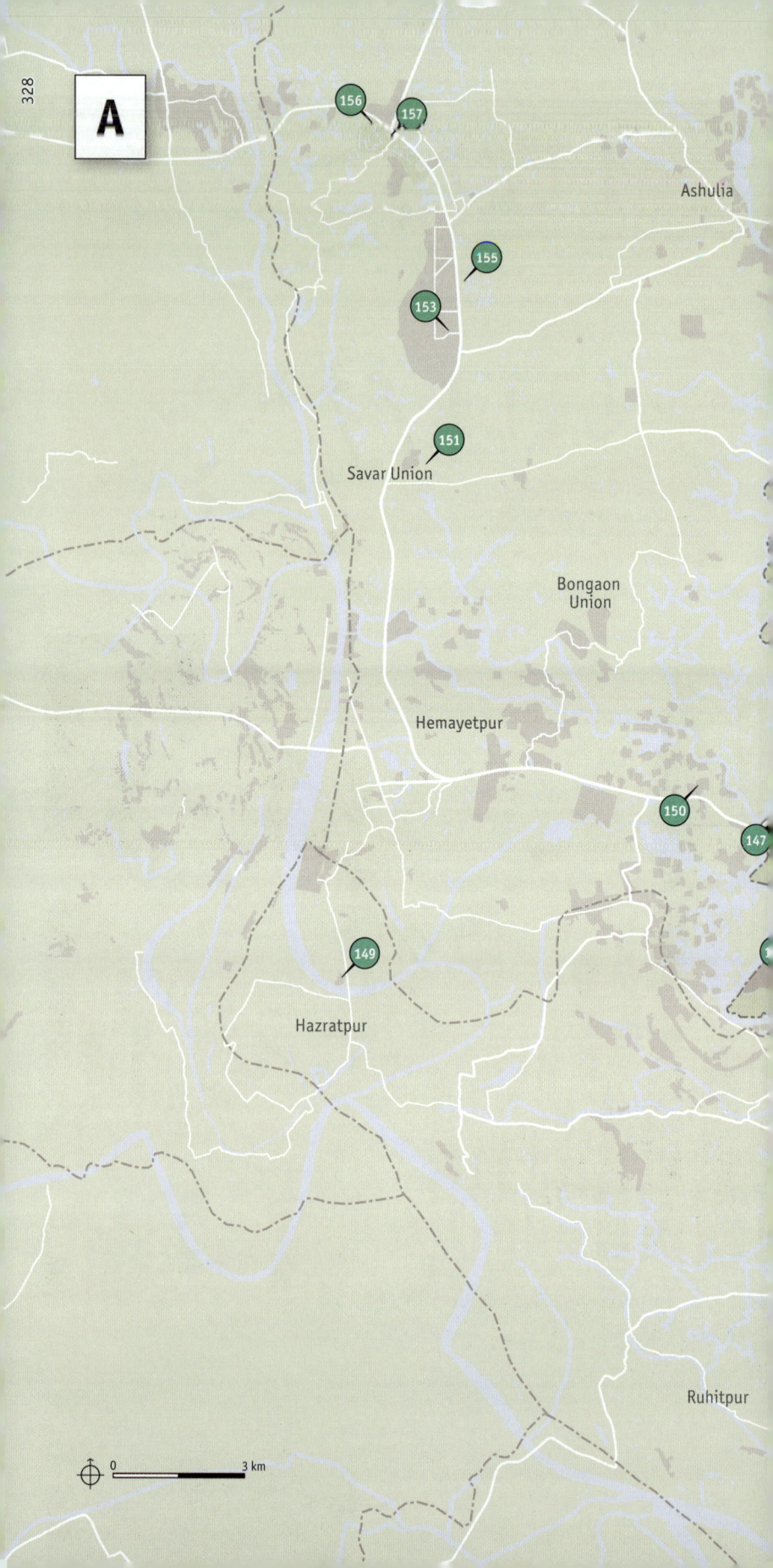

A

156
157
Ashulia
155
153
151
Savar Union
Bongaon
Union
Hemayetpur
150
147
149
Hazratpur
Ruhitpur

0   3 km

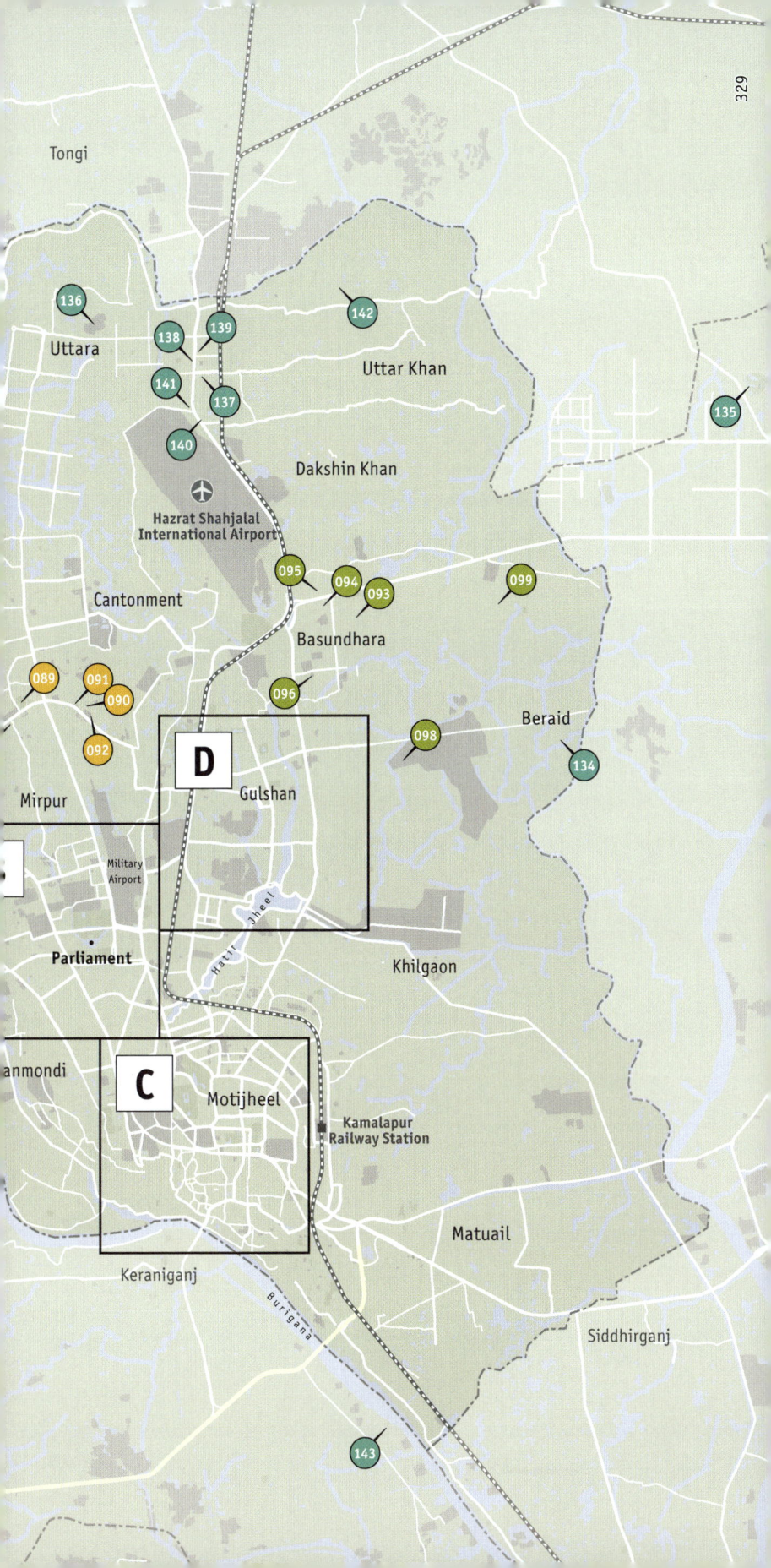

Tongi

Uttara

136

138 139

141

140 137

Uttar Khan

Dakshin Khan

✈ Hazrat Shahjalal
International Airport

Cantonment

095 094 093

Basundhara

089 091

090

092

Mirpur

096

098

134

142

135

099

Beraid

D

Gulshan

Military
Airport

Hatir Jheel

• Parliament

Khilgaon

anmondi

C

Motijheel

Kamalapur
Railway Station

Matuail

Keraniganj

Buriganga

Siddhirganj

143

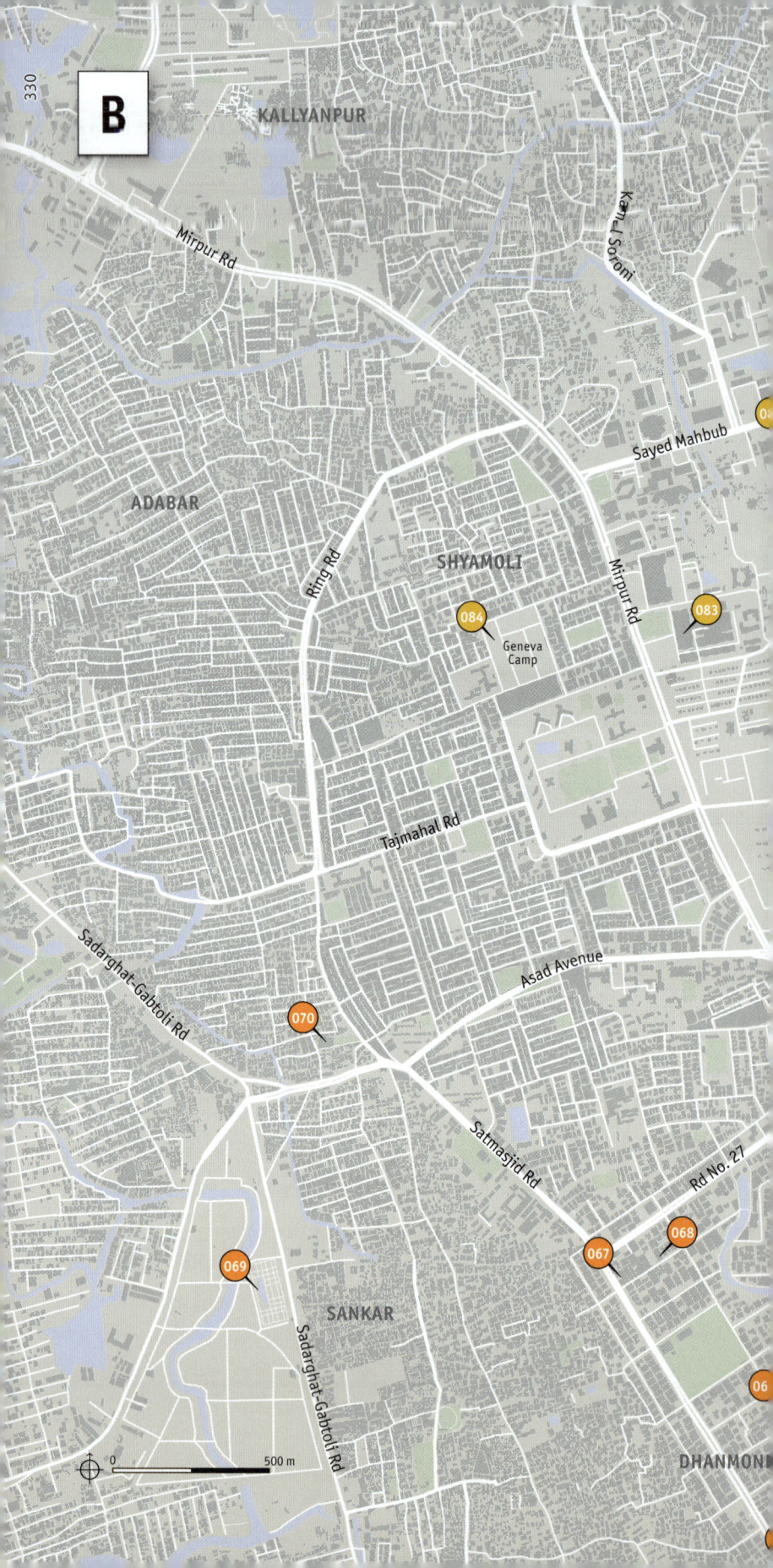

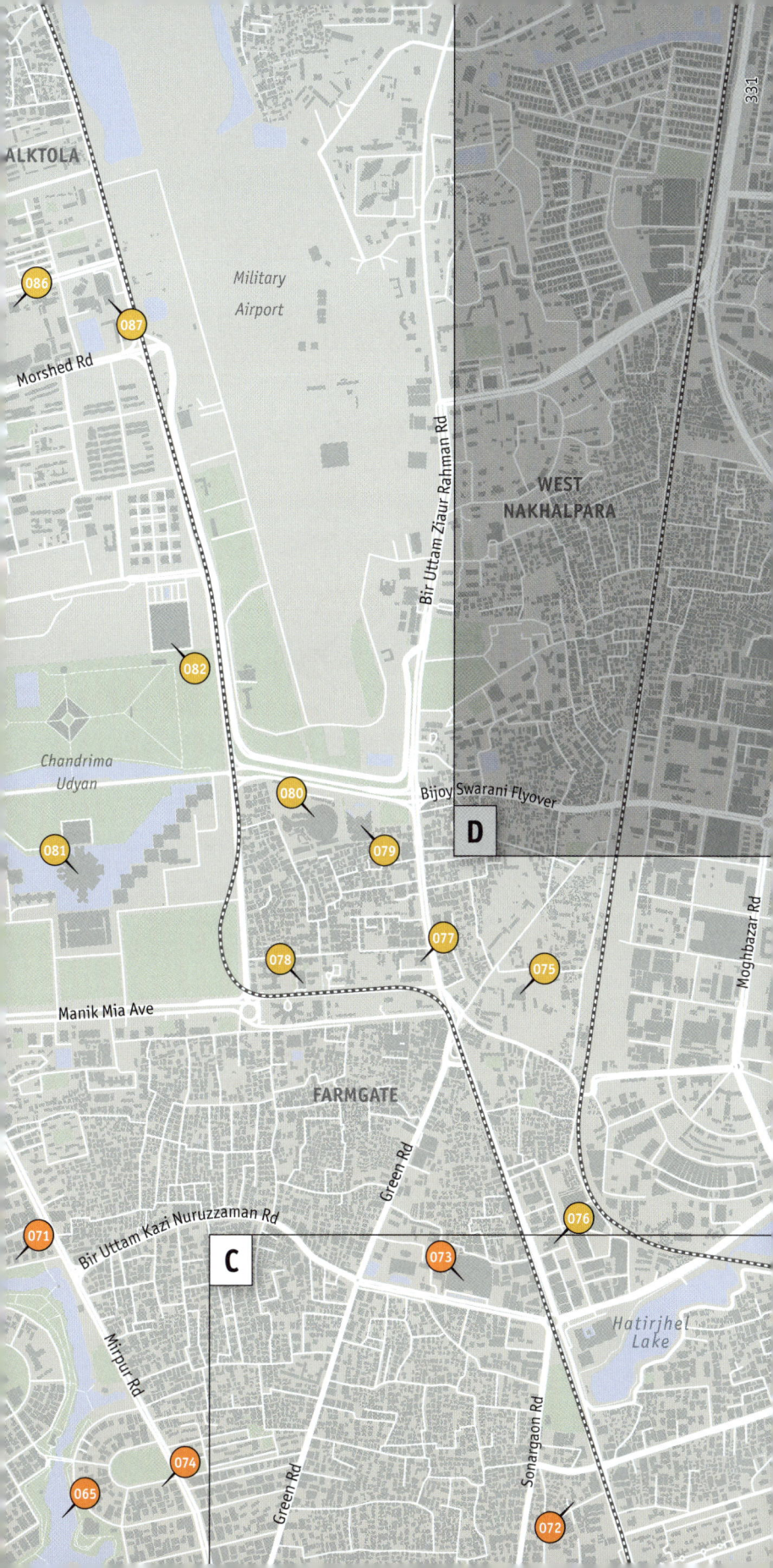

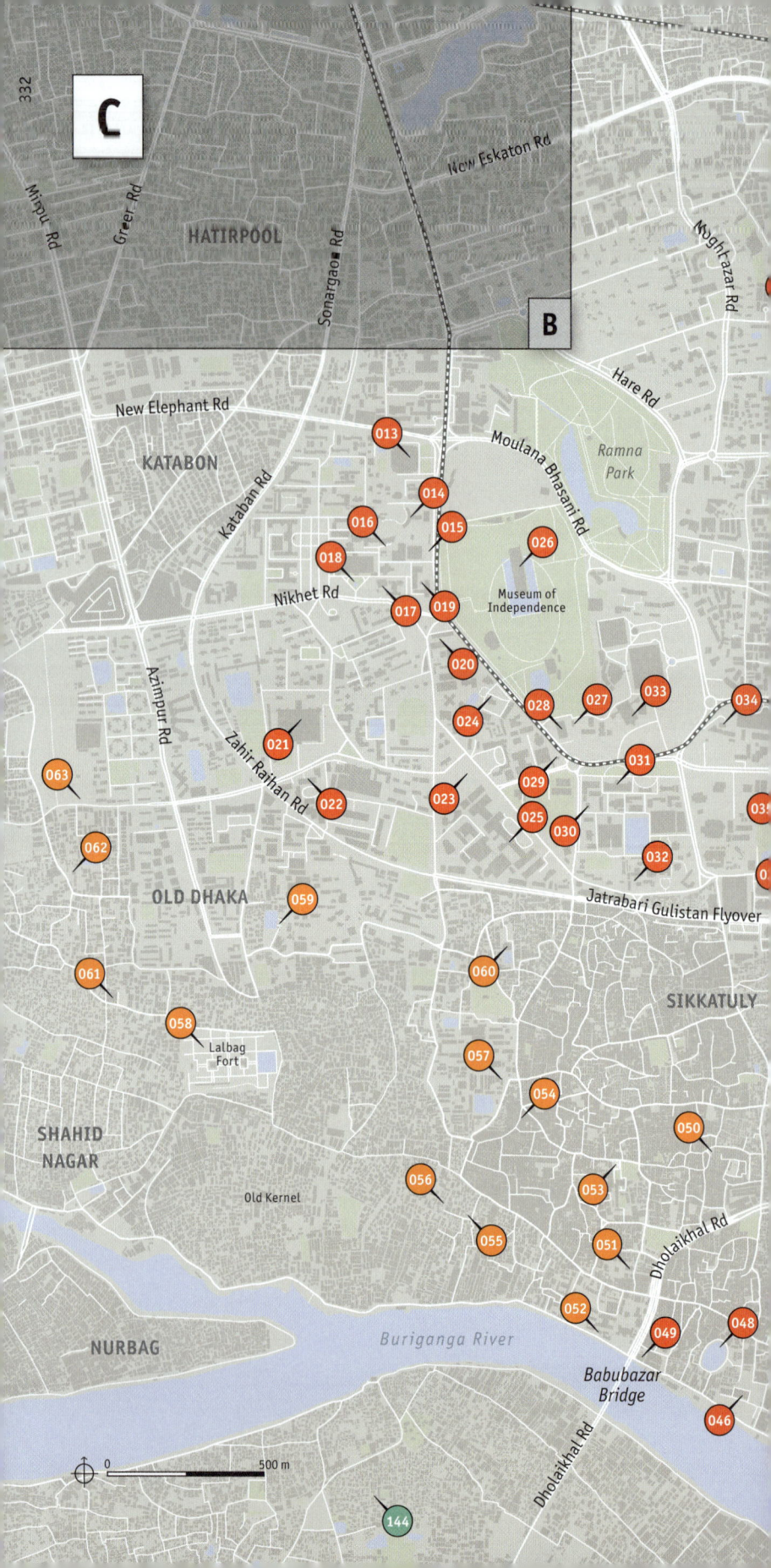

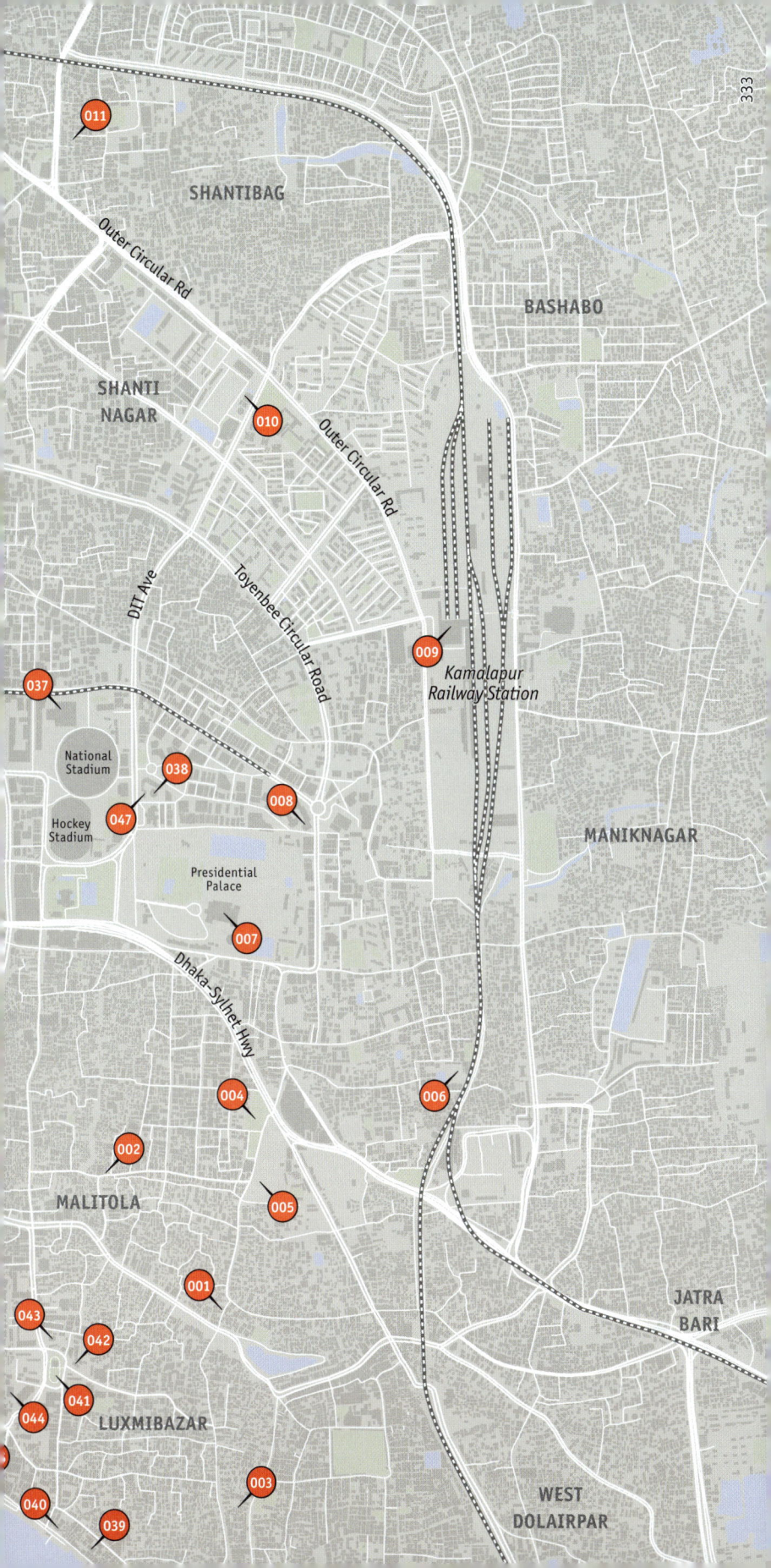

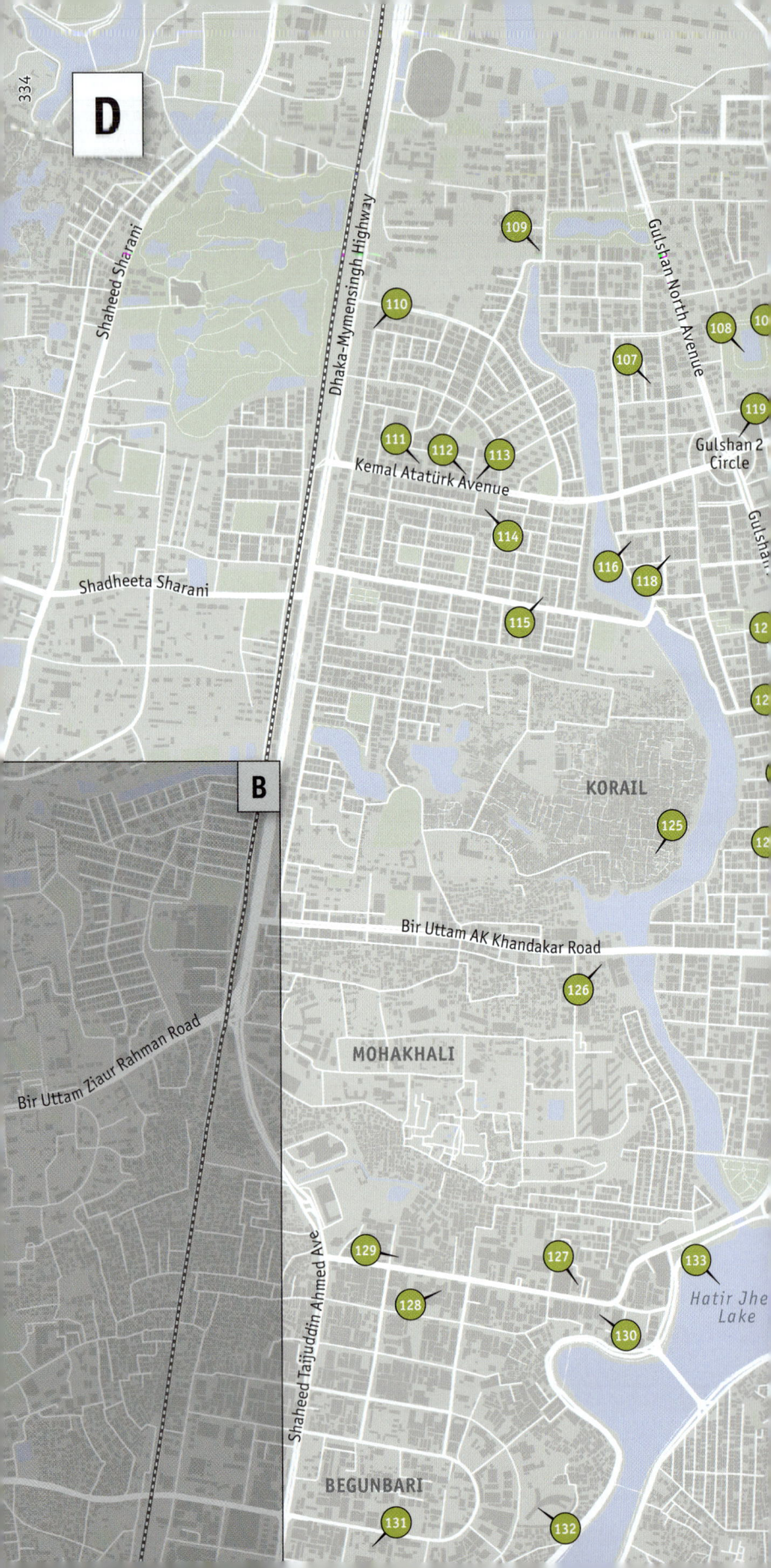

D

Shaheed Sharani

Dhaka-Mymensingh Highway

109

110

Gulshan North Avenue

108

10

107

119

Gulshan 2 Circle

111 112 113

Kemal Atatürk Avenue

114

Gulshan

Shadheeta Sharani

115

116 118

12

12

KORAIL

125

12

B

Bir Uttam AK Khandakar Road

126

Bir Uttam Ziaur Rahman Road

MOHAKHALI

Shaheed Tajjuddin Ahmed Ave

129

127

133

Hatir Jhe Lake

128

130

BEGUNBARI

131

132

SOLMAID

097

100

Madani Ave

103 102 101

104

NURER CHALA

KHILBARI TEK

BAWAILA PARA

Bir Uttam Rafiqul Islam Ave

ADARSHA NAGAR

Gulshan
Lake

UTTAR BADDA

SOUTH BADDA

Jahurul Islam Ave

0   500 m

Nepal

158 159
Dinajpur

India

0   500 km

Bogra

Maimansingh

Sylhet

152 145

Dhaka

146

154

India

Bangladesh

Myanmar

Kolkata

Chittagong

E

Cox's Bazar

Index of Buildings

Residential buildings and hotels

Sacred and cultural buildings

Schools, libraries, and higher education

Index of Architects

Author and Partners

Sayed Ahmed

Sayed Ahmed (born in 1988) is a practising architect and academic from Narayanganj. He graduated from the architecture department at SUST in 2012 with a first-class degree. He was lecturer in the department of architecture at Bangladesh University, Dhaka from 2012 to 2015. He obtained his master's degree in architectural heritage and conservation from Anhalt University of Applied Sciences, known for its world-famous campus at Bauhaus, Dessau in Germany. In 2016 he was the first Bangladeshi architect to take part in World Architecture Festival 2016 in Berlin; his idea was presented as one of eight student group projects for that year's Student Charette. These successes won him a DAAD-Stibet-I scholarship for 'outstanding commitment as an international student'. Sayed specializes in art history, design, cultural studies, philosophy of art, architectural history, urban collective memory, climate and the environment, housing, and vernacular architecture. He has published 27 research articles, three book reviews, and five short notes in journals around the world, including in Argentina, Australia, Austria, Brazil, China, Greece, India, Indonesia, Iran, Iraq, Italy, Kenya, Nigeria, Portugal, South Africa, Thailand, Tunisia, Turkey, UK, and the USA, in addition to Bangladesh. He is also on the editorial boards of the journals *Atinar* (Greece), *Chitrolekha* (India), *Journal of Architecture and Engineering* (Russia) and *International Journal of Culture and History* (USA). He presented his master's thesis paper at the Harvard faculty club and Oxford Brookes University in 2018. He chaired the Common Ground Research conference as one of 11 selected promising urban researchers at Heidelberg University in 2018. He has also been a juror at Inspireli, the world's largest student design competition in the Czech Republic, since 2016. He worked as a junior architect at SWA Group International in Berlin (Germany) until May 2019. Later, he was a short-term volunteer at ASA-Ten Arquitectos in New York (USA) in the latter half of 2019. He came back to Narayanganj in 2020 to work for Nirman Upodeshta. In 2021 he was appointed Assistant Professor at the Department of Architecture at Leading University, Sylhet. Sayed moved to Australia in 2022 to continue his PhD studies in urban design; he was awarded a prestigious scholarship by the University of New England, Armidale/NSW.

photographs were published in *Prothom Alo*, the most popular Bangla daily newspaper, in 2019. He was a member of the cinematography team for the documentary 'Dam Developments at Chandpur supervised by current education minister Dr. Dipu Moni' in 2018. He was shortlisted for Grameenphone Reel Hunt for his short film Lift in 2018. He took all the aerial drone pictures showing Dhaka's historical urban fabric in this book. His hobbies are photography and making short films.

Reza Noor Muin

Reza Noor Muin (born in 1991) graduated from the architecture departure at SUST in 2015. He started working as an architect at J.A. Architects Ltd. in Dhaka in 2016. He won the South Asian Property Awards 2017 for his project for Sajida Foundation's Residential Training Centre at Gazipur in the mixed-use architecture category. He is also the co-founder of Jadukata interior+landscape, which is a 'startup for startups' providing support for young entrepreneurs. His core interests are photography, street life, lifestyles. Travelling and music are his other passions.

Kazi Karar Naier

Special thanks to Kazi Karar Naier, the 'local boy', who was born in old Dhaka's Lakshmibazar neighbourhood in 1998. The team is really indebted to him for extending an eleventh-hour helping hand with the photographs for this book. He passed his SSC exam in 2014 and his HSC exam in 2016 and is currently a fifth-year student at the department of architecture at Khulna University. Along with photography, he loves travelling and cycling. In his future studies he plans to focus on climate change and heritage protection.

Ishtiaque Ahmed

Ishtiaque Ahmed (born in 1995) graduated from the architecture department at SUST in 2019. After working at various renowned firms in Dhaka and Sylhet, he won the commission for visualisation and mould-making for the guard-rail of Padma Bridge in Bangladesh. His

Avijit Barman   **Md. Mohaimin Ali Khan**

Jacob Davies and Chloe Pattinson

Jacob Davies and Chloe Pattinson are a British couple and good friends of Sayed Ahmed, the author of this book. As native speakers of English, they were responsible for initial proofreading of the book. Jacob was born in 1995 in Salisbury (UK); Chloe was born in 1996 in Dorset (UK). The couple currently live in the Jurassic Coast in the south-west of England, an area which is well known for its dinosaur fossils and rolling landscape. Sayed Ahmed first met them at yoga classes during his stay in Berlin, and they have been firm friends since 2019. Jacob and Chloe enjoy travelling to different places around the world, where they exhibit their 'mandala' paintings. The author is very grateful to Jacob and Chloe for their help with the proofreading.

Navid Zaman Dhrubo

Navid Zaman Dhrubo (born in 1994) is from Kishoreganj. He is an architect at UX Design and is also involved in an human-centred design farm, Inked Studios. He is very interested in graphic design. He completed his BA at the architecture department at SUST in 2018. He was cultural secretary of SUST Architecture Society in 2016. His hobbies include puppet dance, cartoon, animation, and board games.

Claudio Gustavo Manzoni

Claudio Gustavo Manzoni (born in 1959 in Argentina) obtained his degree in Architecture from the National University of Córdoba in 1984. His interest in light and its revealing effects on form and space inspires him to use photography as a vehicle for architectural narration. He is a professional freelance photographer; his images have been published internationally.

Faruque Abdullah Shawon
Faruque Abdullah Shawon works as an architect as he pursues his career as a photographer focused primarily on architecture. Self-taught, Shawon is well versed in digital capture. Residing in Dhaka, Shawon has developed a unique vision for landscapes and architecture, with the aim of transforming the simple into the sublime.

H.M. Fozla Rabby Apurbo
H.M. Fozla Rabby Apurbo is a photographer by profession and over the years he has been associated with prestigious business houses and leading corporates in Bangladesh. He has now evolved to specialize in the form of architectural photography. Apurbo is co-founder of *CitySyntax Photography* (together with Faruque Abdullah Shawon).

Acknowledgements
Special thanks to Sazzadur Rasheed, our well-wisher and the Head of the Architecture Department at Prime Asia University, Dhaka, who helped us in gathering information regarding listed heritage in Bangladesh's capital.
Apart from our team members, I also want to thank the wonderful juniors at architecture SUST, without whom it would have been impossible to produce this book and whose support was invaluable for us in selecting contemporary buildings. We are indebted to them for their kind contributions at different stages in the writing. They include: Md. Shafayat Hossain, Akash Karmaker, Koustuv Islam Shreya, Iffat Mahmuda Khan, Fayazul Haque Ashek, Al Amin Abu Ahmed Ashraf Dolon, Ahmed Hasib Bulbul, Latiful Kabir Sujon, Nazmul Asif Rishat, Ferdous Rahman Mugdho, Samia Binte Azhar, Syed Golam Rabbani, and Shadi Murshed Bhuiyan.

We are also indebted to the members of the Facebook groups *Save the Heritages of Bangladesh* and *Contemporary Architecture of Bangladesh*, especially Mohammad Mashiur Rahman Pobitro, who shared photography and information for this architectural guide.

Notes
Pictures and information of featured buildings by Volumezero Ltd. have been taken from the book *Foyez Ullah. Dhaka's Tropical Expressive Architecture* (Oscar Riera Ojeda Publishers, 2022). They have been edited to fit to this layout.
This guide is an attempt to document the architecture of Dhaka. However, it was only sometimes possible to find the complete names of all architects. If readers could provide missing information, please contact the publisher. It would be highly appreciated, and it will be added in subsequent editions of the book.

The *Deutsche Nationalbibliothek* lists this publication in the *Deutsche National-bibliografie*; detailed bibliographic data are available online *http://dnb.d-nb.de*

ISBN 978-3-86922-748-1

© 2023 by DOM publishers, Berlin
www.dom-publishers.com

Editing and final proofreading
John Nicolson

Initial proofreading
Jacob Davies, Chloe Pattinson

Graphic design
Navid Zhaman Drubo

Final artworks
Martina Filippi

Maps
Ee Dong Chen

Printing
Tiger Printing (Hong Kong) Co., Ltd.
www.tigerprinting.hk